TEACHING FOR HISTORICAL LITERACY

Teaching for Historical Literacy combines the elements of historical literacy into a coherent instructional framework for teachers. It identifies the role of historical literacy, analyzes its importance in the evolving educational landscape, and details the action steps necessary for teachers to implement its principles throughout a unit. These steps are drawn from the reflections of real teachers, grounded in educational research, and consistent with the Common Core State Standards. The instructional arc formed by authors Matthew T. Downey and Kelly A. Long takes teachers from start to finish, from managing the prior learning of students to developing their metacognition and creating synthesis at the end of a unit of study. It includes introducing topics by creating a conceptual overview, helping students collect and analyze evidence, and engaging students in multiple kinds of learning, including factual, procedural, conceptual, and metacognitive. This book is a must-have resource for teachers and students of teaching interested in improving their instructional skills, building historical literacy, and being at the forefront of the evolving field of history education.

Matthew T. Downey is Emeritus Professor of History and former Director of the Hewit Institute for History and Social Science Education at the University of Northern Colorado.

Kelly A. Long is an Associate Professor of History and Associate Dean in the College of Liberal Arts at Colorado State University.

TEACHING FOR HISTORICAL LITERACY

Building Knowledge in the History Classroom

Matthew T. Downey and Kelly A. Long

NEW YORK AND LONDON

First published 2016
by Routledge
711 Third Avenue, New York, NY 10017

and by Routledge
2 Park Square, Milton Park, Abingdon, Oxon, OX14 4RN

Routledge is an imprint of the Taylor & Francis Group, an informa business

© 2016 Taylor & Francis

Library of Congress Cataloging in Publication Data
Downey, Matthew T.
Teaching for historical literacy: building knowledge in the history classroom
/ by Matthew T. Downey and Kelly A. Long.
pages cm
Includes bibliographical references and index.
ISBN 978-1-138-85957-9 (hardback) -- ISBN 978-1-138-85958-6 (pbk.)
-- ISBN 978-1-315-71711-1 (e-book) 1. History--Study and teaching--
United States. I. Long, Kelly A., 1957- II. Title.
D16.3.D69 2015
907.1'073--dc23
2015005060

ISBN: 978-1-138-85957-9 (hbk)
ISBN: 978-1-138-85958-6 (pbk)
ISBN: 978-1-315-71711-1 (ebk)

Typeset in Bembo
by Saxon Graphics Ltd, Derby

Printed and bound in the United States of America by Publishers Graphics,
LLC on sustainably sourced paper.

For our students
from whom we have learned so much
over so many years.

CONTENTS

ILLUSTRATIONS

Figures

Tables

ACKNOWLEDGMENTS

We are indebted to many people who have contributed to our thinking and research during the years that have led to the publication of this book.

After working with a pilot group of teachers selected from a Teaching American History grant in which we had been involved, we formed the first Historical Literacy Partnership (HLP) in 2006. The project out of which this book has grown began as a quest for a different kind of in-service teacher education model than we had experienced in the past. The professional development model that took shape was a partnership with teachers that focused on common problems in history teaching. It brought small groups of teachers together for extended periods of time. We have worked with small cohorts of teachers from five school districts over periods lasting from eighteen months to three years.

The Historical Literacy Partnership was an expanding collaborative. The Historical Literacy Partnership incorporated after-school seminars, week-long curriculum-development institutes during the summer, and conversations in which we shared experiences about implementing the changes that we designed together. We read and discussed professional articles about history teaching. In our classrooms we applied the theory and research explored during the seminars by designing units, lessons, and activities. Collectively the partners critiqued the activities for historical authenticity, debriefed each other's classroom experiences, and discussed unforeseen or unresolved problems of teaching and learning. We consulted with the HLP teachers as they developed classroom units and we observed many of them in their classrooms. Several of our partners presented their HLP-related work at professional conferences. Eventually, we discussed the drafts of this manuscript extensively with these partners and incorporated their experiences, along with our own, into the book. They played a significant role in shaping this final outcome of our work together.

Our partners have influenced our thinking, challenged our assumptions, helped us to maintain our focus, and contributed in other meaningful ways. While we have included examples of several partners' work in the pages of this book, we are indebted to all of them. We identify them in the book followed by the initials HLP to indicate their participation in the Partnership. The tradition in scholarly literature is to identify authors by their last names. Because these people are our friends, we frequently refer to them by first name. This may help readers distinguish between our partners' work and examples drawn from the literature. We are pleased to introduce them here as the colleagues and friends we have come to know. They are Kortney Arrington, Carin Barrett, Karen Beitler, Nita Bitner, Tracy Brady, Russ Brown, Deann Bucher, Andrew Bushe, Mandy Byrd, Jody Connelly, Josh Cox, Lori Davis, David Farrell, Trudy Gesin, Mack Holly, Aaron Jackson, Marty Jaskin, Christopher Kline, Christine Matthie, Liz Melahn, Michelle Pearson, Ann Putsche, Shelley Reffner, Cory Reinking, Dan Rypma, Mark Sass, Arleen Schilling, Elaine Kim Spadling, Tom Sweeney, Brooke Tomalchof, Mike Weber, Gabrielle Wymore, and John Valdez. All are teachers from Colorado who teach or taught in Denver, suburban Denver, Loveland, Fort Collins, and Boulder-area schools.

We owe an enormous debt of gratitude to Jaime Donahue, the project's research assistant. We set out to do a search in the published literature for innovative teaching ideas and strategies. We had no idea what a substantial task this would turn out to be. As will be obvious from even a quick perusal of the Reference sections, the scholarship of history teaching and learning is an international and interdisciplinary endeavor. The substantial and growing body of research completed since the 1990s is one of the most promising changes in history education. The skills of a capable research assistant can make undertaking a project of this type a most rewarding experience. To work with an assistant who responded promptly, did meticulous work, and rose to this challenge with a caring, cheerful presence made this work more than simply an intellectual endeavor, but a rewarding experience of friendship as well. Jaime provided us with a great deal more than just a comprehensive survey of this research.

We also are grateful to administrators and their staffs at all levels in each of the districts with which we worked for their support and cooperation. In particular, we are appreciative of the assistance offered by key figures in the area of social studies by leaders in three districts: Margo Walsh and Donna O'Brien, Adams 12 Five Star Schools; Diane Lauer, Thompson School District; and Andrea Delorey, Poudre School District. Without their help in welcoming this project in their districts and sending capable classroom teachers our way, this project would not have been possible. We are most appreciative of the guidance and editorial judgment of Catherine Bernard and Trevor Gori at Routledge.

PART I
Historical Literacy

We are grateful also to Colorado State University and the University of Northern Colorado, at which we have been privileged to teach, for the institutional support and encouragement of the research connected with this book. That support included the invaluable service of Valerie Ashton, Administrative Assistant in the UNC Social Science Program, which was consistently way above and far beyond the call of duty. We also benefitted from the expertise of Bette Rathe, research librarian at UNC's James A. Michener Library. This project also could not have been possible without funding from UNC's Hewit Institute for History and Social Science Education, which is endowed by a generous gift from the estate of William E. Hewit.

1

HISTORICAL LITERACY

History teaching in the schools is not what it used to be. School reform in recent years has altered the routine of classroom teachers everywhere. They face state-imposed curriculum changes, new assessment or testing requirements, and demanding procedures for teacher evaluation. Others spend more time implementing new standards such as the Common Core, mastering the latest classroom technology, and coping with students' second-language learning issues. While such changes attract the most attention, others are transforming history teaching in more fundamental ways. This book is about some of the undercurrents of change in history teaching and learning often obscured by the storms that roil the surface. They are likely to have a more enduring impact on history education than those that seem more newsworthy and controversial today.

A major rethinking of how best to teach history in schools has been underway for at least two decades. In one sense, it represents the collective response of history teachers and teacher educators to Peter Seixas' (1996) call for a "new pedagogy for history," which he hoped "might promote students' ability to develop meaningful, critical historical understanding" (p. 777). More practically speaking, it is the result of individual teachers and scholars' efforts to align history teaching with their own changing assumptions about how students learn and how best to engage students in meaningful learning.

In the not too distant past, the history curriculum in place virtually everywhere was content-driven and focused on teaching and learning factual information. To be sure, many, if not most, history classrooms are still teacher centered and textbook focused, with students spending much of their time as passive listeners who occasionally participate in recitation-like discussions. But these classrooms do not represent, as they once did, a nearly uniform lay of the land in history education. New models for history teaching have emerged that look distinctly different from those of the past and that offer teachers clear alternatives to the "traditional" instruction described above. Teachers are relying less on textbooks and more on primary sources, emphasizing historical thinking over rote learning, and integrating literacy instruction.

While the changes underway promote the meaningful, critical historical understanding that Seixas called for, they do not yet add up to a coherent pedagogy. They do not yet represent a paradigm shift for history education. It may even be that paradigm shifts or tipping points are not useful metaphors for change in history education, especially given the way public education is organized in the United States. Despite national standards and reform agendas, most decisions about what to teach and how to do it are made at the state department of education and local school district levels. Change tends to take place in piecemeal fashion. A broad consensus about how best to teach history may be even less likely, as history in the United States has no single, powerful voice to promote and guide curricular or pedagogical change. Instead, history has two professional associations that promote competing standards and curricular guidelines, the National Council for the Social Studies and the National Council for History Education. Change in history classrooms tends to happen one teacher or district or, at most, one state at a time. As we all know, some teachers in a school district or building embrace change while others resist. Even individuals adopt specific reform measures in piecemeal fashion, accepting one while hesitating about another. While one should be cautious about making claims for paradigm shifts, that significant pedagogical changes are underway is clearly evident.

The changes that we describe and the positions we advocate in the following chapters have implications beyond what teachers and students do in history classrooms. The newly emerging pedagogy is also prompting a rethinking of the purpose or rationale for history education. The two are intimately related. A pedagogy that once emphasized committing names, dates, and events to memory, especially key developments in national history, had its purpose. In schools in the United States, it promoted a shared body of information about the alleged manifest destiny of Anglo-Americans at home and abroad. It was a pedagogy well designed to acculturate young people into an expanding industrial society, Americanize immigrants, and provide the glue thought to be needed to hold a heterogeneous society together. A pedagogy that promotes "meaningful, critical historical understanding" is hardly compatible with that approach. Teaching history for citizenship education has more or less taken its place, at least among social studies educators, but is unnecessarily restrictive. While critical historical thinking and understanding surely are civic assets, they have implications for many other aspects of life as well. The parameters for a more encompassing rationale for history education are only beginning to take shape, to which we will return later. First, we must more closely examine the shifting landscape of history education.

At least the broad outlines of a new pedagogy of history education are discernible. Teachers have shifted their attention from factual knowledge to be regurgitated on tests to a different order of learning outcomes. They emphasize conceptual learning and thinking grounded in the discipline of history. They are more likely to involve students in authentic historical investigations, engage them in analyzing primary sources, and help them think critically about historical accounts. They are more concerned about disciplinary literacy or whether students can read for understanding, construct documents-based accounts and understand the interpretative nature of history. The new pedagogy also represents history's piecemeal implementation of the "thinking curriculum" advocated by Lauren B. Resnick and Leopold E. Klopfer (1989). The teachers pursuing it want to know whether their students can think historically, develop conceptual understandings about what happened in the past, and connect what happened to their own lives today. It is not that factual knowledge is unimportant, but that without the context of conceptual understanding such knowledge is meaningless, useless, and fleeting.

Yet, what innovative teachers are doing is not a clean break from the past. Their teaching retains elements of continuity with what came before, as changes invariably do. In the United States, even innovative teachers continue to implement a standard curriculum consisting of national and world history. More ethnic, women's, and social history have been added over the years, but the traditional curricular framework remains largely in place. That is true elsewhere as well. The history curriculum in Britain, where bold experiments were underway in the 1970s, has returned to an emphasis on national history (National Curriculum for England, 1999, 2007). Jesus Dominguez and Ignacio Pozo (1998) have described generally what is happening as "a balanced approach between traditional content, i.e., historians' accounts of past facts and events, and procedures or methods concerned both with the interpretation of evidence and the understanding and explanation of past actions and events." While the resulting curriculum values historical knowledge, it also recognizes that students "need to acquire some familiarity with the skills and methods required to construct that knowledge" (p. 344). The new approach strikes a balance between history content and historical thinking, factual knowledge, and conceptual understanding.

The Cognitive Revolution

The changes taking place in history classrooms are not unique to history instruction. They are history educators' response to the earlier shift from behaviorist to cognitivist modes of thinking within academic psychology that Howard Gardner (1985) called the Cognitive Revolution. The new cognitivist view of learning assumed that knowledge is not transmitted intact from teacher or text to learner, but is something the learner must actively construct. The new emphasis on cognitive processes has had far-ranging implications for teaching and learning in the schools, first in mathematics, science, and reading instruction (Royer, 2005), and later in history (Wineburg, 2000). Among the Cognitive Revolution's major contributions to content area instruction is the idea that academic knowledge and thinking are discipline specific. "No longer are the disciplines perceived as shells that encase domain-general processes," Sam Wineburg and Pamela Grossman (2001) note. "Rather, there is an awareness that mathematics, biology, history, physics, and the other subjects of the school curriculum are distinctive ways of thinking and talking" (p. 480). Gardner (1999) described disciplines as the different lenses through which biologists, mathematicians, or historians view and make sense of the world. Consequently, for students to be knowledgeable in any subject area, they must know how those who work in that area think as well as understand the subject-matter content that is the product of that thinking. The challenge is to introduce students to disciplined ways of thinking without expecting them to become junior biologists, mathematicians, or historians. "Our goal," Gardner continued, "should not be to telescope graduate training but rather to give students access to the 'intellectual heart' or 'experiential soul' of a discipline. Education succeeds if it furnishes students with a sense of how the world appears to individuals sporting quite different kinds of glasses" (p. 157). We need to outfit students with these disciplinary lenses, he concluded, to give them a better view of the world in which they live.

Historical Literacy

The pedagogical changes that are the focus of this book have the potential to help students see themselves and the world in which they live more clearly. For them to do so, we must help them become historically literate. What does that mean? Although the term "historical literacy" has been used in history education circles for at least three decades, its meaning has shifted over time. It was the title of an earlier book, *Historical Literacy: The Case for History in American Education* (1989), edited by Paul Gagnon and the Bradley Commission. Neither the editor nor his contributors bothered to define the term, likely assuming that readers would recognize its allusion to the title of E. D. Hirsch's *Cultural Literacy* (1987), a then best-seller that emphasized core knowledge that all American citizens should know. While the term was briefly associated with the notion of core historical knowledge (Ahonen, 2005; Partington, 1994; Zinsser, 1995), it soon lost that ideologically tinted connotation.

In time, the term "historical literacy" was adopted and redefined by history education reformers. It has largely come to represent a set of student competencies and instructional outcomes associated with the pedagogy that we briefly outlined above. Tony Taylor (2003) used it as the covering term for a variety of learning outcomes, including knowledge of historical concepts, knowing how to connect historical learning to life outside the school, and the ability to engage effectively in public debate. For Jeffrey Nokes (2013), historical literacies are the strategies and skills that historians use to construct meaning from texts and other sources. Others have used the term to emphasize conceptual historical knowledge as well as an understanding of the discipline of history (Lee, 2007; Mandell & Malone, 2008; Metzger, 2007; Rodrigo, 1994). To the above outcomes, Peter Lee (2011) has added a set of dispositions that includes respect for evidence, willingness to follow where it leads despite one's preconceptions, and respecting people in the past as human beings. The term also is used to define the larger goals of history education (Lee, 2011; Perfetti, Britt, & Georgi, 1995). History educators, Lee (2011) noted, need "a sense of what history education should add up to. We need a concept of *historical literacy* to enable us to tell others, and perhaps more importantly to remind ourselves, what is central to history education" (p. 64). It is primarily in this goals-oriented sense that we use the term in the title of this book and in the chapters that follow. The goals of historical literacy merit a brief introduction here, although we will revisit them periodically throughout the book.

In the first place, to be historically literate, a person must be knowledgeable about the past. Our *American Heritage Dictionary* defines the word "literate" as "knowledgeable, educated" (adjective) and being "a well-informed, educated person" (noun), as well as being able to read and write. While factual content has often assumed the guise of historical knowledge, it is only the raw material from which historical understanding is constructed. Historical knowledge is what people make of those facts. It also is, Perfetti, Britt, and Georgi (1995) argue, more than learning stories about the past. Knowing a narrative is merely the minimum standard for judging whether a student is competent in history. They stress that, "Beyond this minimum, we look to a higher standard—historical literacy" (p. 4). In other words, knowledge that qualifies a person as historically literate is coherent, conceptual, and meaningful knowledge about the past that is grounded in the critical use of evidence. "We assume that historical literacy … is a reasonable goal for high-school students, and certainly for college students" (p. 5). It also is a reasonable goal for elementary students, when outcomes are adjusted to the appropriate age level.

The goal of historical literacy includes helping students become literate about the discipline as well as the subject matter of history. Students should understand at increasingly more sophisticated levels that historical knowledge is not a body of facts waiting to be memorized. It consists of understandings about the past that they must construct from various sources of information. A historically literate person who encounters a primary source understands that the document is a fragment from the past. It may or may not mean that the source is useful evidence in making an argument about what happened and why. It does mean that historical learning is not a passive process. Historical literacy requires an active engagement with facts, the goal being a conceptual understanding about the past and about how the past is related to the present. To build historical knowledge, students must also know what historical texts are, and how and why they are created. A historically literate person knows that a history book or television documentary is someone's interpretation and not the whole truth about the past and nothing but the truth.

Historical literacy also can be defined in the traditional sense of a person being able to read and write. In this respect, the goal of historical literacy is to enable students to read history texts critically, to write thoughtfully, and to engage in meaningful discussions about the past. Like teachers in many subject areas, history teachers have come to recognize the importance of integrating content and reading instruction. The old adage that "every teacher is a teacher of reading" (Manzo, Manzo, & Thomas, 2004, p. 7) is more applicable than ever. Teachers' concern about literacy is partly an artifact of our times, when students typically read and write less, struggle to make up for fewer childhood encounters with print, and frequently speak a language at home that is different from the language of the school. For the history classroom, it also reflects the central role that texts play in history instruction.

History is the most text-rich subject in the school curriculum, except for literature and language arts. Much of what history students learn comes from textbooks, supplementary readings, primary sources, and teacher handouts. However, history texts pose a distinctive set of challenges, especially for younger students. As Jean Fritz (1982) wrote about her first encounter with a history textbook, "I skimmed through the pages but couldn't find any mention of people at all. There was talk about dates and square miles and cultivation and population growth and immigration and the Western movement, but it was as if the forest had lain down and given way to farmland without anyone being brave or scared or tired or sad, without babies being born, without people dying" (p. 153). Many of the literary conventions that young students have come to expect from reading stories are absent from history texts. Their transition to a variety of nonfiction texts accounts in part for the leveling off of student achievement in reading at the fourth grade. Early progress in reading, as measured by test scores and grades, reaches a "fourth-grade slump" as students encounter this content-area reading barrier (Best, Floyd, & McNamara, 2008).

Even fluent readers being introduced to history are likely to find the vocabulary, word usage, and the structure of history texts unfamiliar and at times perplexing. "Historical thinking," Wineburg (2005) notes, "is a powerful form of literacy that has the potential to teach us about text in ways that no other area of the school curriculum can offer" (p. 662). Teaching reading in the content areas has broadened into a more comprehensive effort to teach "disciplinary literacy," as teachers have recognized that vocabulary, text structure, and grammar differ from one subject matter to another (Shanahan & Shanahan, 2008).

Writing, too, has always played a major role in history instruction. "History would not exist without writing," Henry Steffens (1987) notes, "for 'doing history' means writing history" (p. 219). In recent years, teachers across the curriculum have placed increased emphasis on "writing to learn," which is writing that is central to the learning process itself (Tierney & Shanahan, 1991). "Writing helps me understand more what I don't understand about something," Jennifer, a sixteen-year-old student in B. M. Mulholland's classroom, explained.

"When I write something out, it clears my mind. … You have more than facts. You have what you thought about it" (Mulholland, 1987, p. 235). Writing to learn as well as more conventional report writing is an essential tool for building historical knowledge.

Discussion is another important tool in the history classroom, especially when it is student- rather than teacher-centered. Teachers find that student discussions focused on what they are reading and writing is even more productive. Emily Schell and Douglas Fisher (2007) label this "accountable talk." It is accountable because it encourages students to listen carefully, cite statements accurately, build on the comments of peers, and use methods of reasoning appropriate to the discipline. Like writing, a thoughtful discussion helps students understand what they know and don't know. As the old adage has it, "'I know what I think once I hear what I say'" (Parker, 2001, p. 113). Reading, writing, speaking, and listening are reciprocal processes that help students build historical knowledge. They should be literate in this sense as well.

The Common Core State Standards adopted by many schools in the United States have increased teachers' awareness of disciplinary literacy. The Common Core subject-area standards for grades 6–12 are more discipline-specific than the basic standards for English Language Arts. (Standards below grade 6 are incorporated into the Common Core K-5 Reading Standards.) To meet the history/social studies standards, students should be able to analyze primary and secondary sources, understand key terms and how they are used in a text, and be able to critically evaluate multiple sources of information (Common Core State Standards Initiative, 2012). While not a comprehensive approach to disciplinary literacy, the Common Core Standards are a step in a positive direction.

Historical literacy is a relative term and a work in progress. The professional historian's level of expertise is not a realistic goal for a high school student. The goal is to help students reach more sophisticated levels of historical literacy as they progress through the grades. What counts as acceptable progress will differ from grades 5 to 8 to 11 to college undergraduates. Our task as teachers is not to train young historians or to transform novice history students into experts. We could not do that even if we wanted to. School history classrooms have little in common with graduate history seminars that help prepare the historians of the future. While students' work with primary sources is widely acclaimed as an entrée to historical thinking, it is only a distant relative to the authentic source work of historians (Barton, 2005). As Chris Husbands (1996) notes, "the place of historical evidence in the classroom is subtly different from its place in the work of historians. Unlike historians, school pupils will not claim to generate 'new' public knowledge from the study of (selected) historical evidence; they will generate new private understandings" (p. 26). These private understandings will help students become critical historical thinkers.

A Framework for Historical Literacy

What would classroom instruction look like if historical literacy were the goal of history education? One can catch glimpses of it in schools where different components of the new pedagogy are already in place. They are brief sightings because teachers tend to use them in a highly eclectic fashion, interspersed with more traditional strategies (Brophy, 2006). This is not inappropriate. It does mean that the new methods do not yet add up to an integrated approach to teaching history that has historical literacy as its goal.

Still missing is a framework that organizes these instructional elements into a coherent pedagogy. This book is an attempt to address that need. It proposes an organizational framework that we hope teachers will find useful as a guide for instruction. While it is not the only possible framework, we think that it is a viable option. In putting it together, we have drawn extensively from the recent published literature about new directions in history education. It also is the product of our interaction with teachers. It took shape during a succession of seminars and workshops with our Historical Literacy Partnership teachers, who also designed many of the accompanying activities and tried them out in their classrooms. Before presenting it in detail, we want to make explicit the underlying principles on which we think any framework for teaching for historical literacy should rest.

In the first place, any set of recommendations for helping students become historically literate must honor teachers as professional educators. They are not educational assembly-line workers. Consequently, it should be an open framework, not a sealed container. It should free teachers to be creative, not confine them to a lock-step sequence of instruction. We disagree with those who regard teachers merely as deliverers of instruction prescribed by outside authorities. Standards, pacing guides, and frameworks can be useful, but they should not become straitjackets. Teachers have professional responsibilities as curriculum gatekeepers, instructional planners, and classroom decision-makers. They must have sufficient autonomy within the classroom to meet those obligations.

Teaching for historical literacy also has implications for students. To become historically literate, students must be engaged in their own learning. Historical knowledge is constructed by students, not prefabricated and delivered at regular intervals by teachers. This means that the goal of history instruction is a student-created synthesis in which students pull together the pieces and arrive at their own interpretations. While the final outcome depends on the students, getting them there is a shared responsibility. Teachers must help students become and stay engaged. Motivating students, posing challenging questions, and helping them see that history is relevant to their own lives must play a large role in teaching for historical literacy.

Whether students become engaged depends, in turn, on how we present history to them. They need to see history as an inquiry into the past, not as subject matter to be memorized for a test. Focusing on inquiry places more responsibility on the student, challenging them to become engaged investigators rather than passive learners. It invites historical thinking rather than rote learning. It also enables history teachers to do more than "stand and deliver" factual knowledge. In an inquiry classroom, teachers are overseers of knowledge construction rather than deliverers of information. It is the role most consistent with helping students become historically literate.

Instruction for historical literacy must facilitate learning about the discipline as well as knowing historical content. This includes history's singular approach to critical thinking, reflected, for example, in the way historians analyze sources and weigh conflicting evidence. But disciplined historical thinking goes well beyond that. History also has a set of conceptual lenses that focus historical inquiry to help make sense of the past. History's unique conceptual structure distinguishes it from biology and mathematics as much as does its subject matter. Historical thinkers do not ask questions about evolution or number sequences, but about change and continuity or cause and effect. Therein also lies the principal justification for history as a core subject in the school curriculum. A historical literacy classroom should be a classroom engaged in critical historical analysis and historical thinking.

In teaching for historical literacy, we must think of disciplinary literacy as a goal of student learning as well as a means of instruction. Most teachers were introduced to literacy instruction as a set of strategies or tools that help students engage with text. These are important, as students must be able to read with comprehension and to write coherent historical accounts. We must also think about literacy more broadly and as an inseparable aspect of subject matter learning (Moje, 2008; Schleppegrell, Achugar, & Oteiza, 2004). To be historically literate, students must become fluent in the academic language of history, which is not the same as the language of the home or of the playground. It is also different from the language of mathematicians or scientists or poets, as each of us constructs meaning with words in different ways.

A framework for historical literacy must address the role of history in the school curriculum. Much has been made of the value of history and the social studies as education for citizenship. Knowledge of history or economics or civics certainly should contribute to better civic decision-making. Yet, so should an understanding of accounting, environmental science, or urban planning. In certain circumstances, the latter may be more valuable. This is only to say that democratic citizenship depends on well and broadly informed voters and officials. But it hardly makes the case for history as a core academic subject, one as indispensable to students as the language arts, mathematics, and science.

Teaching for historical literacy provides a rationale for history education that is grounded in the discipline itself. History is the only discipline and school subject primarily concerned about how societies change. Science explores change in the physical world. Social science and humanities subjects incidentally deal with social change, but their focus is elsewhere. History is all about change in human affairs. The history classroom should be the laboratory in which students investigate change in the past. Why and how did the American Revolution or the Civil Rights Movement come about? How did people respond to the Great Depression and how did it affect their lives? By inviting comparisons between then and now, focusing on change also helps teachers link the past and the present.

Finally, a pedagogy for historical literacy should help students understand that the past has relevance for the present. It should provide students with what Lee (2011) calls a "usable historical past," one that is applicable to their own lives today. Too often, he notes, students feel separated from the past "by a kind of *temporal* apartheid" (p. 65). Breaking down this wall does not mean blurring differences or assuming that people then were just like us, a fallacy known as "presentism." It means knowing how the past was both similar and different from the present, and how such comparisons can help us better understand the world in which we live. A historically literate individual is one who learns about the past in order to learn from the past.

The successful teaching of historical literacy gives students the tools they need to think conceptually about society, analyze present-day events and their connection to those in the past, critically interpret primary sources, and much more. But that doesn't mean it is easy. Teaching for historical literacy demands an accurate and up-to-date appreciation of its intricacies and its role in the current educational context, as well as the understanding of a specific pedagogical framework to guide instruction. This book provides teachers with specific activities and approaches to employ in promoting historical literacy in their classrooms. Teachers will find the tools they need to take historical literacy from theory to implementation. Ultimately, the book helps educators understand the importance of historical literacy and their role in it. The following chapter-by-chapter overview describes the order in which this book will address these goals.

Looking Ahead

We follow this introduction to teaching for historical literacy by taking a closer look at history as a discipline, as a school subject (Chapter 2). In the first place, history is a way of thinking. Seeing the world through history's disciplinary lens is to view it through a set of concepts. These include the ideas of change and continuity, significance, causation and agency, time and chronology, perspective analysis, and accounts and evidence. A pedagogy for historical literacy uses these conceptual filters to ask: What happened in the past? How did it happen? Why did it take place?

As the above questions suggest, history is an inquiry into the past, both as a discipline and as a school subject (Chapter 3). It is an evidence-based investigation about what happened and its significance for us rather than a received body of information to be learned and committed to memory. Teachers guide their students' historical inquiry by the kinds of questions they ask and by the classroom materials and activities they use. An inquiry classroom is like a construction site, with the teacher and students assigned various and sometimes interchangeable occupational roles.

History also is knowledge about the past, including factual, procedural, cognitive, and metacognitive understandings (Chapter 4). We have created a conceptual model to demonstrate how students build historical knowledge in the classroom, which begins with a Big Question and concludes with a consideration of past-present connections. We conclude these introductory chapters by exploring the implications of history as inquiry for instructional planning (Chapter 5). Teachers must play a major role in deciding what to teach, how to teach it, and how to assess student learning.

In the third part of the book, we look at how effective teachers get historical learning underway. Successful teachers spend time before instruction begins by activating their students' prior learning, addressing their misconceptions, and getting them interested and engaged in the topic (Chapter 6). Teachers have created a variety of K-W-L and Anticipation Guide strategies to make this "up-front" time productive.

Students must also know the gist of a topic to be able to meaningfully learn more about it (Chapter 7). Many teachers use graphic overviews to preview learning, including structured overviews, and concept webs, maps, and murals. Some have their students preview texts to create their own unit or topic overviews. Still others use the direct teaching of vocabulary to create a conceptual overview of the learning to come.

The next series of chapters focuses on building historical knowledge in the classroom. Students begin this process by looking for and collecting evidence that addresses the Big Question they have posed. While this necessarily involves gathering factual information, we are not proposing a "facts-first," lockstep approach to learning. Building historical knowledge is a recursive process that engages students in multiple kinds of learning (factual, procedural, conceptual, and metacognitive) at virtually the same time. That being said, factual learning is important, as it provides students with the boards, bricks, and building blocks of conceptual knowledge (Chapter 8). As they collect evidence, students must also analyze and evaluate what they are learning. This involves at least three kinds of reasoning: comparative analysis, textual analysis, and perspective analysis (Chapter 9). Students must critically evaluate evidence to be able to use it effectively and to understand how it is temporally or causally connected. Making connections and seeing patterns is the bridge between factual and conceptual knowledge. Students make connections through written, verbal or graphic historical accounts (Chapter 10). In doing so, they bring separate elements of understanding together into a synthesis or coherent whole, which is the capstone of historical learning.

Teachers have created a variety of culminating assignments that lead to such evidence-based student accounts (Chapter 11).

If a history unit begins by activating students' prior knowledge, how should it end? We conclude by suggesting that teachers provide time at the end of a unit of instruction to invite students to apply what they learned to their own lives (Chapter 12). Some teachers do this by looking for historical analogies or similarities between the past and the present. Others use the past as a distant mirror to help students understand the time in which they live by seeing how different it is from the past. Students can also apply what they have learned about analyzing the perspectives of historical actors to better understand people today. Having students to be able to use historical knowledge to address the challenges and opportunities of the present is a worthwhile goal of teaching for historical literacy.

References

Ahonen, S. (2005). Historical consciousness: A viable paradigm for history education? *Journal of Curriculum Studies, 37*(6), 697–707.

Barton, K. C. (2005). Primary sources in history: Breaking through the myths. *Phi Delta Kappan*, 86(10), 745–753.

Best, R. M., Floyd, R. G., & McNamara D. S. (2008). Differential competencies contributing to children's comprehension of narrative and expository texts. *Reading Psychology, 29*(2), 137–164.

Brophy, J. (2006). Observational research on generic aspects of classroom teaching. In P. A. Alexander & P. Winne (eds.) *Handbook of educational psychology* (pp. 755–780). Mahwah, NJ: Lawrence Erlbaum Associates.

Common Core State Standards Initiative. (2012). *Implementing the Common Core State Standards*. www.corestandards.org

Dominguez, J. & Pozo, I. J. (1998). Promoting the learning of causal explanations in history through different teaching strategies. In J. F. Voss & M. Carretero (eds.) *International review of history education, Vol. 2: Learning and reasoning in history* (pp. 344–359). London and Portland, OR: Woburn Press.

Fritz, J. (1982). *Homesick: My own story*. New York, NY: Dell.

Gagnon, P. & The Bradley Commission on History in Schools (eds.) (1989). *Historical literacy: The case for history in American education*. New York, NY: Macmillan Publishing Company.

Gardner, H. (1985). *The mind's new science*. New York, NY: Basic Books.

Gardner, H. (1999). *The disciplined mind: Beyond facts and standardized tests, the K-12 education that every child deserves*. New York, NY: Simon and Schuster.

Hirsch, E. D. (1987). *Cultural literacy: What every American needs to know*. Boston, MA: Houghton Mifflin Company.

Husbands, C. (1996). *Historical forms: Narratives and stories. What is history teaching? Language, ideas and meaning in learning about the past*. Buckingham, UK: Open University Press.

Lee, P. (2007). From national canon to historical literacy. In M. Grever & S. Stuurman (eds.) *Beyond the canon: History for the twenty-first century*. New York, NY: Palgrave Macmillan.

Lee, P. (2011). History education and historical literacy. In I. Davies (ed.) *Debates in history teaching* (pp. 63–72). London and New York, NY: Routledge.

Mandell, N. & Malone, B. (2008). *Thinking like a historian: Rethinking history instruction.* Madison, WI: Wisconsin Historical Society Press.

Manzo, A. V., Manzo, U. C., & Thomas, M. M. (2004). *Content area literacy: Strategic teaching for strategic learning.* New York, NY: John Wiley and Sons.

Metzger, S. A. (2007). Pedagogy and the historical feature film: Toward historical literacy. *Film & History,* 37(2), 67–75.

Moje, E. B. (2008). Foregrounding the disciplines in secondary literacy teaching and learning: A call for change. *Journal of Adolescent & Adult Literacy,* 52(2), 96–107.

Mulholland, B. M. (1987). It's not just the writing. In Toby Fulwiler (ed.) *The journal book* (pp. 227–238). Portsmouth, NH: Boynton/Cook Publisher.

National Curriculum for England. (1999, 2007). History. www.nc.uk.net

Nokes, J. D. (2013). *Building students' historical literacies: Learning to read and reason with historical texts and evidence.* New York, NY: Routledge.

Parker, W. C. (2001). Classroom discussion: Models for leading seminars and deliberations. *Social Education,* 65(2), 111–115.

Partington, G. (1994). Historical literacy. *International Journal of Social Education,* 9(1), 41–54.

Perfetti, C. A., Britt, M. A., & Georgi, M. C. (1995). *Text-based learning and reasoning: Studies in history.* Hillsdale, NJ and Hove, UK: Lawrence Erlbaum Associates.

Resnick, L. & Klopfer, L. (1989). *Toward the thinking curriculum: Current cognitive research.* Alexandria, VA: Association for Supervision and Curriculum Development.

Rodrigo, M. J. (1994). Discussion of chapters 10–12: Promoting narrative literacy and historical literacy. In M. Carretero & J. F. Voss (eds.) *Cognitive and instructional processes in history and the social sciences* (pp. 309–320). Hillsdale, NJ and Hove, UK: Lawrence Erlbaum Associates.

Royer, J. M. (2005) *The cognitive revolution in educational psychology.* Greenwich, CT: Information Age Publishing.

Schell, E. & Fisher, D. (2007). *Teaching social studies: A literacy-based approach.* Upper Saddle River, NJ: Pearson, Merrill Prentice Hall.

Schleppegrell, M. J., Achugar, M. & Oteiza, T. (2004). The grammar of history: Enhancing content-based instruction through a functional focus on language. *TESOL Quarterly,* 38(1), 67–93.

Seixas, P. (1996). Conceptualizing the growth of historical understanding. In D. R. Olson & N. Torrance (eds.) *The handbook of education and human development: New models of learning, teaching and schooling* (pp. 165–783). Cambridge, MA and Oxford, UK: Blackwell Publishers.

Shanahan, T. & Shanahan, C. (2008). Teaching disciplinary literacy to adolescents: Rethinking content-area literacy. *Harvard Educational Review,* 78(1), 40–59.

Steffens, H. (1987). Journal in the teaching of history. In T. Fulwiler (ed.) *The journal book* (pp. 219–226). Portsmouth, NH: Boynton/Cook Publisher.

Taylor, T. (2003). Trying to connect: Moving from bad history to historical literacy in schools. *Australian Cultural History,* 23, 175–190.

Tierney, R. J. & Shanahan, T. (1991) Research on the reading-writing relationship: Interactions, transactions and outcomes. In M. L. Kamil, P. B. Mosenthal, P. D. Pearson, & R. Barr (eds.) *Handbook of reading research, Vol. II* (pp. 246–280). Mahwah, NJ: Lawrence Erlbaum Associates.

Wineburg, S. (2000). Making historical sense. In P. N. Stearns, P. Seixas, & S. Wineburg (eds.) *Knowing teaching and learning history: National and international perspectives* (pp. 306–329). New York, NY and London: New York University Press.

Wineburg, S. (2005). What does NCATE have to say to future history teachers? Not much, *Phi Delta Kappan*, 86(9), 658–665.

Wineburg, S. & Grossman, P. (2001). Affect and effect in cognitive approaches to instruction. In S. A. Carver & D. Klahr (eds.) *Cognition and instruction: Twenty-five years of progress* (pp. 479–492). Mahwah, NJ and London: Lawrence Erlbaum Associates.

Zinsser, J. P. (1995). Real history, real education, real merit: Or why is "Forrest Gump" so popular? *Journal of Social History*, 29(1), Supplement, 91–97.

2

HISTORICAL THINKING

A historically literate person must be able to think historically. At some level of proficiency, he or she must be able to view the world through what Howard Gardner (1999) called history's disciplinary lens. Students will not be able to do it as well as professional historians, for whom historical thinking is a well-established habit of mind. Young people lack the experts' background knowledge, archival experience, and critical acumen when confronting historical texts. However, students can understand at various levels of sophistication the concepts that provide the framework for historical thinking. They also can acquire some measure of facility in using them. For that to happen, history teachers must pay as much attention to the discipline of history as to historical content. In modern-day pedagogical thinking the two have become virtually inseparable.

The principle that school subjects are grounded in their respective disciplines has been a hallmark of most recent pedagogical reforms. Jerome Bruner's influential book, *The Process of Education* (1960), argued that the most effective way to teach a subject was to organize instruction around the "underlying principles that give structure to that subject." Unless instruction was organized around "the structure of the disciplines," the content was likely to be poorly learned and quickly forgotten (p. 31). Most curriculum reformers have followed Bruner's lead, identifying a set of principles unique to their disciplines and building curriculum around that conceptual structure.

A major history curriculum reform effort got underway in the United Kingdom in 1972, led by the Schools Council History 13–16 Project, which we will refer to hereafter as the Schools History Project, using the principles of the discipline approach. It identified a conceptual structure for history that was initially anchored in two sets of concepts—continuity and change, and cause and consequence (Boddington, 1984; Shemilt, 1980). When eventually approved as an alternative national history curriculum, the list also included the concepts of empathy and evidence (Steel, 1989). Britain's current national history curriculum has added the concepts of chronological understanding, diversity, significance, and interpretation, while dropping empathy from the list (National Curriculum for England, 2007).

The idea that history has a conceptual structure has become widely accepted by history educators. Peter Seixas (1996) developed a slightly modified version of the Schools History Project's structure, which has driven much of the discussion of historical thinking in the United States and Canada. Under Seixas' leadership, curriculum reformers in Canada adopted six "concepts of historical thinking" based on that structure for their Benchmarks of Historical Thinking Framework (Peck & Seixas, 2008; Seixas & Peck, 2004). Stéphane Lévesque's book *Thinking Historically* (2008) explores these concepts in greater depth. Other history educators have proposed still other variations (Limon, 2002; Van Sledright, 2011; Zarnowski, 2006).

This conceptual structure of history is subject to various interpretations. In this book, we propose a conceptual structure that we think provides a coherent and encompassing version of history's disciplinary concepts (Figure 2.1). We also have made a minor change in nomenclature. To distinguish between subject matter and disciplinary concepts, British history educators described the former as "first order" concepts and the latter as "second order" concepts. That terminology is still widely used (Lee, 2005; Van Sledright, 2011). We refer to the former as "substantive" and the latter as "disciplinary" concepts, as the term second order seems to relegate disciplinary thinking to second place. Disciplinary concepts are different from, but no less important than, substantive concepts, when constructing historical knowledge. We devote the remainder of this chapter to a brief examination of each of these underlying concepts of historical thinking.

Change and continuity	Many things were different afterward than they were before, although not everything, and some of the differences were greater than others.
Significance	Some changes had a bigger and more enduring impact than others.
Causation and agency	We can explain why things changed or did not change and the role individuals and groups played in bringing about change.
Time and chronology	Change happens over time, in a particular sequence of events, and requires different lengths of time.
Perspective analysis	People in the past saw changes that were happening from different points of view.
Accounts and evidence	Historical thinkers create written or graphic explanations of why things changed based on information from the past.

FIGURE 2.1 History's Disciplinary Concepts

Change and Continuity

The idea of change is fundamental to historical thinking. "The primary purpose of the study of history," historian Peter Stearns (1998a) has argued, "is to understand the phenomenon of change over time" (p. 281). It surely follows from this that history instruction in the classroom likewise should focus on teaching and learning about change. As Stearns adds, "the primary responsibility of history teachers is to use their subject to give students as full and sophisticated an understanding as possible of what change may involve and what problems must be handled in interpreting it" (p. 281). One of the purposes of this book is to explore the implications for teachers and students of thinking about history as change.

Change, in turn, implies continuity. However, continuity is not the absence of change, just as change is not the end of all that preceded it. As Frances Blow (2011) notes, "If students are to understand that the past is not dead and gone, and that a change is not an end to what went before, but that as Heraclitus says—'everything flows'—then they need to understand how historical change is about connections between things—change *from* and change *to*" (p. 55). While continuity is the opposite of change, few things remain for long exactly the same. It may be more useful to think of continuity as a dragging anchor that affects the rate and extent of change. "The ability to identify partial continuities even amid seemingly massive upheavals," Stearns (1998a) notes, "constitutes a vital component of the capacity to analyze change" (p. 282). In other words, one grasps the magnitude of a change by judging how much or how little the tug of old ways of doing things helped shape what happened.

The operative question about change is whether or how much did events or developments make institutions, cultural practices, or people's lives different than before? As change agents, events were not created equal. The Navigation Acts passed by Parliament in the seventeenth century were easily evaded and poorly enforced. They did not make much of a difference. The Tea Act of 1773 made a huge difference because it triggered a series of events in North America that culminated in the Declaration of Independence. Teaching about change means evaluating which events or developments made a difference and how much of a difference.

Viewing history as the study of change and continuity also helps students link the past to the present. Students today should be able "to connect the kinds of changes they experience in the society around them, with the better-defined instances of change available from the past. And they will need to understand how factors shaped in the past continue to influence the balance of change and continuity around them" Stearns noted (1998a, p. 282). We will argue that understanding change and continuity in human societies is a fundamental reason for studying history.

Significance

Most lists of key historical concepts include the idea of significance, although history educators do not necessarily agree about the meaning of the term. To Myra Zarnowski (2006), it is a property inherent either in a past event or in people's reaction to it. That is, an event is significant depending on how important it was to people at the time, how many people were affected by it and how deeply, and how long lasting its effects. By such an objective standard, the Holocaust was historically more significant than the Armenian genocide, although both atrocities would overshadow a terrorist bombing or the Ludlow Massacre as a subject meriting historical study. This objective standard is problematic, Seixas (1996) points out, as the significance of historical events "is ultimately tied to their relationship to the present" (p. 768). Thus, an event that may have touched relatively few people could have great significance to us if it has in some way impinged upon our lives.

We define significance here as a way to assess the past and present impact of change. In the first place, how big a difference did an action or event make then? Changes are more or less significant depending on how big a difference they made to the people who lived through them. Historians often refer to really significant events as turning points. Significance also depends on how changes in the past continue to affect us today. A highly significant event, such as the ratification of the US Constitution, made a difference then that continues to reverberate through time. The Articles of Confederation are another matter. They made a difference to eighteenth-century Americans, especially those who chafed under their limitations. They matter little to most of us today, except as a causal factor that led to the US Constitution. Our judgment about historical significance includes its relevance to our lives today.

What role should the concept of significance play in history instruction? The idea of significance, Seixas (1997) argues, should be included "as an explicit component of history instruction. … Indeed, it seems remarkable that curriculum documents do not make teaching about the question of historical significance a central focus of history instruction" (p. 27). The idea of significance probably has been the component of historical thinking least explicitly addressed in the classroom. It may be that students naively view everything that gets included in the curriculum or textbook as significant. However, fourth-grade teachers in a Greeley, Colorado elementary school found that their students added a reverse spin to the concept of significance. They ascribed historical significance by how life in the past differed from their own lives (Fertig, Rios-Alers, & Seilbach, 2005). In a classroom in which history teaching is conceptually focused, raising questions about significance is inescapable.

Significance as a component of causal thinking deserves more explicit attention in the classroom. Asking what things are significant or which are more significant than others is essential for explaining why things happened. In accounting for change over time, we necessarily give greater significance to some developments than to others. Likewise, in reading a historical text, we decide that some information is more significant than other information depending on the question we have posed. To make judgments about significance is to decide about what is relevant or not given their purpose for reading. Ascribing significance can also help students compose their own historical accounts. These more commonplace, operational dimensions of historical significance are the ones that students are most likely to encounter.

Causation and Agency

The concept of causation likewise is central to historical thinking. This idea, Stephen J. Thornton (1997) notes, lies "at the heart of historical understanding" (p. 11). We use the notion of causation to explain why things change or resist change. The concept of cause and effect is not unique to history, but historical thinking uses it in a distinctive way. In a scientist's laboratory, cause and effect can be replicated or proven by repeated observations. In history, causation is an attempt to explain the relationships between multiple antecedents that led to an event. In other words, causation is the key to historical interpretation. A historian's explanation about what caused something to happen is what interpretative history is all about.

While historical explanations can be complex and convoluted, the ideas of cause and consequence are concepts within the reach even of young students. Its most accessible form is the notion of human agency. That is, people are actors, or agents, who make things happen. Young students are most likely to understand causation in terms of people interacting with each other. The major agents for changes are those people who had the most power and influence at any given time. They end up becoming history's "famous people." One limitation of such reasoning is that these movers and shakers are most likely to be identified with the social elites of past societies rather than more anonymous and less privileged groups.

The challenge for teachers is to help students incorporate the idea of human agency while looking beyond individual human actors as explanations for change. One alternative is what Seixas (1996) called "a democratic sense of historical causation" (p. 777). He points to groups such as racial and ethnic minorities, women, and blue-collar workers that have assumed more important causal roles in recent historiography. They also figure more largely in history textbooks than they once did. Even more difficult to pin down are so-called structural causes, which may include economic depressions, the movement to cities, and immigration. Older students are more able and likely to attribute causation to such larger, underlying developments than younger students.

Time and Chronology

As historical change happens over time, the concept of time is as basic to history as space is to geography. It is expressed in various ways: as dates of when things happened, as the chronological sequence of events, and as the duration of historical periods or eras. Dates are the temporal hooks on which we hang events and the way we keep track of duration. Chronology establishes the temporal relationship between events. Chronological sequence also helps explain why they happened, as it is the nexus in which causation is located. As Martha Howell and Walter Prevenier (2001) note, "to produce a chronology of any kind is in some way to locate causality in chronology. That is, historians select information and order it chronologically precisely to demonstrate ... the causal relationships between events described" (p. 128).

The dimension of time that we probably pay the least attention to in the classroom is that of historical period and periodization. When we think of a curriculum in terms of content, we are most likely to see historical periods simply as convenient ways to compartmentalize a course. Periods identify the topics to which we must allocate classroom time. The Age of Exploration is followed by the Colonial Period, which comes before the American Revolution. In fact, periodization is also essential to the conceptual organization of a course or curriculum. "The categorization of change in roughly coherent segments is what distinguishes an analytical approach to the factor of time—what historians call *periodization*—from the memorized dates of a mindless chronology" (Stearns, 1993, p. 157). The labels that we give to periods also represent "colligatory" concepts (Hallden, 1997; Walsh, 1974) or ideas that we use to bring otherwise isolated facts together to see larger developments. That is, periodization is one way that we identify, describe, and organize instruction around major historical changes. For example, the period label "Renaissance" helps establish connections between innovations in art, music, and literature. We need to keep the significance of historical periods more clearly in mind and to make it more explicit to our students.

Perspective Analysis

The idea that the past is different from the present is critical to historical thinking. "The past is a foreign country: they do things differently there" David Lowenthal (1985, p. xvi) noted, quoting a line from L. P. Hartley's novel, *The Go-Between* (1953). People in the past also *thought* differently than we do. Attempting to understand how these people thought is what we call perspective analysis. Identifying multiple perspectives is implied in this term, as people in the past did not necessarily think alike. We also assume that the perspectives of people of the past can be accounted for, whether by individual experience, social position, economic interests, political loyalties, and religious or ideological identification. In that sense, perspective analysis is also a component of causal reasoning.

By analyzing historical perspectives, we are trying to reconstruct the point of view of someone or a group of people that we have never known, never observed, and may have only bits of evidence about. We need to acknowledge at the outset that this is problematic and open to question. We actually cannot get into the minds of other people, even people today who we may know well. Knowing what they say, how they respond to our questions, and how we see them behave takes us only part way there. Our understanding is necessarily incomplete. Trying to account for why that person held those views is even more problematic, even though we may have a document explaining it in their own words. We do not know what they chose not to say and kept to themselves. However, given these many degrees of uncertainty, we must still try to approximately reconstruct their perspective and to attempt to explain why they thought that way. Doing so serves several useful purposes.

In the first place, perspective analysis is a tool for critical historical reasoning. It gets us beyond the concepts of bias and detecting bias in historical accounts, which have little or no explanatory value. Bias, as Keith Jenkins (1991) points out, "makes sense only if it is used in opposition to unbiased; i.e. some sort of objectivity" (p. 37) that does not exist. That all people view the world from particular perspectives means that all people are biased. If everyone is biased, objectivity in the "unbiased" sense of the term is meaningless. Looking critically at a text does not mean detecting where it is not objective, but rather, trying to find the perspective from which it was written. Perspective analysis, in short, is where critical historical thinking begins.

Analyzing perspectives is also essential for causal analysis. Trying to understand how people thought or what motivated them helps us understand why things happened. Identifying multiple and different points of view helps us understand the dynamics of conflict. In the 1850s, northern free soil advocates and pro-slavery southern politicians held very different views about the expansion of slavery into the western territories. When these views clashed in public meetings, in Congress, and in the Kansas Territory, they produced political and sometimes violent physical conflicts. The sequence and increasing severity of these conflicts help us explain how conflicting political perspectives led to civil war.

Accounts and Evidence

History is not the past. It is what historians and other historical thinkers make of the past. This fundamental historical understanding is embodied in the notion of accounts. An account is a later interpretation of what happened during some past event or episode or era. It is usually a written narrative or exposition, but can also be an oral account, an enactment, or a film or other graphic presentation. Whether the account is persuasive or not depends upon the evidence the historian has collected to support her interpretation and how well she has used it. Evidence is not the sum of all information available, but that information on which an interpretative account is based.

That history is an interpretation of what happened in the past is one of the most fundamental concepts of history education. That history is, if not the whole past, at least fragmentary remains of the past, is a common student misconception. In a thinking-based history curriculum, this distinction should be made clear from the very outset of instruction.

In a historical thinking curriculum, instruction revolves around historical accounts that are based on evidence from the past. We speak of "evidence-based accounts," which typically means accounts grounded in primary sources. However, we need to distinguish between evidence and sources. "Evidence is not a category of objects or anything physical in the world," Rosalyn Ashby (2011) writes. "Sources yield evidence but only when they are used as such, to support a claim, back up a theory, establish a fact or to generate a hypothesis" (p. 140). This distinction is important lest students assume that primary sources have some magical quality that lends support to a historical argument. The question they must ask is whether a source does or does not provide evidence for that argument.

Sources that provide evidence necessarily occupy a central place in the classroom. Students who are engaged in historical inquiry by gleaning information from textbooks and secondary sources are using accounts that historians and others have constructed on the basis of evidence. The primary sources that they read closely and with a critical eye are sources of evidence that they can put to their own use. The object of their investigations is to produce their own historical accounts to better understand what happened in the past and why.

While the series of concepts outlined above represent important aspects of historical thinking, they also are interrelated in complex ways. These entwined and mutually supportive concepts represent what we consider to be the core of historical thinking. To return to Howard Gardner's analogy, these concepts are

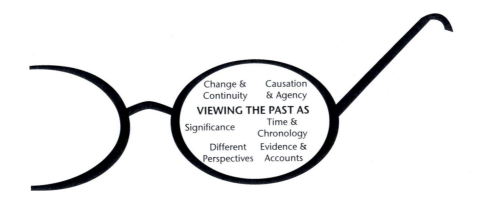

FIGURE 2.2 History's Multifocal Disciplinary Lens

essential components of history's disciplinary lens. To fine-tune the metaphor, the lens is like a multifocal eyeglass, with each viewing area bringing a different aspect of historical perspective into focus (Figure 2.2). Such a template should help students understand what we mean by historical thinking. We think it should be introduced early in the school year or semester and given a conspicuous place as a handout or a wall graphic in the history classroom.

References

Ashby, R. (2011). Understanding historical evidence: Teaching and learning challenges. In I. Davies (ed.) *Debates in history teaching* (pp. 137–147). London: Routledge.

Blow, F. (2011). "Everything flows and nothing stays:" How students make sense of the historical concepts of change, continuity and development. *Teaching History*, 145, 47–55.

Boddington, T. (1984). The Schools Council History 13–16 Project. *History and Social Science Teacher*, 19(3), 129–137.

Bruner, J. S. (1960). *The process of education*. Cambridge, MA: Harvard University Press.

Fertig, G., Rios-Alers, J., & Seilbach, K. (2005). What's important about the past: American fourth graders' interpretations of historical significance. *Educational Action Research*, 13(3), 435–451.

Gardner, H. (1999). *The disciplined mind: Beyond facts and standardized tests, the K-12 education that every child deserves*. New York, NY: Simon and Schuster.

Hallden, O. (1997). Conceptual change and the learning of history. *International Journal of Educational Research*, 27(3), 201–210.

Hartley, L. P. (1953). *The go-between*. London: Hamish Hamilton.

Howell, H. & Prevenier, W. (2001). *From reliable sources: An introduction to historical methods*. Ithaca, NY: Cornell University Press.

Jenkins, K. (1991). *Re-thinking history*. London: Routledge.

Lee P. (2005) Putting principles into practice: Understanding history. In M. S. Donovan & J. D. Bransford (eds.) *How students learn: History in the classroom* (pp. 31–78). Washington, DC: National Academies Press.

Lévesque, S. (2008). *Thinking historically: Educating students for the twenty-first century*. Toronto: University of Toronto Press.

Limon, M. (2002). Conceptual change in history. In M. Limon & L. Mason (eds.) *Reconsidering conceptual change* (pp. 259–289). Dordrecht, The Netherlands: Kluwer Academic Publishers.

Lowenthal, D. (1985). *The past is a foreign country*. New York, NY: Press Syndicate of the University of Cambridge.

National Curriculum for England. (2007). History. www.nc.uk.net

Peck, C. & Seixas, P. (2008). Benchmarks of historical thinking: First steps. *Canadian Journal of Education*, 31(4), 1015–1038.

Seixas, P. (1996). Conceptualizing the growth of historical understanding. In D. R. Olson & N. Torrance (eds.) *The handbook of education and human development: New models of learning, teaching and schooling* (pp. 765–783). Cambridge, MA and Oxford, UK: Blackwell Publishers.

Seixas, P. (1997). Teaching history in a changing world: Mapping the terrain of historical significance. *Social Education*, 61(1), 22–27.

Seixas, P. & Peck, C. (2004). Teaching historical thinking. In A. Sears & I. Wright (eds.) *Challenges and prospects for Canadian social studies* (pp. 109–117). Vancouver: Pacific Educational Press.

Shemilt, D. (1980). *History 13–16: Evaluation study.* Edinburgh: Holmes McDougall.

Stearns, P. N. (1998a). Goals in history teaching. In J. F. Voss & M. Carretero (eds.) *International review of history education, Vol. 2: Learning and reasoning in history* (pp. 281–293). London and Portland, OR: Woburn Press.

Stearns, P. N. (1993). *Meaning over memory: Recasting the teaching of culture and history.* Chapel Hill, NC: University of North Carolina Press.

Steel, D. (1989). The teaching of history - new history 1968-88. *History Resource,* 2 (3), 3-9.

Thornton, S. J. (1997). First-hand study: Teaching history for understanding. *Social Education,* 61(1), 11–12.

Van Sledright, B. (2011). *The challenge of rethinking history education: On practices, theories, and policy.* New York, NY: Routledge.

Walsh, W. H. (1974). Colligatory concepts in history. In P. Gardiner (ed.) *The philosophy of history* (pp. 127–144). Oxford: Oxford University Press.

Zarnowski, M. (2006). *Making sense of history: Using high-quality literature and hands-on experiences to build content knowledge.* New York, NY: Scholastic.

PART II

Historical Inquiry and Instructional Design

3
HISTORY AS INQUIRY

As teachers, we often think of inquiry as a pedagogical strategy. Will we lecture today or use an inquiry activity? What inquiry strategy will work best? While engaging students in historical inquiry involves pedagogical choices, we have concluded that whether or not to do inquiry is not one of them. We believe that we cannot have an effective history classroom without inquiry at its heart. History is by definition an inquiry into the past. "History, in short, is a problem-solving discipline," David Hackett Fischer (1970) notes, "A historian is someone (anyone) who asks an open-ended question about past events and answers it with selected facts which are arranged in the form of an explanatory paradigm." The point is not to teach history as a recitation of past events, to "go a-wandering in the dark forest of the past, gathering facts like nuts and berries" (pp. xv, 4). Inquiry must be an evidence-based investigation of what happened and its significance for us.

We have opted for the above alternative, as we consider history to be an interpretation of what happened in the past rather than a received body of knowledge to be learned and committed to memory. Historical inquiry, then, is an essential element in a history classroom and it involves questioning, investigating, understanding, and interpreting past development and events. Inquiry can be broadly designed to find out generally what happened at some time in the past or it can be targeted to particular events and issues. From this perspective, the question is not whether to involve students in historical inquiry, but how?

The most obvious characteristic of an inquiry classroom is a questioning stance by the teacher. Simply put, courses, units of instruction, even lessons should begin with a question, ether direct or implied. "I wonder why the colonists decided to declare independence and go it alone. Let's try to find out." That is a question-asking stance toward the study of the American Revolution. Or, to provide a sharper focus: "Why were the colonists and Parliament unable to find a middle ground on the question of taxation?" The instruction to follow would be guided by these questions and might well end by posing still other questions. "So, the Patriots signed the Declaration of Independence to protect their lives, property, and right to self-government. Does that mean they agreed on the kind of government best able to secure those rights?" That question, of course, would foreshadow the next unit of this US history course—the Confederation period and the making of the US Constitution.

A classroom in which questions are the order of the day provides students with a purpose for learning about the past. By answering the questions they ask together, students become a community of learners. Questions also will help them understand the tentative nature of historical knowledge. Whatever we conclude about an event or episode is tentative and provisional. We may approach it tomorrow from a different perspective or purpose or question, look at other evidence, and find different answers.

The pedagogy of inquiry includes a range of instructional possibilities. It can be done in various ways and at different levels. Inquiry can be an open-ended exploration or a carefully structured investigation pursuing answers to specific questions (Aulls & Shore, 2008; Banchi & Bell, 2008). Open-ended inquiry is a student-centered approach that is guided by student questions. It is the opposite of highly structured inquiry, which is directed by the teacher with students following along. What we describe as guided inquiry is a balance between the two, in which the teacher chooses the question, but students participate in deciding how the investigation should proceed (Martin-Hansen, 2002).

A strong case can be made for a teacher-guided approach to inquiry (Kuhlthau, Maniotes, & Caspari, 2007). In the first place, it keeps the teacher in control of instruction. Free-wheeling, open-ended inquiry that places students in charge is more difficult to implement or may even be intimidating. It can also present a problem in preparing students for externally designed common assessment. Students' questions can quickly range beyond a teacher's area of expertise or the materials available to address the questions (Alder, 1975; Aulls, 2008; Beyer, 1994). Moreover, minimally guided instruction, as Paul Kirschner, John Sweller, and Richard Clark (2006) argue, is less likely than more structured instruction to result in effective learning. The latter unduly emphasizes methods and processes at the expense of content learning. On the other hand, overly structured inquiry can result in what Lisa Martin-Hansen (2002) calls "cookbook lessons" or inquiry learning "in which students follow teacher directions to come up with a specific end point or product" (p. 37). Such activities do not lead to the kind of generative, open exploration that leads to important and multiple interpretations and perspectives (Hartzler-Miller, 2001). Effective classroom inquiry is guided by the questions teachers ask, the materials they provide the students, and the activities they create.

Inquiry Questions and Materials

The kinds of questions that teachers ask help to move students forward toward more sophisticated levels of thinking and deeper knowledge. Guided inquiry is managed to a large extent by the kind of questions teachers ask. Historical study is so big and broad that historical inquiry must have a well-defined sense of direction. This dictates that inquiry should at least be initiated by questions posed by the teacher. The teacher can also help keep the progression of questions closely aligned with the unit's Big Ideas and with the end-point assessments toward which students are preparing. They should provide students with a focus as they learn more about the topic, yet be sufficiently open ended to invite students to contribute their own ideas. By open ended, we mean more than questions that cannot be answered by a "right" answer or a yes or no response. They must also invite students to explore a range of possible answers and to allow them to construct their own individual interpretations. Questions that strike such a balance also are more likely to engage and maintain a student's interest. Did pioneers move westward because of lack of opportunities in the east or because of land companies promoting the riches of land and resources in the west, or for other reasons?

Teacher questions, at least initially, are likely to be derived from the Big Idea of a course or unit. A new topic or unit of instruction typically begins with broad, overarching questions. For Mr. Lyle, a teacher observed by Chauncey Monte-Sano (2011), the question "Why did the Civil War happen?" provided the unifying theme that tied together units on the US Constitution, the rise of the slavery issue, and the politics of sectionalism. How key developments within each unit contributed to the disruption of the Union became the basis for unit-level Big Questions. These overarching or Big Idea-related questions served as touchstones that students kept coming back to as they investigated individual topics.

Teachers' questions also help clarify student understandings, extend their observations, and help them become attentive to details and distinctions. That is, while keeping Big Idea-centered questions in mind, students also need to focus on more factual or event-level questions as inquiry gets underway. These are the kind of questions that journalists ask—who, what, when, and where (Kohlmeier, 2005; Mandell & Malone, 2007). Such factually oriented questions have the advantage of being familiar to students and typically can be answered in a straight-forward way. While both Big Questions and factual questions play a role in classroom inquiry, queries that bridge the two levels are equally critical.

In an inquiry classroom, the gap between broad, Big Questions and more narrow factual questions is bridged by what Grant Wiggins and Jay McTighe (2005) call Essential Questions. Such questions, they emphasize, "point to and highlight the Big Ideas. They serve as doorways through which learners explore the key concepts, themes, theories, issues, and problems that reside within the content, perhaps as yet unseen" (p. 106). They are the kind of questions that Jannet van Drie and Carla van Boxtel (2003) had in mind in noting that "Historical questions are often shaped by meta-concepts, as, for instance, causation, change, and continuity" (van Drie & van Boxtel, p. 91; Counsell, 2000). In history they necessarily are change-related questions. They allow teachers to shift their focus from one kind of thinking about change to another by the questions they pose. They also direct students toward the kind of information that is called for at a particular point in the unit or lesson. Students can use these questions to guide their investigation of and building knowledge about a historical topic. Teachers may want to provide students with the chart Essential Historical Questions (Table 3.1) as a handout or by posting it centrally in the classroom and referring to it frequently.

While Essential Questions can help guide students during instruction, they also can be posed at the outset of a unit. To scaffold student learning in their tenth-grade history class, Becky Coustan and Ed Abbott posed two Essential Questions at the very beginning of their immigration unit (McConachie, et al., 2006). The questions were these: (1) What are some of the forces pushing people away from their homelands and pulling people to immigrate to the United States? (2) What were the attitudes toward immigration in different historical periods? The questions helped students focus their reading and research by providing them with criteria for comparing four periods of immigration.

The middle-level or Essential Questions posed above helped Coustan and Abbott's students decide what factual information they needed to look for. They needed to know not only where the immigrants came from, but also about the conditions in those countries that spurred or caused emigration to other places. They needed to know something about the perspectives and aspirations of the individuals who became immigrants. The second question focused on the perspectives of the native-born Americans and the reception they gave the immigrants upon their arrival. In this instance, these middle-level questions provided the link between whatever larger ideas about the role of immigration in shaping American society that the teacher-authors had in mind and the stories of the particular immigrants the students were studying. Such Essential Questions help students make connections and see patterns that make the past meaningful.

TABLE 3.1 Essential Historical Questions

Essential questions	*Historical thinking*
• What changed or remained the same?	• Change and Continuity
• How important was it then and is it now?	• Significance
• Who or what made it happen?	• Causation and Agency
• When did it happen and in what sequence?	• Time and Chronology
• How did different people view it?	• Perspective Analysis
• What information about it is most relevant?	• Evidence
• What is the best way to present an explanation?	• Account

Teachers also manage inquiry by the information they make accessible to their students. This usually involves a textbook, at least at the beginning of an inquiry unit, but of course can expand to include a wide variety of teaching materials. Although textbooks have limitations, they also have the virtue of providing the class with a common and reasonably authoritative source of information. In an inquiry classroom, that should be their principal function. Thinking of textbooks as reference tools helps keep them from driving instruction. Inquiry classrooms also need to have an appropriate selection of resources other than the textbook available, including secondary and primary sources. While a scarcity of supplementary materials limits opportunities for inquiry, an overabundance of print or online information can be overwhelming. Teachers can solve both problems by bringing handouts, computer-based presentations, pre-screened Internet web-quests, and other resources into the classroom. Managing the information sources with which students will work is essential for guiding historical inquiry.

Inquiry Activities

Finally, teachers guide instruction by the activities they create to engage students in inquiry. Mark W. Aulls (2008) observed a teacher he identified only as Paul, and found that some strategies that Paul used were more effective than others in breaking down the barriers to inquiry learning. The most effective were project-type assignments that engaged students in finding, manipulating, and presenting information to the rest of the class. They involved students in research, in creating timelines and posters demonstrating what they had learned, and in presenting their work to the class. Such activities helped promote inquiry by allowing students to develop expertise and by reversing student and teacher roles. So did classroom situations in which the teacher took on some of the characteristics of a student by becoming learners in their own classrooms (Aulls, 2008, p. 40). Effective inquiry is likely to depend less on the depth or duration of the activity than on whether it involves students as engaged learners, and that may mean empowering them as the main providers of information from time to time. This requires teachers to act as facilitators of students' inquiry and learning, helping students to make their own learning visible. We think of inquiry classrooms as places where teachers spend less time standing and delivering in front of the class and more time being guides-on-the-side.

Student-centered discussions can be an effective way to get students engaged in their own learning. "All students need opportunities to talk about what they're learning: to test their ideas, reveal their assumptions, talk through the places where new knowledge clashes with ingrained belief," Mike Rose notes (1989, pp. 192–193). To engage students, discussions must go beyond recitation–type teacher dialogues with the most articulate students. For discussions to become what Louise B. Jennings and Heidi Mills (2009) call "a discourse of inquiry"

(p. 1583) they must be student-centered and collaborative. Quoting Ben Brabson, they explain that "'Most productive efforts are always collaborative. We stimulate each others thoughts that don't occur in ourselves and then try to get a perspective that is broader. You get feedback to fine tune your ideas with the knowledge of the group (leading to) an extended mind'" (p. 1588). As Maria Rodrigo concurs, in such discussions, students engage in a shared construction of knowledge, "construct[ing] their knowledge in the presence of others who are also engaged in the same task" (1994, p. 318).

This does not mean that teachers should abandon their traditional roles as instructors. Direct instruction retains an important place in inquiry learning. Mini-lectures, computer-facilitated presentations, and informal teacher talks are efficient ways to provide information that the entire class needs to know. Patricia A. Collins (1990) began an inquiry activity with an "overview lecture" in her Medieval Europe history unit. It provided a shared content that "allowed students' individual projects to fit into the whole, and their own writing was enriched because they could see relationships among aspects of the total Medieval culture" (p. 20). The point is not that teachers in inquiry classrooms should abdicate their responsibilities, but that students should also be encouraged to step into the role of "explainer."

Research Papers

While inquiry activities include a broad spectrum of assignments, the old standby in history classrooms is the research or term paper. Many teachers equate a traditional research paper with inquiry because it calls on students to ask a research question that they must answer. This practice remains alive, especially in the secondary grades, with students choosing a project to be researched in the library or, more likely today, in the computer lab. The students' task is to report on a topic of such-and-such length with some minimum number of reference citations. Not surprisingly, the research paper assignment is often justified as much for its value for teaching research and report writing as for its contribution to content learning. While research projects can play a useful role in inquiry classrooms, we offer the following caveat: assigning a research paper should be the icing on the cake, not the cake itself. That is, the assignment of a research paper does not transform traditional instruction into inquiry learning.

In fact, designing research paper assignments that allow students freedom of selection to provide motivation pose a dilemma. The aim of sustaining student interest by allowing them considerable latitude in choosing topics sometimes makes it hard for the topic to support the course or unit goals of instruction. If given too much freedom, their research projects may diverge in a dozen or more different directions, distracting students' attention from a unit's Big Ideas. The guidelines for authentic historical inquiry created by Stuart Foster and Charles Padgett (1999) address this issue. They suggest that teachers place thematic or chronological limits on students' freedom of choice. Focusing the research helps the teacher identify appropriate resources ahead of time and gives students a common topic for discussion about their research and for collaborative problem solving. The guidelines also provide good advice to teachers about helping students devise researchable questions, monitoring the progress of their research, and presenting the results of their study.

Before assigning a major research project, teachers need to do a cost-benefit analysis. Several weeks spent on a narrow topic or obscure historical character or event may have a lower yield in historical understanding than multiple, less in-depth inquiries. What students learn about research methods also may have limited transfer value, except for another similar historical topic. After all, research methods as well as knowledge are discipline specific. Also, research papers typically require students to work largely in isolation, despite all that we know about the value of collaborative learning. Except for giving the assignment and reviewing a draft or two, even the teacher may have little input into the student's learning process.

Project-based Activities

While research papers remain popular assignments, teachers also use a variety of alternatives to engage students in historical investigations. These are often referred to as project-based learning activities. They involve in-class as well as out-of-class investigations, group work, and alternatives to formal reports. For young students, projects consisting of a one-page poster, an illustrated drawing, or an alphabet-book promote useful learning. "The more I have explored Investigations with learners," Linda Hoyt (2002) writes about elementary school students, "the more convinced I have become of their power for synthesizing learning and teaching the craft of informational writing" (p. 289). Hoyt's model integrates inquiry with project planning, writing activities, and student self-assessment.

Inquiry activities that involve group work can be very effective. Unit-level inquiry typically can be divided into topics, with the topics assigned to student teams. For an inquiry project on the Holocaust, eighth-grade teachers in Middletown, PA combined their social studies and language arts classes and divided the students into small groups (Tunnell & Ammon, 1993). Each of the six groups worked on a separate topic. The teachers brought together a collection of trade books in the classroom for each topic. A similar project on the Civil War created by Eric Jensen and LeAnn Nickelsen (2008) divided students into six groups based on the War's critical turning points. Their task was to research that event and create a product to share what they had learned with the class. No matter how teachers choose to incorporate it, inquiry is a powerful instructional approach and one that is absolutely central to the history classroom.

The Classroom as Construction Site

When we think of the inquiry-based history classroom, the analogy of a construction site comes to mind. In that classroom, a new edifice is rising from the ground up, building on a foundation of prior knowledge. The students are workers busily engaged, using scaffoldings (a construction-site metaphor adopted by educators) that the teacher has provided to achieve various tasks. Books and Internet sites deliver a steady supply of factual building blocks. The workers sort through them, test them for reliability, select some, and reject others. Within the emerging structure, the conceptual floors rest on columns of factual knowledge. Cross-beams of generalization and interpretation bridge empty spaces to help tie the structure together. Periodically, teachers and learners pause to review the architect's blueprints and to assess their progress. When topped off as a finished historical account, the structure will stand as a new and creative synthesis. This image helps remind us that historical knowledge is a construct to be assembled in the classroom, not a prefabricated product packaged as a textbook chapter or a multi-media or lecture presentation.

In this classroom-as-construction-site, the participants have various roles. The teacher typically is the principal architect, general contractor, project manager, and foreperson. The students are the construction workers, although they may also have managerial roles. Occasionally they even serve as consulting architects. The roles open to them depend partly on the teacher's willingness to yield authority. Does she want students to do their own architectural drawings or find their own building materials? It also depends on the teacher's understanding of how historical knowledge is constructed. Is it one coherent structure to which each student contributes or is each student building his own historical truth? Is the goal one historical reality on which everyone agrees or is it many individual interpretations of the past?

The Cognitive Revolution allows teachers to answer those questions in different ways. The most conservative or "cognitivist" response is that the teachers' role is to help students understand the structure of the discipline's current or prevailing interpretations. That is, the class is not likely to deviate much from the design provided by the teacher-as-architect. Historical learning, in this sense, is a re-construction of the prevailing interpretation. The more radical or "constructivist" position assumes that each student's understanding of a past event is bound to be different, given each student's unique experiences and background knowledge. If history is individually constructed, each student will make sense of the past somewhat differently. That is not necessarily true, the "social constructivist" will reply. Knowledge is more likely to be socially constructed in collaboration within one's peer group rather than individually. Of course, any interpretation of the past must be evidence based and accountable to standards of historical investigation. Teachers have a range of choices about how they want students to construct knowledge.

Like real-life construction projects, knowledge building takes time and effort. It does not spring spontaneously from the pages of a textbook, a primary source, class activities, or a teacher's presentation. It includes a progression of steps in which students gather factual information, think critically about and evaluate what they are learning, see how the pieces are related, and bring them together in meaningful ways. Historical inquiry is not a linear sequence in which students proceed in lockstep fashion from beginning to end. Inquiry is reiterative and recursive, with students retracing their steps to learn new information in order to leap forward to new understanding. This is how the inquiry process works.

References

Alder, D. (1975). Why am I teaching history anyway? (And how should I teach it?). In G. M. Linden & M. T. Downey (eds.) *Teaching American history: Structured inquiry approaches* (pp. 1–9). Boulder, CO: ERIC Clearinghouse for Social Studies/Social Science Education and Social Science Education Consortium, Inc.

Aulls, M. W. (2008). Developing students' inquiry strategies: a case study of teaching history in the middle grades. In B. M. Shore, M. W. Aulls, & M. A. B. Delcourt (eds.) *Inquiry in education, Vol. II: Overcoming barriers to successful implementation* (pp. 1–49). New York and London: Lawrence Erlbaum Associates.

Aulls, M. W. & Shore, B. M. (2008). *Inquiry in education, Vol. I.* New York and Oxon: Lawrence Erlbaum Associates, Taylor and Francis Group.

Banchi, H. & Bell, R. (2008). The many levels of inquiry. *Science and Children*, 46(2), 26–29.

Beyer, B. K. (1994). Gone but not forgotten: Reflections on the new social studies movement. *Social Studies*, 85, 251–255.

Collins, P. J. (1990). Bridging the gap. In Nancie Atwell (ed.) *Coming to know: Writing to learn in the intermediate grades* (pp. 17–31). Portsmouth, NH: Heinemann.

Counsell, C. (2000). Historical knowledge and historical skills: A distracting dichotomy. In S. Capel, J. Lori Davison, J. Arthur, & J. Moss (series eds.), & J. Arthur & R. Philips (vol. eds.) *Issues in subject teaching series* (pp. 54–71). London: Routledge.

Fischer, D. H. (1970). *Historians' fallacies: Toward a logic of historical thought.* New York: Harper & Row, Publishers.

Foster, S. J. & Padgett, C. S. (1999) Authentic historical inquiry in the social studies classroom. *Clearing House*, 72(6), 357–363.

Hartzler-Miller, C. (2001). Making sense of "Best Practice" in teaching history. *Theory and Research in Social Education*, 29(4), 672–695.

Hoyt, L. (2002). *Make it real: Strategies for success with informational texts.* Portsmouth, NH: Heinemann.

Jennings, L. B. & Mills, H. (2009). Constructing a discourse of inquiry: Findings from a five-year ethnography at one elementary school. *Teachers College Record*, 111(7), 1583–1618.

Jensen, E. & Nickelsen, L. (2008). *Deeper learning: 7 powerful strategies for in-depth and longer-lasting learning.* Thousand Oaks, CA: Corwin Press.

Kirschner, P. A., Sweller, J., & Clark, R. E. (2006). Why minimal guidance during instruction does not work: An analysis of the failure of constructivist, discovery, problem-based, experiential, and inquiry-based teaching. *Educational Psychologist*, 41(2), 75–86.

Kohlmeier, J. (2005). The impact of having 9th graders "Do History." *History Teacher*, 38(4), 499–516.

Kuhlthau, C. C., Maniotes, L. K., & Caspari, A. K. (2007). *Guided inquiry: Learning in the 21st century*. Westport, CT: Libraries Unlimited.

Mandell, N. & Malone, B. (2007). *Thinking like a historian: Rethinking history instruction*. Madison, WI: Wisconsin Historical Society Press.

Martin-Hansen, L. (2002). Defining inquiry. *Science Teacher*, 69(2), 34–37.

McConachie, S., Hall, M., Resnick, L., Ravi, A. K., Bill, V. L., Bintz, J., & Taylor, J. A. (2006). Task, text, and talk. *Educational Leadership*, 64(2), 8–14.

Monte-Sano, C. (2011). Beyond reading comprehension and summary: Learning to read and write in history by focusing on evidence, perspective, and interpretation. *Curriculum Inquiry*, 41(2), 212–249.

Rodrigo, M. J. (1994). Discussion of chapters 10–12: Promoting narrative literacy and historical literacy. In M. Carretero & J. F. Voss (eds.) *Cognitive and instructional processes in history and the social sciences* (pp. 309–320). Hillsdale, NJ and Hove, UK: Lawrence Erlbaum Associates.

Rose, M. (1989). *Lives on the boundary*. New York: Viking Penguin.

Tunnell, G. & Ammon, J. (1993). Teaching the Holocaust through trade books. In M. O. Tunnell & R. Ammon (eds.) *The story of ourselves: Teaching history through children's literature* (pp. 115–134). Portsmouth, NH: Heinemann Educational Books, Inc.

Van Drie, J. & van Boxtel, C. (2003). Developing conceptual understanding through talk and mapping. *Teaching History*, 110, 27–31.

Wiggins, G. & McTighe, J. (2005). *Understanding by design* (expanded 2nd edn.). Upper Saddle River, NJ and Alexandria, VA: Pearson Education/Association for Supervision & Curriculum Development.

4

HISTORICAL KNOWLEDGE

Knowledge plays a central role in disciplinary literacy. While that may seem self-evident, it often gets overlooked in the discussion about disciplinary literacy. Literacy researchers and teacher educators have focused on methodology rather than content. They have deemphasized information and knowledge, Moje (2008) suspects, "in an attempt to avoid communicating the idea that knowledge should be simply transferred from teacher to learner." A fear of "reifying knowledge" may have led them to downplay its importance (p. 102). The professional literature about teaching historical thinking has also emphasized process rather than product. That may simply be the result of the larger role that literacy researchers and methods specialists have played in both conversations. While not absent from the discussion, content specialists have had relatively less input. In this chapter, we will try to bring the knowledge component of historical literacy more clearly into focus.

We must first explain what we mean by knowledge. In our research for this book, we looked for conceptual models that might help teachers distinguish between levels of understanding and kinds of knowledge. Perhaps the best known is Bloom's Taxonomy of Educational Objectives, created some sixty years ago by a committee chaired by Benjamin S. Bloom, and revised more recently (Anderson & Krathwohl, 2001; Bloom, Engelhart, Furst, Hill, and Krathwohl, 1956). We found other possible candidates by several scholars who had found the Bloom taxonomy lacking in various respects (Biggs & Collis, 1982; Jensen & Nickelsen, 2008; Marzano & Kendall, 2007). However, these are generic models that assume that thinking and knowing is the same across disciplines and academic subject areas. None of them speak explicitly to history teachers. If knowledge is discipline specific, as we believe it is, ways of understanding will vary from one subject area to another. Also, these constructs are more or less static models that mask the fluid, back and forth process of thinking through a problem or addressing a question. They provide little insight into the processes involved in the construction of historical knowledge in the classroom. To better describe what happens with students engaged in historical inquiry, we created the model below (Figure 4.1).

This concept web presents historical reasoning in two dimensions. The outlying cells represent the cognitive tasks involved. They include Activate Prior Learning, Collect Evidence, Analyze and Evaluate, Make Connections, Synthesize, and Apply Knowledge. The inner cell and the arrows leading from it as well as those connecting the outer cells demonstrate the process of historical inquiry. Historical inquiry in the classroom begins with a Big Question, which is the central cell in the diagram. The outer cells represent the cognitive tasks that are involved in answering it. They are arranged by levels of complexity moving counter clockwise from Activate Prior Learning to Apply Knowledge. We will examine each of these cognitive tasks at greater length in the chapters that follow.

The Activate Prior Learning and Collect Evidence cells represent the basic information that students need to begin to respond to the Big Question. Their investigation could begin at either cell, depending on whether students have prior knowledge about the topic. If they do, learning begins with recalling what they already know or think they know. It is likely to be learning either from a

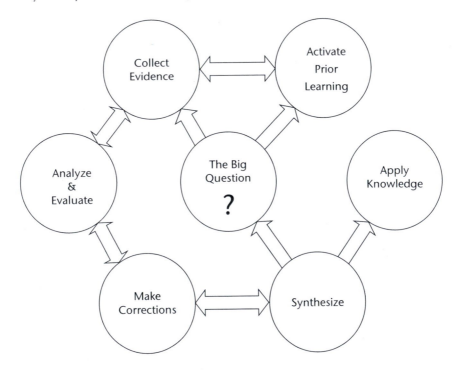

FIGURE 4.1 Classroom Historical Inquiry Concept Web

previous classroom encounter with history or from out-of-school experiences. This learning must be examined critically, as it may or may not be valid knowledge. Learning either continues or begins, if they lack such knowledge, by gathering evidence. The double arrow between the cells suggests that new information may trigger memories of prior learning.

The new information must be critically analyzed and evaluated, for its usefulness as evidence, as the Analyze and Evaluate cell indicates. A moment's thought may suggest that some information can be discarded as irrelevant to the Big Question or that it may not be sufficient to account for what students think happened in the past. That, in turn, may prompt students to follow the reverse arrow back to find new information. In fact, the reverse arrows from any of the succeeding cells may lead all the way back to a search for new information. The thinking represented by the Analyze and Evaluate cell, as we will see later, also involves comparison, textual and perspective analysis, and students otherwise sorting through what they have learned.

The Make Connections cell asks the students to think about how what they have learned is related. They may well have begun to do so already, as thinking is not necessarily a linear progression. The point is that making connections is the student's entrée to conceptual knowledge. As John Biggs (1999) notes, "what is separate in ignorance is connected in knowing" (p. 73). This cell also is a midway point between getting information and thinking about it critically and using it as evidence to create a synthesis. We do not think of the latter as an "ah–ha!" moment when the answers to questions magically fall into place. They are the result of patterns that emerge through the thoughtful connecting of different strands of information.

Nevertheless, Synthesis, the next cell in the diagram, is the near-term goal of historical learning. It is an interpretative historical account or argument that uses evidence to explain how and why something happened or changed. In an inquiry classroom, it is the best answer students can come up with to the Big Question posed at the outset of instruction. We call it near-term because it leaves the larger question, what does all this mean for us, unanswered.

The most complex task involved in historical inquiry is represented by the final cell, the application of what we have learned to better understand the world around us. "What does knowing about the past have to do with me?" Responding to that Essential Question is a step beyond creating a synthesis, as it asks us to relate that synthesis to still another set of understandings—to what we know about the present. It asks us to think about how the past and present are similar and different and how change in the past compares with change taking place today.

The Varieties of Knowledge

While the model in Figure 4.1 describes levels of reasoning and the process of inquiry, it does not account for the varieties of knowledge included in history instruction. As we are concerned here not only with *what* students should know about the past, but what *kinds* of knowledge are essential to historical understanding, we needed a categorical description of knowledge. A major fault of traditional pedagogy is its narrow focus on factual learning at the expense of other kinds of understanding. We settled on the four kinds of knowledge: factual, conceptual, procedural, and metacognitive, described by Lorin W. Anderson and David R. Krathwohl (2001). We took the liberty of arranging these in the diagram below (Figure 4.2), which includes the first three in the inner circles. They overlap, as factual, procedural, and conceptual knowledge have a reciprocal relationship in real learning situations. The overlap between the inner circles suggests these interactions. We include metacognitive knowledge as the background awareness that allows students to monitor other kinds of learning. While these categories are generic, the content is unique to the subject matter and its parent discipline.

Factual Knowledge

Much of what students initially learn about a new topic is factual learning. Facts are the essential building blocks of any structure of knowledge, including the specific

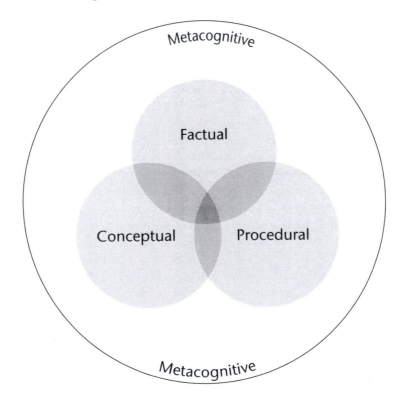

FIGURE 4.2 Varieties of Knowledge

information that experts believe represent important knowledge about a subject matter. They may consist of discrete bits of information or details, such as events, places, names, and dates. Or they may be terms that are central to the discipline or to a body of content. The latter, Anderson and Krathwohl (2001) explain, "are the basic language of the discipline—the shorthand used by experts to express what they know" (p. 45). For history, these include such disciplinary labels as "primary source" or "historical interpretation" and subject matter terms such as "imperialism" or "civil war." Traditional history teaching has often been criticized for relying too much on factual learning, especially of the names and dates variety. While that criticism is merited, it is not an indictment of factual knowledge.

History instruction has also been criticized for relying too much on memorization, which is usually associated with factual learning. The criticism, too, is warranted when memorization is all that happens to factual learning. However, memorization does play a role in building factual knowledge. Students who cannot remember what the Fugitive Slave Law or the Kansas–Nebraska Act were about will not be able to link them to the rise of the Republican Party. At the outset of learning, memorization requires time and repetition. In an integrated history/science unit on Antarctica, Graham Nuthall (2000) found that three to four repetitions were required for the students' new knowledge to be created in working memory and from there transferred to long-term memory. Memorization is an aid to understanding, but not a substitute for it. Experts assimilate and retrieve information by integrating facts into more complex knowledge. The point is that while factual learning and memorization are essential to historical understanding, they are not sufficient. Factual information needs to become part of more complex structures of conceptual knowledge.

Procedural Knowledge

Procedural knowledge is knowledge about how to do something. Recent history reform efforts have emphasized procedural knowledge, especially document and source analysis. We prefer to label procedures as "knowledge" rather than "skills," as they are domain-specific strategies rather than generic skills. "Because of the subject-specific nature of these procedures," Anderson and Krathwohl (2001) note, "knowledge of them also reflects specific disciplinary knowledge or specific disciplinary ways of thinking in contrast to general strategies for problem solving that can be applied across many disciplines" (p. 53). Procedural knowledge strategies in historical learning are different from critical thinking skills that may be applied to multiple subjects.

The procedural knowledge especially relevant to history education includes text and document analysis, identifying perspectives, and critical historical thinking. Each has received a good deal of attention in the literature of history/ social studies reform in recent years. The set of heuristics that Sam Wineburg (1991) created for analyzing primary sources is a notable case in point. So are

Isabelle L. Beck and Margaret G. McKeown's (2002) Questioning the Author (QTA) strategies, which are useful procedures for critiquing historical accounts. Virtually every historical document or account invites perspective analysis, as authors necessarily bring their own point of view to bear. Critical historical thinking helps students understand how perspectives help shape a document or a narrative. Collectively, procedural knowledge based in the discipline of history enables students engaged in conceptual learning to guard against making unfounded conclusions and unwarranted connections.

Procedural knowledge also includes a variety of strategies that help students organize and access what they are learning. These include knowing and being able to "do history," which can include weighing evidence, gathering source materials, comparing accounts, organizing events chronologically, explaining relationships, identifying cause–effect relationships, interpreting historical data, and forming an interpretation of events based on the scrutiny of sources. It is the kind of knowledge that state content standards have come to emphasize. For example, Colorado's history standards (Colorado Department of Education, 2010) includes the ability to use the historical method of inquiry to ask questions, evaluate primary and secondary sources, critically analyze and interpret data, and develop interpretations defended by evidence from a variety of primary and secondary sources. It also emphasizes analyzing the key concepts of continuity, change, and causation.

Conceptual Knowledge

Conceptual understanding builds upon factual knowledge, but it is more than the sum of factual learning. It consists of the patterns that one finds among those discrete facts. It may also include ideas or concepts, but it goes well beyond lists of abstract terms. Students may memorize concepts and learn their definitions, but still have a poorly organized understanding of the subject matter that they represent. Gaining a conceptual understanding of a topic involves making connections between things that one knows about it. "Yes, of course! That's why Parliament taxed the colonies," a student may say, connecting the Stamp Act of 1765 to the financial burdens of Britain's newly expanded empire. The growth of conceptual knowledge also helps guide the acquisition of new factual information because it helps us understand not only what we know, but also what we still need to know.

Conceptual understanding represents a significant step beyond factual learning and remembering by repetition. In the history classroom, James F. Voss and Jennifer Wiley (1997) note, "what and how much one remembers from the contents of a history chapter would define what the person has learned." Understanding, on the other hand, refers to "the knowledge a person has about the underlying conceptual relations of a given topic" (p. 256). Conceptual knowledge also involves making sense of what one is learning. To make sense of something is to make it meaningful. According to Robert S. Siegler (2001), "meaningful understanding implies [the] … ability to integrate facts, concepts, and procedures" (p. 201). Meaningful knowledge helps make past events resonate for us today. Knowing the problem that budget shortfalls lead to, a meaning-making student might say, "I can't say I blame Parliament for raising revenue to keep Britain from falling deeper into debt." Helping students construct conceptual knowledge is, we believe, the major challenge facing history teachers.

Conceptual knowledge has pay-offs both in the quality of student learning and in their ability to retrieve and use what they have learned. Generally speaking, the more individual facts someone learns about a subject, the more difficult it is to retrieve any one of them from memory. This so-called "fan effect" applies primarily to novice learners, while experts tend to be immune from its effects (Anderson, 1974; Anderson, & Reder, 1999; Bunting, Conway, & Heitz, 2004; Radvansky, 1999). "Since experts do not exhibit fan-effect difficulties in their own domains of expertise, it is likely that they integrate individual pieces of knowledge into organized structures that aid retrieval" (Spoehr, 1994, p. 76). Novices, on the other hand, lack the conceptual structures that provide cohesiveness and integration. Although we do not expect students to operate at expert levels in the domain of history, we must help them create as richly textured a network of conceptual understanding as possible.

Research on learning and memory has clearly demonstrated the connection between conceptual understanding and retention. The ability to retrieve information from memory, according to Fergus I. M. Craik and Robert S. Lockhart (1972), depends on the strength of memory traces or how deeply information has been processed. Depth of processing involves "enrichment" or "elaboration," so that after a vocabulary word, for example, is recognized, "it may trigger associations, images or stories on the basis of the subject's past experience with the word" (p. 675). These connectors, in turn, strengthen the memory trace. While strength of memory is different from the complex linkages of in-depth historical knowledge, the two do have striking similarities. In either case, the more elaborated the knowledge the more meaningful as well as memorable it is likely to be.

Metacognitive Knowledge

Metacognitive knowledge is knowledge about thinking and knowing, including an awareness of one's own cognition (Pintrich, 2002). "Metacognition is thinking about thinking; knowing what we know and what we don't know" (Callison, 1998, p. 43). Metacognition is a relative newcomer to the pantheon of knowledge that educators emphasize, reflecting the increased emphasis on students learning independently and assessing their own progress. Attending to students' metacognitive understanding is an important task facing history teachers, second only to helping them develop conceptual knowledge.

What is involved in metacognitive knowing? Introductions to the subject usually divide the task into three parts, which include self-knowledge, knowledge of the task at hand, and knowledge of strategies. The strategies usually are presented as a checklist that include having students talk about their thinking, keep a thinking journal, monitor comprehension by summarizing, and the like (Callison, 1998). While such generic activities may help students understand what metacognition involves, research strongly suggests that metacognitive knowledge is subject matter or domain specific (Baker, 2010; Donovan, Bransford, & Pellegrino, 1999; Pellegrino, 2008). History teachers engage students in thinking about their own learning almost routinely, especially through informal formative assessments. They ask students to check for comprehension when reading and to be aware of their own judgments and perspectives in written assignments. Teachers play an important role in their students' metacognitive thinking, as they are not likely to internalize such thinking and monitor their understanding on their own.

Reflection journals are useful for monitoring students' metacognitive understanding. Pamela Derson, a fourth-grade history teacher observed by Bruce Van Sledright and Lisa Frankes (2000), had her students keep a journal in which they identified the tasks they were engaged in each day. She established categories for three task phases, which included gathering information (G), organizing it (O), and presenting it to the class (P). The students' daily reflections about where they were in the learning process helped them understand how as well as what they were learning. The journals enabled Derson to monitor both their historical learning and their metacognitive awareness.

To summarize the above, successful history instruction involves students in a balanced approach to historical learning. At times they should direct much of their energy to factual learning, while other lessons might emphasize procedural understanding. Both may be happening at the same time. The historical-literacy focused classroom would differ from the stereotypical traditional classrooms by a much greater emphasis on conceptual learning. That is what gives factual and procedural knowledge their principal reason for being. The classroom also would attend to metacognitive understanding more systematically than most classrooms probably do today. Finally, we needed to address a third dimension of knowledge to which history educators have paid a great deal of attention. This is the dichotomy between depth vs. coverage or, as we prefer to state it, the choice between depth and breadth.

Depth vs. Coverage

Much of the criticism of traditional history instruction has focused on the coverage issue. "We are addicted to coverage," Fred M. Newmann (1988) wrote some thirty years ago. He added, "This addiction seems endemic in high schools—where it runs rampant, especially in history" (p. 346). Howard Gardner (2006) weighed in even more strongly in asserting that, "the greatest enemy of understanding is coverage. ... If you're determined to cover a lot of things, you are guaranteeing that most kids will not understand" (p. 148). Coverage involves more than cramming too much content into an already tight academic schedule. Producing a curriculum that is "a mile wide and half an inch deep" (Biggs, 1999, p. 45), it places a premium on rote learning, relies on low-level cognitive skills, and involves learning tasks that require little effort (Biggs, 2001; Rosie, 2000).

The inevitable result of coverage as an instructional goal is an over-emphasis on factual learning, with too little attention to conceptual understanding. Teaching history for coverage, as Peter Seixas (1996) points out, "proceeds too frequently on the implicit assumption that students learning more historical facts means understanding more history" (p. 777). Michael Wolfe and Susan Goldman (2005) agree that "history and social studies curricula rarely go beyond the presentation, memorization and recitation of other people's facts. … Well into early adolescence, students learn lists of facts and acquire minimal understanding of important causal principles and relations" (pp. 205, 472). Joseph Onosko (1991) found pressure for content coverage to be the single most important obstacle to the introduction of higher order thinking tasks in social studies classrooms.

Earlier generations of history educators in the United States devised what they hoped would be a solution to the coverage problem by restructuring the history curriculum. By dividing up the survey courses in US and world history, they hoped to limit the span of historical time covered at each grade level. This idea first surfaced in a 1944 joint report by the American Historical Association, the Mississippi Valley Historical Association (now the Organization of American Historians), and the National Council for the Social Studies (*American History in Schools and Colleges*, 1944). It recommended weighting the American history survey course toward the early periods in the elementary grades, emphasizing the 1776–1876 period in the junior high grades, and the post-Civil War period in high school. Curriculum restructuring has gained significant ground in the United States since the mid-1980s. Texas divided up its US survey course between junior high school and high school, with the Civil War as the watershed (Downey, 1988). California took this a step further with its 1987 History–Social Science Framework, which divided both the US and world history survey courses among three grades. Different periods of US history were recommended for grades 5, 8, and 11, with world history from grades 6, 7, and 10. The courses were linked together by introductory reviews that refreshed the students' memories about what they had previously learned and by conclusions that foreshadowed historical developments yet to come. Other states and school districts have adopted similar period-focused survey courses since then.

Despite these curriculum changes, teachers still complain that they have too much to cover in too little time. The high school teacher in S. G. Grant's (2005) case study is a good example: "Like every history teacher, Paula views time as her enemy." Grant observed, "Even under the best circumstances teachers find themselves with far more content to teach than the time to teach it" (p. 123). Why has restructuring failed to resolve the problem? It may be that just as work is said to expand to fill the time available, so does a factual-knowledge-based curriculum. We think there are two less facile reasons, each operating at different levels of the curriculum and both the unintended consequences of other school reforms. In the first place, the standards movement "has created the expectation that US educators will teach more content than is possible within the time currently available" (Marzano, 2004, p. 121), especially at the secondary school level. For high school teachers, the recent emphasis on high-stakes testing also has added to that pressure (van Hover & Heinecke, 2005). A study by David Gerwin and Francesco Visone (2006) of two sets of courses offered in a high school in New York state, one set tested by the state, the other consisting of elective courses, illustrates the dumbing-down impact of high-stakes testing. These researchers found "ambitious history teaching activities in the electives, and rote-learning emphasizing coverage and facts in the state-tested course" (p. 259). Additionally, in the elementary grades in the United States, high stakes testing in reading, mathematics, and science has shifted time away from history and social studies. Although elementary teachers may have less material to cover at any grade level, they have even less time in which to do it. The implication is either to further segment the history curriculum, as some have advocated, or to encourage teachers rethinking of the ways they teach the assigned content.

The solution that critics most commonly offer to the superficial coverage of content is in-depth teaching and learning. Newmann (1988) defined in-depth learning as "the sustained study of a given topic that leads students beyond superficial exposure to rich, complex understanding" (p. 346). Such a prescription for change usually requires teachers to make choices, as it "focuses on in-depth treatment of fewer topics rather than shallow coverage of many" (Yeager, 2005, p. 4). When the choice is between depth vs. coverage, teachers face an either/or situation. They cannot have it both ways. As a result, do teachers who wonder whether they have time to teach history as inquiry have a legitimate concern? We think the answer depends less on the limitations of time than on how the choice is presented.

Depth and Breadth

We need to rethink the problem posed by the depth vs. coverage alternative. In the first place, it is a false dichotomy. The antonym for depth is breadth, not coverage; and depth and breadth are not mutually exclusive (Pearcy & Duplass 2011; Seixas & Peck, 2004). Rephrasing the choice gives teachers the freedom to decide how to weight the choice between depth and breadth for any instructional unit or topic. Think of it as selecting any number of points along a continuum from greater depth to greater breadth. Secondly, the choice is not only about the focus or chronological sweep of instruction or how much content should be included. It is also a matter of the kind of conceptual reasoning in which students will be involved. That is, the choice involves not only what or how much students will learn, but also how they will learn it. To make such a choice, teachers must know how to differentiate between the two. What is involved in teaching for depth or for breadth, and how are they different?

First, let's take a look at depth. The term often is used to mean digging deeper into a topic or knowing more about something. This sometimes is called "post-holing" (Scheurman, 2008, p. 350). However, acquiring more factual knowledge about a topic does not necessarily result in greater depth of understanding. "Excessive and exclusive depth is no better than excessive coverage," Grant Wiggins and Jay McTighe (1998) observe, "that is, it isn't effective to focus on a single idea, digging deeper in the same hole" (p. 101). That is, it may only result in deeper holes of disconnected factual knowledge. In his definition of depth, Newmann (1988) was careful to include both the sustained study of a topic *and* exposure to rich, complex understanding. We prefer his understanding of depth, especially its emphasis on understanding, to that of digging deeper holes.

The difference between factual post-holing and teaching for conceptual depth was demonstrated by two high school teachers whom Bruce Van Sledright (1997) observed. During her eight-week unit on Colonial America, Nancy Kerwin confronted her students with "a detailed stream of facts and textbook interpretation. … In many ways she appeared to be postholing [sic], the practice of focusing in depth on a particular aspect of history for an extended time" (p. 38). The second teacher, Bob Jansen, taught the same unit using a different approach to depth, "one constructed around a disciplinary matrix that considered regional colonial development in the context of changing economics, politics, and sociocultural life" (p. 38). His students constructed a wall chart that allowed them to compare similarities and differences between colonial life in New England, the Middle Colonies, and the Southern Colonies, and to propose explanations for these different regional ways of life. Jansen spent fewer weeks on the unit than Kerwin, but provided his students with richer and more meaningful and conceptually integrated historical learning. By engaging his students in analytical and causal thinking as well as factual learning, he helped them arrive at Newmann's rich and complex understanding.

By breadth we do not mean treating a topic in a quick or superficial way. The weakness of the coverage approach was that it resulted in factual learning that merely skimmed the surface. Instead, we think of breadth in terms of the conceptual demands of a learning task. A narrative is conceptually less complex than an expository synthesis. A student who weaves events together in a story treats them in less depth than one who makes a well-reasoned explanation or argument. While the student's story provides a thin veneer rather than rich and complex learning, it meets the minimum requirement of historical understanding. It is not the rote, factual, quickly forgotten learning of the coverage syndrome, even though it may permit a broader survey of a period and require less classroom time than conceptually more demanding learning. It is a question of the kind of knowledge that results, not whether it has value at all.

Approaches to Teaching Breadth

There may be other useful ways to think about breadth. As Peter Lee (2005) has suggested, teachers could provide breadth by teaching an overview of a course at the very beginning of instruction. "To provide something students can use and think about, we may need to teach a big picture quite quickly, in a matter of two or three weeks, and keep coming back to it. Such a framework focuses on large-scale patterns of change, encompassing students' in-depth studies so they are not simply isolated topics" (p. 68). It would provide a broader context within which individual topics would be situated. Another proposed alternative is to have students preview the textbook at the beginning of the year. Karen Garner-Miller (2007), a high school teacher, suggested having pairs or small groups of students prepare reports on individual chapters, addressing the question: What's old and what's new? Using a two-column chart, they could list the chapter's primary content topics and concepts as to whether they are new or have been encountered in past classes. Each group then leads the class on a "chapter walk," pointing out what is familiar and new in the chapter.

Building on Lee's idea, during a four-week summer session, Kelly Long began her university-level US History survey course by exploring Big Questions about US history after Reconstruction. She began by asking students to write a one-page narrative of US history from Reconstruction to the present. Thereafter, she drew a timeline and projected it on a document projector, with 1877 at one end and the current date at the other end and then asked students to tell her the big events that belonged in a narrative of US history spanning this period. After writing down student suggestions, she asked them to assess the types of events or categories they illuminated, indicating whether they reflected political, economic, social/cultural, or international aspects of history. She then drew timelines that represented those categories of analysis above and below the major timeline. This allowed her to show intersections between the various categories while offering breadth-based overview of the sweep of US history. As the course progressed, Long engaged students in more in-depth study of units within that longer historical chronology. Offering an overview of the breadth of history tapped in to students' prior learning and from an early point in the course directed their attention to change, continuity, and causation.

Teachers in the Historical Literacy Partnership also engaged students in several topics at a broader content level that resulted in useful student learning. Shelley Reffner (HLP) addressed the need for depth and breadth by using a compare and contrast strategy in her ninth grade unit on the Middle Ages in Europe. Examining a few case studies in detail allowed her to shorten the unit, and later to use it to compare Western and Eastern Medieval empires. Her students ended up with a large number of examples of Medieval life, while they also benefitted from exploring the contrasts between cultures. When a topic has relevance to what is happening in the world today, Carin Barrett (HLP) provides breadth by comparing past and present-day situations. For example, she had students compare the presidential speeches of Herbert Hoover and Franklin Delano Roosevelt to the campaign pledges of more recent presidential candidates.

Liz Melahn (HLP) provided breadth by allowing students to select individual books on which they became subject "experts." She provided structured reading time after which students shared about a topic from a book they selected from a classroom set. Melahn provided a wall chart that gave her students reading targets so that they would be prepared to contribute to the class discussion by a designated time. In reporting about their books, students provided historical breadth as they shared their knowledge of the historical topic treated in the book.

How a teacher makes that choice between depth and breadth will likely depend on her interests and knowledge and the needs of her students. Let us return briefly to Paula, the teacher who S. G. Grant described as struggling against the clock and calendar while negotiating the competing demands of a state test, the state curriculum's scope and sequence, the needs of her students, and her own academic interests (Grant, 2005). Within this negotiation, she made decisions about depth and breadth. She changed the pace of instruction to place more emphasis on topics her students found engaging, backed off others that she thought the state curriculum overemphasized, and highlighted themes such as nationalism that she found interesting. All the while, she remained attuned to the factual knowledge that her students needed to know for a good performance on the state test.

Whether to teach for depth or breadth of understanding has obvious implications for instructional planning. It is not an either-or choice for teachers, but one of weighting instruction in favor of one or the other. The more in-depth an investigation, the greater is the likelihood that it will require more classroom time. The intellectual work required of in-depth learning is likely to be more demanding than that for breadth. Instruction that emphasizes breadth can be either more inclusive in terms of content or require less classroom time. There is no optimal balance. A teacher may select one unit for in-depth treatment and another for more surface-level teaching and learning. Making such choices reinforces the autonomy of teachers as curriculum planners and developers.

References

American History in Schools and Colleges (1944). Report of the Committee on American History in Schools and Colleges of the American Historical Association, the Mississippi Valley Historical Association, the National Council for the Social Studies. New York: Macmillan.

Anderson, J. R. (1974). Retrieval of propositional information from long-term memory. *Cognitive Psychology*, 6, 451–474.

Anderson, J. R. & Reder, L. M. (1999). The fan effect: New results and new theories. *Journal of Experimental Psychology*, 128(2), 186–197.

Anderson, L. W. & Krathwohl, D. R. (eds.) (2001). *A taxonomy for learning, teaching and assessing: A revision of Bloom's Taxonomy of educational objectives* (complete edition). New York, NY: Longman.

Baker, L. (2010). Metacognition. In P. Peterson, E. Baker, & B. McGaw (eds.) *International Encyclopedia of Education, Vol. 5* (pp. 204–209). Amsterdam: Academic Press.

Beck, I. L. & McKeown, M. G. (2002). Questioning the author: Making sense of social studies. *Educational Leadership*, 60(4), 44–47.

Biggs, J. (1999). *Teaching for quality learning at university: What the student does.* Buckingham, UK: SRHE and Open University Press.

Biggs, J. (2001). Enhancing learning: A matter of style or approach? In R. J. Sternberg & L., Zhang (eds.) *Perspectives on thinking, learning, and cognitive styles* (pp. 73–102). Mahwah, NJ and London: Lawrence Erlbaum Associates.

Biggs, J. B. & Collis, K. F. (1982). *Evaluating the quality of learning: The SOLO Taxonomy.* New York, NY: Academic Press, Inc.

Bloom, B. S., Engelhart, M. D., Furst, E. J., Hill, W. H., & Krathwohl, D. R. (1956). *Taxonomy of educational objectives: The classification of educational goals. Handbook I Cognitive Domain.* New York, NY: David McKay Company, Inc.

Bunting, M.F., Conway, A. R. A., & Heitz, R. P. (2004). Individual differences in the fan effect and working memory capacity. *Journal of Memory and Language*, 51, 604–622.

Callison, D. (1998). Metacognition. *School Library Media Activities Monthly*, 14(7), 43–44.

Colorado Department of Education. (2010). http://www.cde.state.co.us/standardsandinstruction/index.asp

Craik, F. I. M. & Lockhart, R. S. (1972). Levels of processing: A framework for memory research. *Journal of Verbal Learning and Verbal Behavior*, 11, 671–684.

Donovan, M. S., Bransford, J. D., & Pellegrino, J. W. (eds.) (1999). *How people learn: Bridging research and practice.* Washington, DC: National Academy Press.

Downey, M. T. (1988). Reforming the history curriculum. In B. R. Gifford (ed.). *History in the schools: What shall we teach?* (pp. 198–213). New York: Macmillan Publishing.

Gardner, H. (2006). *The development and education of the mind: The selected works of Howard Gardner.* London and New York, NY: Routledge Taylor and Francis.

Garner-Miller, K. (2007). Playful textbook previews: Letting go of familiar mustache monologues. *Journal of Adolescent and Adult Literacy*, 50(4), 284–288.

Gerwin, D. & Visone, F. (2006). The freedom to teach: Contrasting history teaching in elective and state-tested courses. *Theory and Research in Social Education*, 34(2), 259–282.

Grant, S. G. (2005). More journey than end: A case study of ambitious teaching. In E. A. Yeager & O. L. Davis, Jr. (eds.) *Wise social studies teaching in an age of high-stakes testing: Essays on classroom practices and possibilities* (pp. 117–130). Greenwich, CT: Information Age Publishing.

Jensen, E. & Nickelsen, L. (2008). *Deeper learning: 7 powerful strategies for in-depth and longer-lasting learning.* Thousand Oaks, CA: Corwin Press.

Lee P. (2005) Putting principles into practice: Understanding history. In M. S. Donovan & J. D. Bransford (eds.) *How students learn: History in the classroom* (pp. 31–78). Washington, DC: National Academies Press.

Marzano, R. J. (2004). *Building background knowledge for academic achievement.* Alexandria, VA: Association for Supervision and Curriculum Development.

Marzano, R. J. and Kendall, J. S. (2007). *The new taxonomy of educational objectives* (2nd ed.). Thousand Oaks, CA: Corwin Press.

Moje, E. B. (2008). Foregrounding the disciplines in secondary literacy teaching and learning: A call for change. *Journal of Adolescent & Adult Literacy*, 52(2), 96–107.

Newmann, F. W. (1988). Can depth replace coverage in the high school curriculum? *Phi Delta Kappan*, 69(5), 345–348.

Nuthall, G. (2000). The role of memory in the acquisition and retention of knowledge in science and social studies units. *Cognition and Instruction*, 18(1), 83–139.

Onosko, J. J. (1991). Barriers to the promotion of higher order thinking in social studies. *Theory and Research in Social Education*, 19(4), 341–366.

Pearcy, M. & Duplass, J. A. (2011). Teaching history: Strategies for dealing with breadth and depth in the standards and accountability age. *Social Studies*, 102(3), 110–116.

Pellegrino, A. M. (2008). The manifestation of critical thinking and metacognition in secondary American history students through the implementation of lesson plans and activities consistent with historical thinking skills. Doctoral dissertation, Florida State University. *Dissertation Abstracts: International Section A: Humanities and Social Sciences*, 68(9-A), 3793.

Pintrich, P. R. (2002). The role of metacognitive knowledge in learning, teaching, and assessing. *Theory Into Practice*, 41(4), 219–225.

Radvansky, G.A. (1999). The fan effect: a tale of two theories. *Journal of Experimental Psychology*, 128(2), 198-206.

Rosie, A. (2000). Deep learning. *Active Learning In Higher Education*, 1(1), 45–59.

Scheurman, G. (2008). Poetry and postholes: Making history instruction deeper and more personal. *Social Education*, 72(7), 350–353.

Seixas, P. (1996). Conceptualizing the growth of historical understanding. In D. R. Olson & N. Torrance (eds.). *The handbook of education and human development: New models of learning, teaching and schooling* (pp. 165–783). Cambridge, MA and Oxford, UK: Blackwell Publishers.

Seixas, P. & Peck, C. (2004). Teaching historical thinking. In A. Sears & I. Wright (eds.) *Challenges and prospects for Canadian social studies* (pp. 109–117). Vancouver: Pacific Educational Press.

Siegler, R. S. (2001). Cognition, instruction and the quest for meaning. In S. M. Carver & D. Klahr (eds.) *Cognition and instruction: Twenty-five years of progress* (pp. 195-204). Mahway, NJ: Lawrence Erlbaum Associates.

Spoehr, K. T. (1994). Enhancing the acquisition of conceptual structures through hypermedia. In K. McGilly (ed.) *Classroom lessons: Integrating cognitive theory and classroom practice* (pp. 75–101). Cambridge, MA and London: MIT Press.

Van Hover, S. D. & Heinecke, W. F. (2005). The impact of accountability reform on the "Wise Practice" of secondary history teachers: The Virginia experience. In E. A. Yeager & O. L. Davis (eds.) *Wise practice in the teaching and learning of history in an era of high stakes testing* (pp. 89–116). Greenwich, CT: Information Age Publishing.

Van Sledright, B. (1997). Can more be less? The depth-breadth dilemma in teaching American history. *Social Education*, 61(1), 38–41.

Van Sledright, B. & Frankes, L. (2000). Concept-and strategic-knowledge development in historical study: A comparative exploration in tow fourth-grade classrooms. *Cognition and Instruction*, 18(2), 239–283.

Voss, J. F. & Wiley, J. (1997). Developing understanding while writing essays in history. *International Journal of Educational Research*, 27(3), 255–265.

Wiggins, G. & McTighe, J. (1998). *Understanding by design*. Alexandria, VA: Association for Supervision and Curriculum Development.

Wineburg, S. (1991). Historical problem solving: A study of the cognitive processes used in the evaluation of documentary and pictorial evidence. *Journal of Educational Psychology*, 83(1), 73–87.

Wolfe, M. B. W. & Goldman, S. R. (2005). Relations between adolescents' text processing and reasoning. *Cognition and Instruction*, 23(4), 467–502.

Yeager, E. A. (2005). Introduction: The "wisdom of practice" in the challenging context of standards and high-stakes testing. In E. A. Yeager & O. L. Davis, Jr., *Wise social studies teaching in an age of high-stakes testing: Essays on classroom practices and possibilities.* (pp. 1–9). Greenwich, CT: Information Age Publishing.

5

PLAN INSTRUCTION

Planning for instruction is a critically important dimension of teaching. Of course, effective instruction involves a good deal more than that. The teacher's depth of content knowledge is important, as is having a broad repertoire of teaching strategies. Classroom experience helps, as teachers, too, learn by trial and error. Spontaneity plays a role, especially being able to seize upon a teachable moment and pursue it. Yet, few things are as important as thoughtful and purposeful planning. What often appears to an observer as inspired teaching is actually the product of planning that took place well before instruction began.

Some of the teachers with whom we talk see themselves more as deliverers than as planners of instruction. That is understandable in this age of national standards and state curricular guidelines. Some school districts in the United States even impose pacing guides that specify what history teachers should teach on a given day. We think that micromanagement is short sighted on the part of school administrators. While aware that many decisions about what to teach and how it is to be evaluated are made beyond the classroom, teachers can, should, and still do play a critical role in designing content instruction. It is a role that Stephen Thornton (1991) called a "gatekeeping" function, through which teachers make day-to-day decisions about what is to be taught and how they will teach it. It helps account for the fact that teachers in the same school with the same state guidelines sometimes make widely different instructional decisions (Grant, 2003).

History and social studies teachers are in a better position than teachers of many other subjects to decide what is to be included in instruction. In a survey conducted in the 1990s, Pamela Grossman and Susan Stodolsky (1995) found that secondary social studies teachers had a greater sense of curricular autonomy than either mathematics or foreign language teachers. They felt freer to deviate from externally imposed notions of scope and sequence and were less likely to feel pressure from other members of their departments to coordinate course content. We think that is still true, partly because of the nature of the history curriculum. The history curriculum is more narrative-like and less taxonomic than mathematics, foreign language, science, and even some other social studies subjects. This gives history teachers more latitude about what content to emphasize and what to spend less time with.

Making choices about what to emphasize is a history teacher's professional responsibility. In the first place, content standards, history textbooks, and many curriculum guides prescribe both more and less subject matter content than teachers can use. They tend to include too many topics for in-depth learning and provide too little information. Responsible teachers have to pick and choose what to give a broad brush to and what to investigate in depth. In doing so, they need to play to their own strengths and passions as well as to the perceived needs and interests of their students. Curriculum guides, as Jeffrey Nokes (2013) observes, "typically leave much room for interpretation as history teachers determine the depth of coverage." While a state standard might call for teaching about the causes and consequences of the Crusades, "the world history teacher decides whether the students spend 20 minutes or six days working toward that standard" (p. 195). Whether or not to participate in instructional planning is not an option for history teachers. To do otherwise violates everything that we know about effective teaching and how students learn.

The instructional planning approach that we recommend, which is widely used in school districts in the United States, is Grant Wiggins and Jay McTighe's (1998) Understanding by Design (UbD). It is a goals-driven approach based on a systems model developed more than thirty years ago (Dick & Carey, 1978). It is different from traditional instructional design by its emphasis on establishing goals and on creating assessments prior to planning instruction. It often is described as a Backward Design approach because of the priority given to assessment planning (Figure 5.1).

Setting Instructional Goals

In the systems model of instructional design, planning begins with determining needs of students and setting goals for instruction. In K–12 education in the United States, needs assessment has been pre-empted by district decisions about scope and sequence. Presumably students "need" United States history at grades 5, 8, and 11 or wherever a state or school district places it. Setting goals of instruction is a shared responsibility in which teachers and district decision-makers both have a say. By goals we mean academic goals or specific learning outcomes. The question is what do we want students to know or be able to do as a result of instruction? Teachers help answer that question by deciding what content and procedural knowledge to emphasize, what to leave out, and how to

Drivetrain sequence for traditional instruction

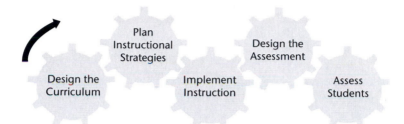

Drivetrain sequence for goals-driven instruction

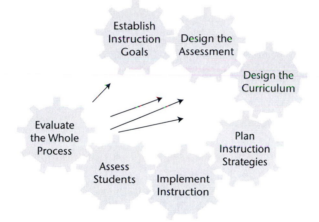

FIGURE 5.1 Drivetrain Sequence

engage their students. In this model, everything else—creating assessments, choosing instructional strategies, selecting materials—follows from the definition of goals.

The knowledge most worth knowing about any school subject, Wiggins and McTighe (2005) argue, are its Big Ideas. A Big Idea, they point out, "is not just another fact or a vague abstraction but a conceptual tool for sharpening thinking, connecting discrepant pieces of knowledge, and equipping learners for transferable applications" (p. 70). The Big Ideas of content instruction, John T. Guthrie (2003) notes, provide the conceptual knowledge structures and relationships that students are most likely to remember. Science's Big Ideas include physics' model of the atom, chemistry's periodic law, astronomy's big bang theory, geology's plate tectonics model, and biology's theory of evolution (Wynn & Wiggins,

1997, cited in Wiggins & McTighe, 2005, pp. 66–67). These are foundational understandings about the physical and natural world that are the result of years of scientific investigations and theory building. While the Big Ideas of history are analogous to those of physics or chemistry, they come from a very different kind of discipline.

History's Big Ideas are different because of the interpretative nature of this discipline. Its biggest idea of all is that history is not the past. It is what people today make of the past. This means that history's Big Ideas are subject to change. Historical thinkers may agree that Abraham Lincoln and Franklin D. Roosevelt were exceptional presidents. But their judgments or Big Ideas about these major characters in the past may be quite different and may change over time. History's Big Ideas are malleable, are likely to be transient, and frequently are controversial.

What constitutes a big historical idea? It is a statement that characterizes a period or development in the past, but not one so vast as to be meaningless. A Big Idea, Wiggins and McTighe caution, is "not necessarily vast in the sense of a vague phrase covering lots of content" (p. 67). It is big in the sense of helping learners connect many of the dots of factual content. Big Ideas are "'conceptual Velcro'—they help the facts and skills stick together and stick in our minds!" (p. 66). The idea that "Americans are freedom loving people" is too amorphous to be useful as a Big Idea. That Manifest Destiny was a driving force behind American expansion in the nineteenth century is a more manageable Big Idea. We think that Big Ideas should be arguable, allowing students to push for or against something. Making an argument also helps students organize and synthesize information, which we will explore in a later chapter. Beyond that, we think that the most useful Big Ideas in a history classroom include two kinds or levels of statements.

The first are the large, overarching ideas that provide unifying themes for a course. The idea that the United States is a nation of immigrants is a classic example. The implication is not only that the nation was populated by immigrants and their descendants, but also that they played key roles at different times in shaping its economic, political, and cultural institutions. In this sense, immigration as a Big Idea or course theme has a causal or explanatory function. Others simply may be generalizations that warrant investigation. A district-level curriculum guide in New York State posed the following overarching question for its fourth-grade history course: "Has the history of New York State been a history of progress for all?" Each unit in the course broke it down into a topic specific question, such as "Did colonization of New York state result in progress for all?" (Libresco, 2005). Both kinds of broad statements serve a useful purpose in getting students to take a position.

The second are unit-level Big Ideas. While overarching ideas at the course level are useful, helping to provide a thread of continuity, Big Ideas at the unit-level are absolutely essential. They help students make sense of the blocks of content into which history courses are traditionally organized. History courses, at least in the United States, typically are organized chronologically into units of instruction. Often, a unit title itself embodies a Big Idea, such as the Age of Exploration or the Progressive Era. The Agricultural Revolution, the Rise of European Nation States, or Western Imperialism would be equivalents for a world history course (Figure 5.2). Whatever periodization scheme a district guide, set of standards, or textbook uses, it is a fertile soil for Big Ideas.

Where else do teachers find Big Ideas? Wiggins and McTighe (2005) recommend looking carefully at state standards. "Many of them either state or imply Big Ideas, especially in the descriptive text that precedes the list of standards" (p. 73). School district guides may also provide either Big Ideas or Big Questions derived from Big Ideas. Teachers also can look to their own classroom resources. Textbooks are a good source for Big Ideas. The historical periods into which textbooks typically are divided are not just arbitrary divisions of time. They often are labels, which William H. Walsh (1974) called "colligatory concepts," which are ideas historians use to cluster events to describe "movements or processes or developments in history" (p. 129). A period label such as the Industrial Revolution, the Enlightenment or the Fall of the Roman Empire is a higher order concept "that implies 'change,' or adds a 'direction' or makes single events 'intelligible'" (Hallden, 1998, p. 135; van Boxtel & van Rijn, 2006). Historians refer to the period in US history from 1820 to 1840 as the "Age of Jackson" to indicate that significant political changes took place then and that Jackson and the party he represented were agents of those changes. Significant changes and what caused them are prime candidates for unit-level Big Ideas. The question remains, how do teachers organize instruction around them?

The Big Idea provides the rationale for deciding what to emphasize and for selecting the content of the unit of instruction. Let's assume that a teacher is planning an eighth-grade unit on the coming of the Civil War. Her district guide states that students will understand causes of this war. She decides to focus on the Big Idea that slavery was its most important cause. This means that she must provide her students multiple opportunities to explore the connection between slavery and the political conflicts of that period. She will allocate a class period each to such topics as the Mexican War acquisitions and Wilmot's Proviso, the Compromise of 1850, and the resistance to the Fugitive Slave Act and the rise of the Republican Party. However, she is quite aware that slavery was not the only divisive issue of the time. So, she will weave secondary themes into the unit, including sectional controversy over states' rights and the role of the federal government, disputes over tariffs and internal improvement policies, as well as cultural differences that divided North and South.

Announcing the Big Idea at the outset rather than arriving there at the conclusion of instruction may seem counterintuitive. It may also seem inconsistent with history as inquiry. Providing students with a general idea about a topic in order to learn more about it is what Ola Hallden (1994) calls the learning paradox. "There seems to be a genuine paradox here if we see learning as being a linear

* COLONIZATION
  While religion was a factor in the settlement of some American colonies, most colonists came in search of economic opportunities.

* COLONIAL AMERICA
  The British colonies in North America developed into three distinctive geographic regions, with different economies, religious traditions, and political interests.

* COMING OF THE AMERICAN REVOLUTION
  Although the Declaration of Independence triggered the American Revolution, the real revolution had already occurred as a change in the hearts and minds of once loyal British subjects.

* THE AGE OF JACKSON
  As a party leader and president, Andrew Jackson was more the product than the cause of change in his time.

* ECONOMIC CHANGE IN ANTEBELLUM AMERICA
  Despite growing sectional differences in the antebellum period, an integrated market economy had developed in the United States by 1850.

* THE SECTIONAL CRISIS
  Slavery was single most important cause of the sectional crisis that threatened to destroy the Union in 1861.

* CIVIL WAR AND RECONSTRUCTION
  The changes brought about by the Civil War and Reconstruction constituted a Second American Revolution.

* WESTWARD EXPANSION AND IMPERIALISM
  During the nineteenth century, Manifest Destiny was the driving force behind the United States' westward expansion and imperialism.

* GILDED AGE AND PROGRESSIVISM
  Progressivism was an effective response to the conditions created by industrialization, urban growth, and unregulated capitalism.

* THE 1920s
  The Jazz Age image is a misleading portrayal of the United States during the 1920s.

* THE GREAT DEPRESSION AND NEW DEAL
  The Great Depression and the New Deal transformed the United States into a modern welfare state.

* WORLD WAR TWO AND THE COLD WAR
  The United States' policy of containment was an effective response to the foreign policy challenges of the Cold War.

* THE CIVIL RIGHTS MOVEMENT
  The Civil Rights Movement is aptly called the Second Reconstruction.

FIGURE 5.2 Some Big Ideas for American History

process that entails the piecemeal building up of a body of knowledge by adding separate bits of information to one another. But such bits and pieces can have no meaning if there is no body of knowledge to give them meaning" (p. 34). In other words, there must be a cognitive structure or a general idea about the subject matter already in place into which the student can fit the fragments of new learning.

The way to resolve the paradox, Hallden contends, is to assume that the structure is in flux; that is, it is open to investigation and subject to change. Big Ideas are jumping off places for inquiry rather than facts to be learned. To introduce the Big Ideas in their Understanding by Design approach, Wiggins and McTighe (2005) use what they call overarching questions. These Big Questions are queries posed about the curriculum's Big Ideas that both proceed from and challenge them. Turning Big Ideas into Big Questions maintains Hallden's "structure in flux," preventing the investigation from being closed off before it has begun. That slavery was the major cause of the Civil War is an appropriate Big Idea for that period in US history. Asking how significant slavery was as a cause of the war keeps the Big Idea from becoming a dogmatic statement and candidate for rote learning. To keep the inquiry honest and open-ended, the question must bring the Big Idea itself into question. What other issues besides slavery may have been involved? What about non-slave owners who supported slavery expansion? To encourage critical historical thinking, the teacher must play devil's advocate with his own explanatory Big Idea (Figure 5.3).

Cory Reinking (HLP) addresses this challenge by turning Big Ideas into questions that organize his community college world history course into seven major sections with an overarching Big Idea question for each. For example, while studying the Medieval period his students considered "Was Europe the most depressed and static region in the world?" This question provided a basis of comparison with other areas in the course, and also established a comparison for later study of Europe during the Modern Era. For the Early Modern Period, he asked about power and class status as students examined the Rise of the Bourgeoisie and investigated which class was the most powerful in Europe, the aristocracy or the bourgeoisie.

In his high school world history course in the IB program, Russ Brown (HLP) poses Big Ideas that align with the mandated course topics and aims of the IB curriculum for that course. For his unit comparing world wars of the twentieth century he asks Big Idea questions: "What causes a war to take place (political, economic, and ideological causes)?" "How are wars fought?" "How do wars impact the countries fighting them?" and "What are the effects of wars?" These questions helped students explore big concept categories including political, economic, ideological, and social developments.

* COLONIZATION
  Big Question
  Was economic opportunity a more important attraction to American colonists than religious freedom?
* COLONIAL AMERICA
  Big Question
  To what extent were the thirteen original colonies three distinctive geographic regions, with differing economies, religious traditions, and political interests?
* COMING OF THE AMERICAN REVOLUTION
  Big Question
  To what extent had a change in the hearts and minds of once loyal British subjects occurred prior to the Declaration of Independence?
* THE AGE OF JACKSON
  Big Question
  Was Andrew Jackson more the product than the cause of change during his time?
* ECONOMIC CHANGE IN THE NEW REPUBLIC
  Big Question
  Did the United States have an integrated market economy by 1850?
* THE SECTIONAL CRISIS
  Big Question
  How important was slavery as a cause of the sectional crisis that threatened to destroy the Union by 1860?
* CIVIL WAR AND RECONSTRUCTION
  Big Question
  In what sense did the Civil War and Reconstruction represent a Second American Revolution?
* GILDED AGE AND PROGRESSIVISM
  Big Question
  To what extent was Progressivism an effective response to the conditions created by industrialization, rapid urban growth, and unregulated capitalism?
* WESTWARD EXPANSION AND IMPERIALISM
  Big Question
  How important was Manifest Destiny as a driving power behind the United States' westward expansion and imperialism during the nineteenth century?
* THE 1920s
  Big Question
  How accurate is the Jazz Age image as a portrait of the United States during the 1920s?
* THE GREAT DEPRESSION AND NEW DEAL
  Big Question
  To what extend did the Great Depression and the New Deal create a modern welfare state?
* WORLD WAR TWO AND THE COLD WAR
  Big Question
  How effective was the United States' effort to contain communism during the Cold War?
* THE CIVIL RIGHTS MOVEMENT
  Big Question
  To what extent was the Civil Rights Movement a Second Reconstruction?

FIGURE 5.3 Some Big Questions

Assessing Learning and Planning Assessment

In the Understanding by Design model, establishing the question-driven goals of instruction is followed by setting a clear slate of assessments that will help teachers and students recognize how well the goals are being met. Decisions about when and how to spend instructional time are closely tied to these assessments. We are aware that history teachers also must prepare their students for standardized tests mandated by their school district or state. While sensitive to these challenges, we focus here on the in-class and end-of-unit assessments that are linked to instruction and are designed by teachers rather than by external testing committees. We also believe that creating good classroom assessments is the most helpful way to prepare students for externally mandated tests. There are two kinds of classroom assessment—formative and summative or end-of-unit assessment. They serve different purposes: assessment *for* learning and assessment *of* learning. Some evaluation specialists add a third purpose, which is assessment *as* learning, when evaluation serves a metacognitive function by helping students learn what they do and do not know. As that purpose is implicit in formative assessment, we will discuss it in that context.

Summative assessment is end-point evaluation. It assesses what students have learned by the end of instruction. Its most common evaluation tools include essays, essay exams, objective tests, and projects intended to demonstrate what students know. A meaningful summative assessment will ask students to pull together the factual, procedural, and conceptual learning that have already taken place, synthesizing what they have learned. In the context of goals-directed instruction, it is the students' understanding of the Big Ideas that were the focus of the unit of instruction. It will provide the teacher with the final verdict on the effectiveness of her instruction. Summative assessments serve a valuable purpose for both the teacher and the students, but they are heavily influenced by the quality and frequency of formative assessments.

Formative assessment is "assessment for learning" rather than "assessment of learning" or evaluation for the purpose of grading, selection, certification, and accountability (Buhagiar, 2007). Formative assessment includes any assignment, task, or intervention that enables a teacher to determine what a student knows about a subject during the course of instruction. It also pinpoints where a student may be struggling, working with misconceptions, or failing to understand key concepts. Good formative assessments allow "each student [to] show the teacher all along the way where his or her understanding is deep, shallow, or stalled" (Brookhart, Moss, & Long, 2008, p. 52). It also serves a metacognitive or "assessment as learning" purpose by providing students feedback about their own learning. Finally, it helps the teacher assess the effectiveness of her own on-going instruction and to make adjustments to her teaching. Formative assessment pays off. An extensive study by Paul Black and Dylan Wiliam (1998) based on 250 journal articles and book chapters found that formative assessments boosted academic achievement. The extent of the payoff depends also on the frequency of assessment. Robert Marzano (2006) reported that assessing students twenty times in a fifteen-week course nearly doubled the knowledge gains produced by a single formative assessment. Teachers use a great variety of formative assessments, both formally and informally. Graphic organizers, timelines, comparison charts, Venn diagrams, summary statements in Cornell-type notes can all be used to assess how new content is being learned. Even short responses to Questions of the Day handed in at the end of class, which are also known as "tickets-out-the-door," work well for some teachers. Others use metacognitive journaling, which is an on-going process of students recording newly gained insights and how they came to acquire them. Perspective taking writing tasks, RAFTS (role, audience, form, topic), I-Am poems, and quick role playing simulations can also work as formative assessments. They range from pre-assessments to in-class discussion responses to prompts for Data Based Questions. Assessments can be quick glances at how students are integrating new concepts or material to longer and more formal measurements. The teacher co-author of one recent study (Brookhart & Durkin, 2003, p. 33) used nine different kinds of formative assessments across five lessons. They included paper-and-pencil tests, a student-made comic book portraying events leading to the Civil War, two different history games, three kinds of individual and group presentations, assessments for which students wrote their own rubrics, a conversation between two philosophers, and a World War Two timeline.

As JoyAnn Morin (2003), a fifth-grade US history teacher stated, "Effective assessment is most often integrated with instruction. ... An eclectic approach to assessment can include observations, student folders, student projects, student presentations, and student essays reactions." The point is to create lesson activities "that allow for assessment that provides the student with immediate feedback and provides the teacher with information to make decisions about the appropriateness of subsequent student activities" (Morin, 2003, p. 72). Judy Willis (2006) also emphasizes the role of summaries and exit cards (little summaries) as tools that both strengthen memory and provide assessment opportunities. Formative assessments on longer projects can take the form of student and teacher conferences or weekly progress updates. Formative assessments also help students keep track of their own learning and progress, thus reinforcing metacognitive understanding.

Formative and summative assessment should be closely linked, as illustrated by Carin Barrett (HLP), whose students evaluated primary documents about US involvement in World War One. They used these documents to create found poetry showing their understanding of the war experience. They also completed maps before writing the final summative assessment paper. To determine if they were on the right track, she assessed these smaller formative assignments before the students wrote their papers. She used an even greater variety of formative assessments during her instruction about the Gilded Age. Her students created a comic book, children's book, or chapter book that told the story of the period, featuring "robber barons" and inventions. Students turned in pages after each topic was covered. For the summative assessment they wrote an explanation of why the changes that occurred during that age were important to the development of the nation.

Let's imagine a teacher who is creating summative and formative assessment plans. Our unit on the American Revolution (1763–1781) would include the events leading up to the War for Independence. As the Big Idea we would present the British and American Tory point of view that Parliament was entirely justified in tightening its administration of colonial affairs in the aftermath of the French and Indian War, asking the American colonists to pay their share of the cost. The textbook the students are using presents the American point of view that Parliament and the King drove the colonists into rebellion by encroaching upon traditional liberties and "natural rights." In planning instruction, we would provide our students with ample opportunities to consider both perspectives. But, first, how will we assess student learning?

Our formative assessments will focus on the students' understanding of the series of events that led from the expulsion of France from Canada up to the break with Britain. These evaluations are listed on the left-hand margin of the matrix in Table 5.1, and include the Proclamation of 1763, the Stamp Act, sending troops to Boston, the Tea Act, the Coercive Acts, and the armed confrontations at Lexington and Concord. We need to know if students understand how each event contributed to the developing conflict and how it was viewed by each side. For example, if many students do not grasp Prime Minister George Grenville's rationale for the Stamp Act and what the protestors meant by "no taxation without representation," we will need to pause and re-teach. As history educators have come to realize, assessments must address students' historical thinking as well as their factual and conceptual understanding (Brown, 2013; Ercikan & Seixas, 2015). This assessment focuses on understanding of the disciplinary concepts of change, causation, and perspective as well as historical content knowledge. The formative assessment that we decide upon is a matrix that includes the name of each event in a column down the left-hand side with four adjacent columns with the following headings (Table 5.1).

Near the end of the class period in which instruction about that event is completed, we will ask students to add their responses to the matrix and turn it in as they leave the classroom. This assignment is their "ticket out the door," which we will review prior to the next class meeting. It will help us know which students did not "get it," and whether so many are off target that re-teaching is needed. We decide that the most appropriate summative assessment is an argumentative essay that students either agree with, modify, or dispute. We do not care which position they take so long as they support it with the critical use of evidence, recognize that different perspectives existed at the time, and write a persuasive argument.

TABLE 5.1 Formative Assessment Matrix

	What was it?	*British argument*	*Colonists' argument*	*Effect on British–colonial relations*
Proclamation of 1763				
Stamp Act				
British Troops sent to Boston				
Tea Act				
Coercive Acts				
Lexington and Concord				

Meaningful Big Ideas and Big Questions set at the beginning of unit planning, and around which instruction is planned, will provide coherence and help students understand the purpose of their study. These ideas and questions tie directly to the assessments by which students, teachers, and the larger public gauge what students are learning. All of these components of instructional planning will serve teachers well as they move forward to engage students in the study of history.

Planning Instruction

With goals set, Big Ideas in place, and assessments in hand, the teacher's next task is to plan the unit of instruction. The question is not what topics will be taught, as the subject matter may already be determined, at least in public schools in the United States. The school district curriculum guide or state framework typically prescribes the content of instruction, with the curriculum at each grade level divided into units of instruction. Still, teachers have a good deal of autonomy in their classroom. They can decide what content within a unit to emphasize and what to pass over more quickly and how to balance depth and breadth. Within limits, they are their own time-keepers, as they can decide how to allocate the time available for a unit of instruction. Finally, they decide how to teach the content.

Planning for instruction in an inquiry classroom is very different than planning for traditional instruction. In a traditional history classroom, instruction is a survey of the content, with students marching through a sequence of historical events. They learn about that content by listening, reading the textbook, and engaging in teacher-led discussions. At the conclusion of the unit, they demonstrate what they have learned by writing an essay or taking a test. In an inquiry classroom, students do more than survey the content. They interact with it and interrogate it in pursuit of answers to questions. These students read about a topic, take and make notes, and periodically review what they are learning. They make connections, look for patterns, and synthesize what they have learned. Finally, they think about what it means to them. Teachers in an inquiry classroom make information available to students, provide direct instruction when needed (especially about textual analysis and other procedures), and intervene when students need help. It is teaching that supports rather than dictates student learning or in Wiggins and McTighe's (2005) terminology, "'Just in time' teaching" (p. 300). That does not mean that instruction in an inquiry classroom is improvised or unstructured, only that it is organized differently than traditional instruction.

In looking for a roadmap to guide instruction in an inquiry classroom, one instructional model in particular caught our attention. It is the framework that reading teachers use to organize instruction for comprehension. To improve reading comprehension, reading specialists developed a variety of strategies based on how proficient readers derive meaning from texts (National Institute of Child Health and Human Development, 2000; Reynolds & Sinatra, 2005; Ryder & Graves, 1998). These include activities that engage students before reading, during reading, and after reading (Figure 5.4). Strategies used before reading activate prior learning, engage students' interest, and give them a purpose for reading. Those employed during reading check for and deepen comprehension. After-reading strategies help students retain and apply what they have learned. While several of the learning strategies are appropriate for history classrooms, it was the three-part division of learning that we found most useful.

READING COMPREHENSION STRATEGIES

Before Reading
- Text Previews
- Predictions
- KWL, Anticipate Guide
- Vocabulary

During Reading
- Note Making
- Partner Conversations
- Reciprocal Teaching
- Semantic Mapping
- Questioning the Author

After Reading
- Summarizing
- Enacting
- Visualizing
- Creating Time Lines

FIGURE 5.4 Reading Comprehension Strategies Chart

Setting aside time before formally beginning instruction and at the end, the before-reading and after-reading phases make good sense for history instruction. In the first place, it gives teachers an opportunity to find out what students know about a topic and what common background teachers need to provide them. It is difficult for students to become a community of learners when large differences exist in their background knowledge. Much of what students think they know may consist of stereotypes, myths, and misunderstandings, which teachers need to address at the outset of instruction. Teachers also can use this time to whet students' interest, and engage them with the subject matter. The pay-off of such "up-front" instruction in terms of facilitating learning is well documented (Jonassen and Grabowski, 1993; Marzano, 2004; Ogle, Klemp, and McBride, 2007). We also think that history students need time at the end of a unit to explore the implications of what they have learned. That instructional time is the history classroom's equivalent to the after-reading phase of literacy instruction. An equivalent history phase would encourage students to make past–present connections, draw analogies, and reflect on historical and present-day changes.

The weakest parallel between the reading model and history instruction is the middle or during-reading phase. For reading instruction, it consists of a variety of text comprehension and generic learning strategies. These can be useful for reading some historical texts, but they fail to address most of the cognitive tasks involved in historical learning. History teachers need a guideline for instruction specific to building historical knowledge. The Building Knowledge phase of our chart (Figure 5.5) serves this purpose. It includes the cognitive tasks involved in creating historical knowledge.

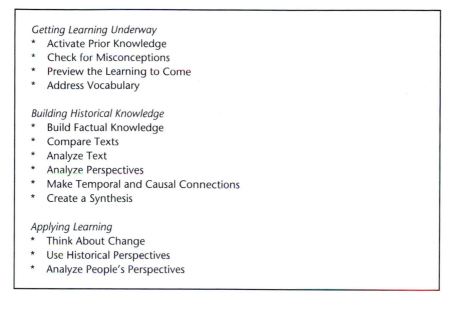

Getting Learning Underway
* Activate Prior Knowledge
* Check for Misconceptions
* Preview the Learning to Come
* Address Vocabulary

Building Historical Knowledge
* Build Factual Knowledge
* Compare Texts
* Analyze Text
* Analyze Perspectives
* Make Temporal and Causal Connections
* Create a Synthesis

Applying Learning
* Think About Change
* Use Historical Perspectives
* Analyze People's Perspectives

FIGURE 5.5 Teaching for Historical Literacy

Integrating the Building Knowledge components into a three-part model creates a structure for guided inquiry in a history classroom. It is both a list of basic components and, proceeding from top to bottom, a sequence of instruction. It is an outline that we will expand in the chapters ahead. The phases of instruction are not proportionate in length to the size of the three lists.

The duration of the three phases vary significantly in length, as the arc of instruction (Figure 5.6) indicates. Getting Learning Underway, the introduction to a unit, provides time for the teacher to prepare the students to become a community of learners. Some teachers will find that spending more time on this phase is essential to moving their students forward. The lion's share of instruction is concentrated in the Building Historical Knowledge phase. Here students use the lens of historical thinking to investigate the past in order to construct historical knowledge called for by the unit's Big Question. The third phase, Apply Historical Learning, is a brief reflection on the present-day significance of what students have learned about the past.

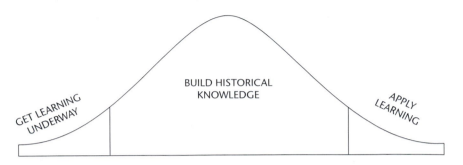

FIGURE 5.6 Arc of Instruction

References

Black, P. & Wiliam, D. (1998). Assessment and classroom learning. *Assessment in Education: Principles, Policy & Practice*, 5(1), 7–71.

Brookhart, S., Moss, C., & Long, B. (2008). Formative assessment. *Educational Leadership*, 66(3), 52–57.

Brookhart, S. M. & Durkin, D. T. (2003). Classroom assessment, student motivation, and achievement in high school social studies classes. *Applied Measurement in Education*, 16(1), 27-54.

Brown, S. D. (2013). Preparing effective history teachers: The assessment gap. *Journal of Social Studies Research*, 37, 167–177.

Buhagiar, M. A. (2007). Classroom assessment within the alternative assessment paradigm: revisiting the territory. *The Curriculum Journal*, 18(1), 39–56.

Dick, W. & Carey, L. (1978). *The systematic design of instruction*. Glenview, IL: Scott, Foresman.

Ercikan, K. & Seixas, P. (2015). *New directions in assessing historical thinking*. New York, NY: Routledge.

Grant, S. G. (2003). *History lessons: Teaching, learning, and testing in U.S. high school classrooms*. Mahwah, NJ: Lawrence Erlbaum Associates.

Grossman, P. L. & Stodolsky, S. S. (1995). Content as context: The role of school subjects in secondary school teaching. *Educational Researcher*, 24(8), 5–23.

Guthrie, J. T. (2003). Concept-oriented reading instruction. In A. P. Sweet & C. E. Snow (Eds.) *Rethinking reading comprehension* (pp. 115-140). New York, London: The Guilford Press.

Hallden, O. (1994). On the paradox of understanding history in an educational setting. In Leinhardt, G., Beck, I. L.,& Stainton, C. (Eds.), *Teaching and learning in history* (pp. 27–46). Hillsdale, New Jersey, and Hove, UK: Lawrence Erlbaum Associates.

Hallden, O. (1998). Personalization in historical descriptions and explanations. *Learning and Instruction*, 8(2), 131-139.

Jonassen, D. H. & Grabowski, B. L. (1993). *Handbook of individual differences, learning, and instruction, Part VII: Prior knowledge*. Hillsdale, NJ: Lawrence Erlbaum Associates.

Libresco, A. S. (2005). How she stopped worrying and learned to love the test … sort of. In E. A. Yeager & O. L. Davis (eds.) *Wise social studies teaching in an age of high-stakes testing: Essays on classroom practices and possibilities* (pp. 33–49). Greenwich, CT: Information Age Publishing.

Marzano, R. J. (2004). *Building background knowledge for academic achievement.* Alexandria, VA: Association for Supervision and Curriculum Development.

Marzano, R. J. (2006). *Classroom assessments and grading that work.* Alexandria, VA: Association for Supervision and Curriculum Development.

Morin, J. H. (2003). *Social studies instruction incorporating the language arts.* Boston, MA: Pearson Education, Inc.

National Institute of Child Health and Human Development. (2000). *Report of the National Reading Panel. Teaching children to read: An evidence-based assessment of the scientific research literature on reading and its implications for reading instruction* (NIH Publication No. 00–4769). Washington, DC: US Government Printing Office.

Nokes, J. D. (2013). *Building students' historical literacies: Learning to read and reason with historical texts and evidence.* New York, NY: Routledge.

Ogle, D., Klemp, R., & McBride, B. (2007). *Building literacy in the social studies.* Alexandria, VA: Association for Supervision and Curriculum Development.

Reynolds, R. E. & Sinatra, G. M. (2005) The cognitive revolution in scientific psychology: Epistemological roots and impact on reading research. In J. M. Royer (ed.) *The cognitive revolution in educational psychology* (pp. 13–39). Greenwich, CT: Information Age Publishing.

Ryder, R. J. & Graves, M. F. (1998). *Reading and learning in content areas* (2nd edn.). New York, NY: John Wiley and Sons.

Thornton, S. J. (1991). Teacher as curricular-instructional gatekeeper in social studies. In J. P. Shaver (ed.) *Handbook of research on social studies teaching and learning* (pp. 237–248). New York, NY: Macmillan Publishing Company.

Van Boxtel, C. A. M. & van Rijn, M. (2006). Picturing colligatory concepts in history: Effects of student–generated versus presented drawings. *Proceedings of the EARLI SIG Text and Graphics Comprehension*, Nottingham University, UK, 5–7.

Walsh, W. H. (1974). Colligatory concepts in history. In P. Gardiner (ed.) *The philosophy of history* (pp. 127–144). Oxford: Oxford University Press.

Wiggins, G. & McTighe, J. (1998). *Understanding by design.* Alexandria, VA: Association for Supervision and Curriculum Development.

Wiggins, G. & McTighe, J. (2005). *Understanding by design* (expanded 2nd edn.). Upper Saddle River, NJ and Alexandria, VA: Pearson Education/Association for Supervision & Curriculum Development.

Willis, J. (2006). *Research-based strategies to ignite student learning.* Alexandria, VA: Association for Supervision and Curriculum Development (ASCD).

PART III
Getting Learning Underway

Getting Learning Underway
* **Activate Prior Knowledge**
* **Check for Misconceptions**
* **Preview the Learning to Come**
* **Address Vocabulary**

Building Historical Knowledge
* Build Factual Knowledge
* Compare Texts
* Analyze Text
* Analyze Perspectives
* Make Temporal and Causal Connections
* Create a Synthesis

Applying Learning
* Think About Change
* Use Historical Perspectives
* Analyze People's Perspectives

FIGURE 6.1 Teaching for Historical Literacy: Getting Learning Underway

6

ACTIVATE PRIOR LEARNING

Activating prior learning helps students connect new learning to knowledge that they may already have about the subject-matter. As illustrated in Figure 6.1, Teaching For Historical Literacy chart, on the facing page, the first phase of historical literacy focuses on the getting learning underway. While effective learning is dependent on many factors, as Robert Marzano (2004) points out, what students already know influences how well they can learn new information. Activating prior knowledge, in turn, helps them store, recall, and process the new information they are learning. Teachers use a variety of activities to activate what students already know or believe they know about a topic. We will examine two of the best known, the Know-Want-to-Know-Learned (K-W-L) sequence and Anticipation Guides (AG). However, activating prior knowledge is less a matter of the kind of activity than the purpose for which it is used. Even the most traditional modes of instruction can accomplish this purpose.

Students enter history classrooms with widely differing kinds and levels of useable prior historical knowledge. It may include general or common-sense knowledge, which is the shared experience and anecdotal background that comes from living in a society. Students may even bring their own personal experiences to bear on historical topics, such as equating a tent camping experience to frontier life (Dulberg, 2002). They learn much of the history they know from parents, relatives, television, and movies (Barton, 2005). This means that students encountering school history for the first time bring with them "beliefs about individuals, myths, and events of history that are not coherently integrated" (Voss & Wiley, 1997, p. 149). While they may know some historical facts, they are unlikely to know how historical knowledge gets created.

Teachers cannot count on prior learning being shared knowledge. Students' background experience is simply too varied. Students whose parents took them to Mount Vernon or Monticello on a family vacation may know a good deal about George Washington and Thomas Jefferson. Yet these students, in turn, may know little that other students have learned from their own out-of-school encounters with the past. Still others may know that George Washington was "the father of our country" without knowing anything else about him or even what that means. To transform a classroom into a community of learners, teachers need to find out what prior learning students do and do not have.

Not all "prior learning" is "prior knowledge" that students can reliably build upon. Misconceptions and flat-out misinformation often arise when students are asked what they know about the past. Spending time prior to instruction working with students to activate their prior learning helps the teacher uncover misunderstandings and stereotypes that they may bring to the classroom (Dochy, Segers, & Buehl, 1999). Helping students confront misconceptions is not a simple task. Previous learning can be intractable; nonetheless, misconceptions have to be confronted deliberately and explicitly. In this chapter, we will examine strategies that teachers have created for activating prior knowledge and grappling with misconceptions.

Another advantage to tapping into preexisting knowledge is that it can help teachers pique student interest in a topic, identifying areas that they might like to know more about. Interest in a topic may also help to reinforce motivation and engagement, which is as essential to learning and as complex a matter as any that we face in education. History teachers use a variety of activities that help engage and motivate students, ranging from script writing (Fertig, 2001), to integrating art activities (Selwyn, 1993), to linking the past to personal experience (Dulberg, 2002; Tobias, 1994).

Students usually are most engaged when the subject has some direct relevance to their own lives and when texts are personally involving. Still, it is not enough for introductory activities to generate interest. They must also help students connect new learning to prior knowledge in order to make connections with content in a broader historical context. Taking time to activate prior knowledge will help students make these connections and set the stage for integrated historical learning.

The K-W-L and Variations

The most commonly used strategy for activating prior learning is the K-W-L activity borrowed from reading instruction. The acronym stands for "What do you Know?" "What do you Want to know?" and "What did you Learn?" It was created by Donna Ogle (1986), a reading specialist and former social studies teacher. It typically is used as a brainstorming activity before students start to read an article or chapter during which the teacher records on the board or overhead their responses to the first question (what do you know). To extend the activity beyond recall, teachers can also ask the class to categorize the information that is on the board. This helps students anticipate the kinds of information they may encounter in the reading. The second or "W" step (want to know) usually is a group activity in which students also write down the items they are most interested in knowing about. This gives them a personal commitment to guide their reading. In the final or "L" step (learned), students review what they learned from the reading and the extent to which their knowledge was confirmed and their questions answered. The K–W–L is widely used as an instructional strategy to introduce new history and other content units (Table 6.1).

Although created as a reading comprehension activity, the K–W–L quickly gained wide application in content instruction (Ogle, 1992). Social studies teachers have found it especially useful (Readence, Moore, & Rickelman, 2000). The first task in a content-area K–W–L is to find out what students already know about the historical subject-matter. Paul, a middle-grades teacher observed by Mark Aulls, began his unit on Egyptian Civilization by asking his students to write down all the words that came to mind when he said "Ancient Egypt." He created a profile of the student's background knowledge from the words most frequently listed (Aulls, 2008). A simple extension of the K–W–L is demonstrated by Robert Bain, who asked his high school students (2000) to respond in their journal to questions such as: What do you know about this topic? What do you think about the topic? What attitudes do you bring to this topic? What questions do you have about it? Making their initial ideas explicit at the outset and revisiting them later, he concluded, "reveals that which is difficult for students to see—the changes in their own thinking" (p. 341). The journal entries provide students and the teacher with a written record of those changes. While whole-class brainstorms are probably the most common approach to the K–W–L, teachers also use small-group sessions in which students report as a group. These tend to engage more students than large-group brainstorms (Downs, 1993; Levstik & Barton, 1997).

The "W" or "What do you want to know?" in the K–W–L formula can present a challenge. We have observed teachers make lists on the board about what students said they wanted to know when they still knew very little about the topic. These questions tend to reflect students' immediate interests rather than aspects of a topic worth exploring further. More or less random questions produced on the spur of the moment are not likely to have much educational value. Yet, these "W" questions can have important educational purposes. They may help motivate students to dig further into the topic, giving them a stake in the instruction that is to follow. They also introduce students to the inquiry

TABLE 6.1 Basic K–W–L Chart

What do you know?	What do you want to know?	What did you learn?
K	W	L

Source: Based on Donna Ogle's K–W–L

process, giving them at least one foot in a door that can open wider in the lessons to come. The challenge is to make the students' "W" questions more thoughtful and more productive.

We believe that, like any good inquiry, the "K" of the K-W-L should be teacher guided to most effectively connect students to prior learning. Rather than asking simply "what do you know," which can lead in unproductive directions because of its vagueness, we suggest tying the "K" to content that has previously been addressed in the course. Teachers can refine the "K" by asking "What do you remember about," and then moving to what do they predict or think probably happened. Another productive way to guide the exploratory "K" for purposes of historical learning is to ask students to recall "what happened when?" For example, the debates during the Constitutional Convention involved the topic of slavery and States rights. In a class where students have studied the Early National Era in US history, and will next study the Civil War, they could be asked "what do you remember happened when the convention members took up the topic of slave ownership?" They could then be asked "what do you predict happened because of that compromise?" Such "predicting what happened" use of the "K" can help students when they later explore questions of causation. Another example of pointing them toward a more specific "K" question that connects with a previous unit of study might be, "What do you know about slavery in the US before the Civil War?" This use of the "K" helps students connect prior learning, link one historical context to other contexts, and provide breadth of knowledge.

Another example of establishing a quick historical context within which to ask the "K" of the K-W-L comes from Kelly Long's US history class that had just completed a unit on American involvement in World War Two. She wanted to ascertain what students already knew about the post-war period. To activate their prior learning, students were asked to recall themes and topics they had explored about the US during their study of the Depression and New Deal. She asked, "What do you recall about the conditions of African Americans during the Depression era?" She moved from this question based on recalling a prior unit to a question aimed at accessing prior learning about the unit to come by next asking students, "What do you think changed or stayed the same with regard to African American rights?"

When the process works well, a K-W-L can create a body of commonly shared background knowledge that allows the class to proceed as a community of learners. However, it does not always work that way, as Janet Allen (2000) noted in a chapter entitled "Am I the only one who can't make a K-W-L work?" in her book on reading strategies. When she opened with the "K," asking her students what they knew about the topic, they typically shrugged off the question. Often, their response was "nothing" (p. 132). She got much the same response when asking what they wanted to know. The problem, she realized, was that they did not know enough about the topic to know what they wanted to know more about.

As Allen discovered, the K–W–L works best with topics that students already know or think they know something about. With many historical topics, students rarely know very much. Most of Paul's middle-grades students could only think of six words or fewer when asked what came to mind when he said "Ancient Egypt." They were predictable responses derived from movies, television, and popular culture, such as "people who built pyramids," "had queens like Cleopatra," or "had mummies." In observing Paul's classroom, Aulls noted that "this absence of prior knowledge of history concepts considerably increased the difficulty students had in learning and understanding new history content" (Aulls, 2008, p. 19). Aulls reinforced the idea that accessing prior knowledge must also emphasize historical concepts and processes. Asking the "K" in conjunction with historical concepts helps to remind students of how history is constructed. "What do you know about what changed after an event" or "what do you know about the causes of the Civil War," helps to focus the "K" and reinforce historical concepts as well.

Extended K-W-Ls

Often, teachers need to explicitly develop background knowledge through sources rather than relying only on verbal prompts to help students connect to their prior learning. To provide essential background knowledge, Allen developed a B–K–W–L–Q format, adding Background Knowledge (B) to the beginning and What New Questions Do I Have (Q) to the end (Table 6.2). To build shared background knowledge in a unit on the Civil Rights movement, she assigned short, well-chosen readings calculated to have an emotional impact that also would help generate student interest in the topic. She began with the poem "Ballad of Birmingham" and a short news write-up of the bombing of the church in Birmingham, Alabama that took the lives of young girls. These led to other readings that further whetted her students' interest while adding background knowledge. Table 6.2 illustrates a simple graphic organizer that can help students as they keep track of the background knowledge they are building.

TABLE 6.2 B–K–W–L–Q Organizer

B	K	W	L	Q
Build background	What do I know?	What do I want to know?	What did I learn?	What new questions do I have?

Source: Adapted from Janet Allen (2000), *Yellow Brick Roads*, pp. 133, 136

In another classroom, Allen and a fifth-grade teacher, Christine Landaker, created a set of strategies for assessing and building background knowledge (Allen & Landaker, 2005). A homework assignment used as an "admit slip" for the next day's class consisted of a single sheet with a column of engaging text on the left-hand side of the paper that introduced the new topic. On the right-hand column were questions that invited the students to predict what they were about to learn and to elicit student questions about the topic. Provided with a basket of books about the topic, students divided into small groups to conduct a "book pass" in which they individually sampled each book, noting the title, author, and one thing they learned about the topic from reading the first few pages. After two to five minutes, the teachers said "book pass," requiring the students to pass their book to another student. In a third activity, students responded to "I wonder?" and "I want to know" prompts in a quick-write after reading five assigned paragraphs of their textbook. Each of these activities engaged students in a quick exploration of the topic, providing them with short installments of background information.

The amount of time spent on "B" in a B-K-W-L-Q depends on the makeup of the class. Better-informed students may need very little background information. In other instances, building this background knowledge may require a good deal of time. Ann Putsche (HLP) worked in a middle school with a low socio-economic demographic and high percentage of English Language Learner (ELL) students. With students who had little to no prior knowledge or shared experience, Ann found that the *before* part of the activity often became a content lesson in itself. She observed that "Many times it feels like teaching the background information is the unit of study." Explaining a difficulty with using the K-W-L strategies with her students, she observed that "They might not have enough background information (or trust the information they do have) to make predictions and inferences from pictures." Ann recognized that without some more concrete ideas about the type of physical terrain and challenges encountered by early colonists, students growing up in the arid western and southwestern part of the United States would be unlikely to understand the types of geographically-related struggles faced by people in those early colonies in the East. Therefore, she had students work in small groups using pictures and posing questions about specific things they saw in order to build concepts and vocabulary before their study of colonial settlement. From those questions students were able to both assert what they knew and pose some further questions that arose from their work with the pictures.

Lori Davis (HLP) found the B-K-W-L-Q most effective when she used it very intentionally to point students toward the Big Questions for the inquiry. Her Essential Questions were linked to disciplinary concepts and Big Ideas of the unit. Lori reported that the "K" works best when it is connected directly to something specific like a text, a film, a photo, or a piece of music used to build background knowledge. After exposing students to the source and asking what they know, she modified the "W" by asking, "What information would help you to better understand this topic?" This sort of question is more likely to garner a productive response rather than a "nothing," and moreover, it keeps attention focused on the Big Question that is the point of the inquiry.

David Farrell (HLP) used a composite of sources to create a B-K-W-L-Q activity prior to opening his unit on the Gilded Age. These included photos and graphs, which he showed students and asked questions about, prior to leading them into a K-W-L activity. High school teachers and HLP partners Mandy Byrd and Brooke Tomalchof worked together to create a B-K-W-L-Q for their unit on Industrial America. It included photos of key players in the Industrial Era, statements by them, and photographs of inventions. After asking students to connect these items, they moved forward into a K-W-L activity. They asked students "What do you think changed in America during this time?" and "What do you predict might have changed?"

Along with problems encountered when students seem to have extremely limited background knowledge, or lack of commonly shared prior learning, another problem with the "K" in a content-area K-W-L is that some of the "learning" being activated is incorrect or riddled with misconceptions and stereotypes. While a publicly recorded brainstorming session is in progress, a teacher has a choice. Either she lists the misconceptions along with the accurate information or she passes judgment on each student's prior learning as she goes. Neither are highly desirable options. Putting misconceptions on the board gives them equal status with valid information, at least for the moment, and that may be long enough for other students to log them into memory. While correcting misconceptions one at a time can be handled tactfully ("Now, Andrew, does that really make sense?"), it interrupts the dynamic of a brainstorm and may discourage students from contributing.

Obviously, misinformation must be addressed. At the very least students must understand that what they think they know is subject to verification. "One way to address students' misconceptions is to alert them that the new information may conflict with their existing ideas," as Felip Dochy, Mien Segers, and Michelle Buehl (1999, p. 153) note. We have seen teachers after a brainstorm raise questions about individual items as they debriefed the information on the board. They pointed out that questionable information would be revisited as the lesson or unit proceeded. A solution consistent with historical thinking would be to explain that all the items on the board and everything else we think we know about the past are tentative. It has to be checked out and verified with evidence. This means that the brainstorming list must become part of the classroom "furniture" for the rest of the unit or lesson and be revisited frequently. We believe that allowing the students themselves to confront misconceptions with evidence will have a larger pay-off than for the teacher to censor the list during the brainstorming. Because wrong information can stick with younger learners, especially if students see it written on the board, we believe that teachers should address or at least raise questions about misinformation before students are allowed to leave a classroom session in which ideas have been made public and put on display. We have seen teachers who make a separate box in which to place questionable items that arise during a brainstorming session, which indicates that these are topics that will need further investigation.

Another alternative is to address misconceptions head-on at the outset of instruction. The following examples offered by Mary Beth Sampson (2002) and Adam Woelders (2007) combine the K-W-L approach with the Anticipation Guide approach, which will be discussed later in this chapter. It is a process that Sampson (2002) describes as "confirming" the prior knowledge of a K-W-L. Sampson used an approach that engaged students in contemplating the importance of "sourcing" their information. Her format started with a column "what we *think* we know" to defuse the illusion of absolute accuracy (Sampson, 2002, p. 529). After confirming initial guesses by surveying at least two sources, students affixed sticky notes to the "think we know" column with the name of the source that affirmed the information. However, the information was verified as "confirmed" only after the full class talked and reached consensus about it. When sources offered conflicting information, students went to the library to conduct further research before they could move something into the "what they learned" column. This approach taught the importance of sourcing information, of seeking multiple sources, and of keeping up to date with recent research (Sampson, 2002).

Similarly, Woelders (2007) modified a Know-Wonder-Learned approach that required students to use written sources to compare accounts presented in historically themed film. Using only a few questions that provided opportunity for disagreement and challenge, Woelders (2007) had students make predictions about where film accounts and documentaries would go in exploring a topic. After viewing, students used written sources to compare how the film treated or did not treat a topic. This strategy encouraged students to compare conflicting accounts of history and to form their own accounts based on use of multiple sources (Woelders, 2007).

Allen found that her B-K-W-L-Q format helped her students ask better "W" questions. She discovered that "many learners need some background knowledge *before* they know enough to want to know more," Allen (2000, p. 132). She began her lesson on the Civil Rights Movement with a Write to Learn Chart that asked students to examine sources and write responses. As they moved from one source to the next, they added facts and "I wonder" questions to their responses. After examining the final source, they added a "What I know now" and "What I'm interested in knowing" column. Delaying the "W" step until after students had a foundation of shared background knowledge had a substantial pay-off for her. This may mean delaying the "W" stage until several days into a new topic or unit and approaching it as only the beginning of a student-directed, question-asking process. The standard university lecture course demands such a delay because classes typically meet only two or three times a week. Some block schedules used in public schools create a similar challenge. In introducing the topic of immigration in her US history survey course, Long wanted students to understand demographic changes and diverse responses to such changes in the late-nineteenth century. To build shared background knowledge as part of a B-K-W-L-Q, she showed students a set of historical photographs depicting people and scenes from the era, a poem, and a census graph reflecting immigration sources and patterns. She projected photographs and asked students to write down what they observed and what they knew or guessed about the people in the photos. Thereafter, students shared their responses in an informal pair-share. While reading a short poem, they recorded observations, key words, and questions in their own learning journals and again engaged in a simple pair-share. As they examined a census graph, students called out comments about data on the graph. Thereafter, students wrote briefly about what they were still wondering about or might now want to know. The homework assignment for the class that met the next week was for students to read a chapter in the textbook along with a set of primary source documents, and then view short online videos. After those exposures to further content background, students wrote down questions about what they wanted to know more about and where they would look to answer them.

The final step in the K-W-L, the "What did you Learn?" also needs to be a fully developed portion of a successful K-W-L strategy. Teachers often address the "L" by asking students to write a paper or take a test in order to demonstrate what they have learned. Just as we advocate returning to the "K" frequently throughout a unit of study, as the unit nears an end we encourage a public enactment of the "L" to help the full class understand what they have learned collectively and individually. Talking about how they went about learning strengthens their metacognitive skills and familiarity with historical procedures. During the last part of the B-K-W-L-Q, the "L" and "Q" phases, teachers can explicitly address the original K that students began with, redress any lingering misconceptions, and help students to firm up their new understandings.

The K-R-A-W-L

As already observed, while K-W-Ls are widely used in elementary and secondary schools, they also are helpful for students in higher education. Matt Downey devised a K-R-A-W-L activity for his university course on Colorado history. The first assignment in his plains Indians unit asked students to list in short, bulleted statements what they knew about several aspects of this high-plains culture: food, clothing, and shelter; work and tools; family life and child rearing; and community and tribal life. He was comfortable leading off with the "K" of the K-W-L, as he suspected that misconceptions were likely to pose a far greater challenge than lack of prior knowledge. Most of his students were native Coloradoans who had been learning about the Cheyenne and Arapaho Indians since elementary school. As homework before the next class meeting, the students checked their statements (K) against a set of primary sources posted on a course-related website, revised (R) any misconceptions, added (A) whatever new background knowledge they had learned, and listed what else they would like to know (W). The end-of-unit assessment would evaluate what they had learned (L) from their investigations. The students took the assignment seriously and came to the next class meeting with well-developed lists for the "R-A-W" sections of the handout. Whether it is adaptable to elementary or secondary classrooms depends on how much knowledge students bring to the task, the availability of resources, and the teacher's expectations for independent student work (Figure 6.2).

COLORADO'S PLAINS INDIANS

K-R-A-W-L CHART

I. ACTIVATING PRIOR KNOWLEDGE (K)

Jot down words or short phrases in the spaces below about what you already know about Colorado's plains Indians and their way of life.

- FOOD, CLOTHING AND SHELTER?
- WORK (MEN & WOMEN'S) AND TOOLS?
- FAMILY LIFE AND CHILD REARING?
- COMMUNITY LIFE?
- RESERVATION LIFE?

II. REVISING PRIOR KNOWLEDGE & ADDING BACKGROUND KNOWLEDGE (R-A)

Visit the assigned website and click on Colorado Indians. After exploring the Colorado Indian topics, indicate below 1) how you have revised (R) your prior knowledge and what new knowledge have you added (A) as a result of your visit. Be specific. Which photographs or first-hand accounts helped you revise or add to your knowledge?

- FOOD, CLOTHING AND SHELTER?
- WORK (MEN & WOMEN's) AND TOOLS?
- FAMILY LIFE AND CHILD REARING?
- COMMUNITY LIFE?
- RESERVATION LIFE?

III. WHAT ELSE WOUD YOU LIKE TO KNOW ABOUT THE PLAINS INDIANS THAT WE MAY BE ABLE TO EXPLORE IN THIS UNIT? (W)

-
-

IV. WHAT DID YOU LEARN ABOUT THE TOPIC? (L)

-
-

FIGURE 6.2 K-R-A-W-L Chart

Any of these approaches to activating and assessing students' prior learning are valuable. Next we explore forms of the Anticipation Guide, which have some similarities to the K-W-L and yet are distinct strategies for working with prior learning.

Anticipation Guides

A second strategy for activating prior knowledge that has crossed over from reading instruction is the Anticipation Guide (AG). Researchers identify three types of Anticipation Guides: a standard AG created to provoke response and prediction; an extended AG that activates prior knowledge by having students explain why they responded as they did; and a confirming AG, which asks students either individually or in groups, to verify their responses by cross-checking against other sources. Regardless of the type or label used, AGs serve as a bridge between prior learning and the Big Question. We recommend their use for purposes of activating prior learning, creating engagement, and perhaps, sparking students' motivation to learn more about the subject at hand.

The basic Anticipation Guide typically consists of five to seven teacher-generated statements to which students respond (Figure 6.3). These are often structured as True or False (or Agree or Disagree) statements. The aim is to allow prior learning and misconceptions to surface before reading or study. Unlike traditional True–False quiz items and pre-tests, in an AG the statements are not just focused on factual knowledge. Instead, they are general statements about major ideas in the content about to be introduced. They should include provocative questions that will elicit student reaction. A Likert scale that offers a range of responses from very low to very high, or do not agree to strongly agree,

---

Directions: Read each statement and write "Agree" in the blank if you believe the statement and can support it. Write "Disagree" if you disagree and cannot support the statement.

_____1. Communism was a real threat to US domestic culture in the 1950s.

_____2. The alignment of government, business, and military into a "military-industrial complex" was a positive development.

_____3. All Americans enjoyed a higher standard of living and prosperity in the 1950s.

_____4. Use of the atomic bomb was necessary in order to bring an end to World War Two in the Pacific.

_____5. The Civil Rights movement of the 1950s corrected decades if not centuries of inequality.

FIGURE 6.3 A Basic or Standard Anticipation Guide

encourages students to respond to a statement and express an opinion that may vary in intensity. Such questions engage students in the learning process by challenging their beliefs and creating conceptual conflicts. In the dissonance that arises students will desire to seek answers that resolve the tension, and thereby, are motivated to verify facts or the accuracy of their beliefs.

As Frederick A. Duffelmeyer (1994) notes, a well-written statement must allow students to confront conflicting information. It is in their further exploration of the topic that they will work toward resolving conflicts and misconceptions they have identified. Questions, therefore, are designed to draw out students' prior knowledge or experience and to elicit and challenge their beliefs about the topic. The statements must be sufficiently provocative to draw forth students' opinions and to evoke emotional responses (Readence, Bean, & Baldwin, 1995). For example, the statement that 'racism is no longer an issue in America', is likely to trigger opinion and impassioned responses today.

A variation of the basic Anticipation Guide is the sticky note response method, which we have seen used with great effect. It allows the teacher to have elective control over which questions and topics to attend to. Students write it anonymously on the sticky notes and do not face jeopardy in addressing their own opinions before the class. This form of an AG is less likely to encourage students to discard misconceptions even though they may come into contact with discrepancies between their answers/beliefs/prior learning and the information presented in the text. Liz Melahn (HLP) used this type of Anticipation Guide with her class. Instead of having individual sheets of paper, the first student dragged an icon on the Smart Board to register her "vote." The next student did the same thing making a public and powerful visual diagram of class values and responses. Once the guide was completed, Melahn saved it on the computer. Later she returned to it to help students see changes in their thinking *after* their study of the unit.

Extended Anticipation Guides

Another form of the Anticipation Guide is sometimes called an extended or reaction guide (Duffelmeyer and Baum, 1992). In this version, students read the standard AG "triggering statements," mark their response, and then explain why they thought what they did. Or, they may talk with a partner about why they made the choice they did. We strongly recommend that teachers use the Anticipation Guide and ask students to explain their reasons for responding as they did. The format of such a guide should include space for students to present their explanations in writing. This, in turn, can lead to a Think–Pair–Share activity in which students check their understanding with a partner. Whether or not this discussion leads to a consensus statement, sharing can raise questions about initial responses that students may not have thought of on their own and will further engage them in the learning process. As reflected in Figure 6.4, Gabrielle Wymore (HLP) provided an example that she used with her middle school students.

Colonization AG   **Name**

Part I- Before we study Colonization read the statements in Part I. If you believe that a statement is true, place a check in the Agree column. If you believe a statement is false, place a check in the Disagree column. Be ready to explain your choice.

Agree   Disagree   Statement

_____   _____   1.   The abundance (surplus) of natural resources in the "New World" made life easier for the colonists.

_____   _____   2.   The colonists were called the Pilgrims.

_____   _____   3.   Native Americans welcomed the colonists.

_____   _____   4.   England was the only country that colonized what we know as the US.

_____   _____   5.   People came to the New World for religious freedom.

_____   _____   6.   The colonists came to the New World to create a new country.

Part II- We will now study Colonization. If the information we learn supports your choices above, place a check in the Yes column in Part II. Then write where you found that information. If the information does not support your choices, place a check in the No column. Then write where you found that information.

Yes   No   Why is my choice correct? (Agree)

                    Why is my choice incorrect? (Disagree)

                    1. _____

                    2. _____

                    3. _____

                    4. _____

                    5. _____

                    6. _____

FIGURE 6.4 Extended Anticipation Guide

Source: Permission of Gabrielle Wynmore (HLP)

Just as with the "K" portion of a K-W-L, the AG is likely to bring misconceptions to the surface. Therefore, it invites follow-up, which can happen in a variety of ways. Martha Head and John E. Readence (1992) argue that the extended Anticipation Guide, which asks students to explain their responses, should be debriefed publicly and used to diagnose misunderstandings and gaps in knowledge. However, even individual reflection on one's preconceptions and confirmation or redirection has a powerful role to play in getting students ready to learn new information. Students can do a Think-Pair-Share, or they can share ideas in a small group, to explain why they made the choices they did.

Confirming Anticipation Guide

Some teachers have enlarged upon the standard Anticipation Guide by expanding the set of sources that students must consult in a "confirming AG" model. As they read to find support for their responses in texts that offer factual information, students must go back to check their initial answers as they learn more about the topic. Returning to their initial responses has metacognitive pay-offs, as it helps students see how their ideas are changing. Finally, their new knowledge is solidified by their being called upon to explain why the new information either affirms or disproves their answers (Duffelmeyer and Baum, 1992). Moreover, the act of summarizing and paraphrasing enhances the likelihood that the new, confirmed information will replace misconceptions.

This approach involves revisiting the guide after instruction in order to confirm or correct students' initial responses by working with sources to determine whether their prior learning and preexisting assumptions were correct or not. They justify in writing where they agree and/or disagree with the text. Such guides help students to scrutinize the authority of a text while also helping them recognize that multiple perspectives exist. It encourages them to work with a variety of short sources to determine the accuracy or validity of their notions, and to compare sources in so doing. A teacher can simply collect this work to determine whether students have adjusted their ideas or confirmed them. This can help to set the direction of the study ahead.

A confirming Anticipation Guide helped Long's students in a teaching methods course in the study of Colonial America. Her students were asked to respond to the statements in the Anticipation Guide individually and then talk about several of their responses with two classmates. This activity generated interest and debates among the students. Thereafter, as homework, she sent them to pre-selected sites on the Internet where they could read and scan for more information on the topics introduced by the guide. During the next class session students turned in their work after they discussed their findings with classmates in small groups of three or four students. Following that, the full class engaged in discussion of their findings and considered how their prior learning had or had not changed. Thereafter, as homework, she sent them to pre-selected sites on the Internet where they could read and scan for more information on the topics introduced by the guide, as reflected in Figure 6.5.

Colonial America Anticipation Guide: Mark T for true and F for false next to the statements below. Then, discuss your responses with one classmate.

___The colonists were all Puritans.

___The small pox vaccine was innovated during this time.

___Strong religious standards help to keep individuals and society in order.

___Quakers and Catholics were excluded from the colonies.

___The Spanish, French, and Russians also established colonies in North America.

Colonial America Confirming Anticipation Guide: Now do a little reading on Internet sites pertaining to the following items. How and why have your responses changed. In the area beneath the statement, write down the new information you have learned that has confirmed or changed your opening views.

William Penn
Cotton Mather
Jonathan Edwards
Salem Witch Trials
Spanish Colonization
French Colonization

The colonists were all Puritans.
Confirming evidence 1, 2, 3
Source

The small pox vaccine was innovated during this time.
Confirming evidence 1, 2, 3
Source

Strong religious standards help to keep individuals and society in order.
Confirming evidence 1, 2, 3
Source

Quakers and Catholics were excluded from the colonies.
Confirming evidence 1, 2, 3
Source

The Spanish, French, and Russians also established colonies in North America.
Confirming evidence 1, 2, 3
Source

FIGURE 6.5 Colonial America Confirming Anticipation Guide

Head and Readence (1992) support this approach of discussing the responses with the students as a way to guide the full class toward broader understandings. This is an opportune time to teach students about cross-checking sources, or about exploring multiple perspectives and using more than one source or site to confirm that prior learning is in fact reliable knowledge. While a standard AG elicits student beliefs, these expansions of the basic guide go a step further by directing students to actively determine where they were correct or incorrect in their answers (Duffelmeyer & Baum, 1992).

Anticipation Guides and the K-W-L have a good deal in common. Both can activate prior knowledge, help engage students with a topic, and provide clues to misconceptions. Both also work best with topics about which students have enough prior knowledge to generate meaningful responses. However, AGs may be the more versatile of the two. Statements that are controversial may evoke emotional responses that enhance motivation. As the statements focus on the major components of the content, they can also serve to help students anticipate future learning.

Anticipation Guides and K-W-L activities serve the purpose of drawing forth and assessing students' prior learning. While activating prior learning, these tools also help to provide students with a sense of what to look for in the unit of study to come. They can also be sources from which, or in which important vocabulary and conceptual terms first come to students' attention. Working with vocabulary is another important part of Getting Learning Underway, as we shall see in the next chapter.

References

Allen, J. (2000). *Yellow brick roads: Shared and guided paths to independent reading*. Portland, ME: Stenhouse Publishers.

Allen, J. & Landaker, C. (2005). *Reading history: A practical guide to improving literacy*. New York, NY: Oxford University Press.

Aulls, M. W. (2008). Developing students' inquiry strategies: A case study of teaching history in the middle grades. In B. M. Shore, M. W. Aulls, & M. A. B. Delcourt (eds.) *Inquiry in education, Vol. II: Overcoming barriers to successful implementation* (pp. 1–49). New York, NY and London: Lawrence Erlbaum Associates.

Bain, R.B. (2000). Into the breach: Using research and theory to shape history instruction. In Stearns, P.N., Seixas, P., & Wineburg, S. (Eds.) *Knowing, teaching, and learning history: National and international perspectives* (pp. 331–352). New York, NY: University Press.

Barton, K. C. (2005). Primary sources in history: Breaking through the myths. *Phi Delta Kappan*, 86(10), 745–753.

Dochy, F. J. R. C., Segers, M., & Buehl, M. M. (1999). The relation between assessment practices and outcomes of studies: The case of research on prior knowledge. *Review of Educational Research*, 69(2), 145–186.

Downs, A. (1993) Breathing life into the past: The creation of history units using trade books. In M. O. Tunnell and R. Ammon (eds.), *The story of ourselves: Teaching history through children's literature* (pp. 137–145). Portsmouth, NH: Heinemann.

Duffelmeyer, F.A. (1994). Effective AG statements for learning from expository prose. *Journal of Reading*, 37(6), 452-457.

Duffelmeyer, F. A. & Baum, D. D. (1992). The extended AG revisited. *Journal of Reading*, 35(8), 654–656.

Dulberg, N. (2002). Engaging in history: Empathy and perspective-taking in children's historical thinking. Paper presented at the Annual Meeting of the American Educational Research Association, New Orleans, LA.

Fertig, G. (2001). Hard times and New Deals: Teaching fifth-graders about the Great Depression. *Social Education*, 65(1), 34–40.

Head, M. H. & Readence, J. E. (1992). AGs: Using prediction to promote learning from text. In E. K. Dishner, T. W. Bean, J. E. Readence, & D. W. Moore (eds.) *Reading in the content areas: Improving classroom instruction* (pp. 227–233). Dubuque, IA: Kendall/ Hunt Publishing Company.

Levstik, L. S. & Barton, K. C. (1997). *Doing history: Investigating with children in elementary and middle schools*. Mahwah, NJ: Lawrence Erlbaum Associates.

Marzano, R. J. (2004). *Building background knowledge for academic achievement*. Alexandria, VA: Association for Supervision and Curriculum Development.

Ogle, D. M. (1986). K-W-L: A teaching model that develops active reading of expository text. *The Reading Teacher*, 39(6), 564–571.

Ogle, D. M. (1992). K-W-L in action: Secondary teachers find applications that work. In E. K. Dishner, T. W. Bean, J. E. Readence, & D. W. Moore. *Reading in the content areas: Improving classroom instruction* (3rd edn.) (pp. 270–282). Dubuque, IA: Kendall/ Hunt Publishing Company.

Readence, J. E., Bean, T. W., & Baldwin, R. S. (1995). *Content area reading: An integrated approach*. Dubuque, IA: Kendall/Hunt Pub. Co.

Readence, J. E., Moore, W. D., & Rickelman, R. J. (2000). *Prereading activities for content area reading and learning*. Newark, DE: International Reading Association.

Sampson, M. B. (2002). Confirming the K-W-L: Considering the source. *The Reading Teacher*, 55(6), 528–532.

Selwyn, D. (1993). *Living history in the classroom: Integrative arts activities for making social studies meaningful*. Tucson, AZ: Zephyr Press.

Tobias, S. (1994). Interest, prior knowledge, and learning. *Review of Educational Research*, 64(1), 37-54.

Voss, J. F. & Wiley, J. (1997). Conceptual understanding in history. *European Journal of Psychology of Education*, 11(2), 147–158.

Woelders, A. (2007). "It makes you think more when you watch things": Scaffolding for historical inquiry using film in the middle school classroom. *Social Studies*, 98(4), 145–152.

7

PREVIEW THE LEARNING TO COME

Previewing the subject-matter that students are about to encounter makes it easier for them to understand it. Learning does not proceed by piling up of bits of information, but rather by relating information to a larger body of knowledge that gives it meaning. That is, students must know the gist of a topic to be able to meaningfully learn more about it. It is one dimension of what Ola Hallden (1994) called "the learning paradox" (p. 34), and its pedagogical implications are well established. Beginning in the 1960s, psychologist David Ausebel and others demonstrated that students need a conceptual framework known as an "advance organizer" to integrate new learning and to link it to what they may already know (Ausubel & Robinson, 1969; Ausubel, Novak & Hanesian, 1978). Cognitive research demonstrated that this was an especially effective way for students who had little background knowledge to learn about a topic, as they would otherwise have had to rely on rote learning. As a great many history students lack background knowledge for most topics they encounter, previews of subject-matter are especially important in history instruction.

Subject-matter previews tend to rely heavily on direct instruction. Teachers traditionally introduce students to a new topic simply by telling them about the material they are about to encounter. That is not inappropriate, even in an inquiry classroom. It gives the teacher an opportunity to introduce the Big Question that will be the focus of instruction or to elaborate on it if that has already happened. She can prepare a lecture that calls out those events or episodes on which the unit will focus and that emphasizes the dimensions of historical thinking that will be involved. Direct instruction is an efficient use of time for what is essentially a survey of the topic about to be explored. Teacher-directed instruction is appropriate and useful when it supports rather than deters student engagement, historical thinking, and meaningful learning.

While we will focus here on overviews of a unit of instruction, previews at the beginning of a course would serve much the same purpose. As we have already seen, Peter Lee (2005) offered one possibility—a proposal to spend two or three weeks to teach the big picture at the outset of a course. It would focus on large-scale patterns of change to provide a context for the events students would explore in depth. The point is to provide students with both a historical and a conceptual context within which to fit the material they will encounter during the course.

Graphic Overviews

Teachers who preview a unit typically find graphic organizers useful. These are charts that display the major events and concepts that a teacher has decided to emphasize in a unit. They come in a variety of formats, as the list below demonstrates (Table 7.1). The structured overview is the most formal and typically the most conceptual of these graphics. It presents a topic in a vertical and hierarchical sequence that consists of boxes representing the topic, its subtopics, and their sub-subtopics. Another is the concept or semantic web, which is a radial chart with the main topic in the middle cell, with lines extending out to subtopic or related cells and beyond. While it also is hierarchical, it tends to be less abstract than a structured overview. The concept map is still more free-form in design, with multiple hubs and sets of connecting lines. The concept mural is a web or map, with the topics represented by images. While such charts add a visual dimension to a teacher's presentation, they can also become an introduction to the interpretative nature of history. Teachers should be explicit that such organizers demonstrate what they have chosen to emphasize about a unit and that other versions are possible. Here we will look at how teachers have used each of these formats to present a graphic overview of history units.

TABLE 7.1 Kinds of Graphic Overviews

Graphic overviews	Basic characteristic
Structured overview	Vertical hierarchy
Concept (semantic) web	Radial hierarchy
Concept map	Free-form, multiple hubs
Concept mural	Web or map with images

Structured Overviews

In their unit on the Industrial Age in the United States after the Civil War, Mandy Byrd and Brooke Tomalchof (HLP) created a structured overview that included topics on immigration, industrialization, and progressive reform (Figure 7.1). They used it at the beginning of the unit to present a brief overview of the

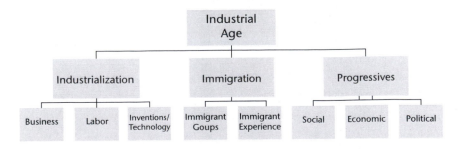

FIGURE 7.1 Industrial Age Structured Overview

Source: Permission of Mandy Bird and Brook Tomalchof (HLP)

content, mounted the structured overview in the classroom, and gave students page-size copies to place in their notebooks. They meant for the overview to be a work in progress. As the unit proceeded, they worked with the students to expand it, adding categories and providing more detail. This helped students keep track of major events and concepts and make new connections. Mandy noted that this approach "demonstrated how the topics flowed together and were not separate ideas." The overview also helped the students to see how "things are progressing simultaneously in history." As they approached the end of the unit, the diagram served as a graphic reminder of how developments during the period fit together. It also helped them prepare for the end-of-unit essay. In this final assessment, students explained how historical developments of the period fit together.

Fordham and her colleagues (Fordham, Wellman, & Sandmann, 2002) created a similar Structured Overview for a unit on the Sectional Crisis of the 1850s (Figure 7.2). It included the key concepts that the unit would cover. "Those ideas are then arranged in graphic form using connecting lines between categories to illustrate the relationship," they explained (pp. 149–150). Students used the graphic as a road map as their journey unfolded. They were able to return to the chart as the unit proceeded, flesh it out, and draw new lines of relationships.

Concept Webs

Like the Structured Overview, the graphic known as a Concept or Semantic Web provides students with an overview of a unit. It organizes the major topics in a radial rather than a vertical chart, which makes it somewhat easier to expand and to add details. The latter can be added as key words in cells linked to the main topic cells. In his Colorado history course for future elementary teachers, Matt Downey also used Concept Webs as a note-taking form (Figure 7.3). Using a projector, he modeled how students could link key words to topic cells to represent and help them recall larger chunks of information. His students also used the web to add details when reading assigned texts.

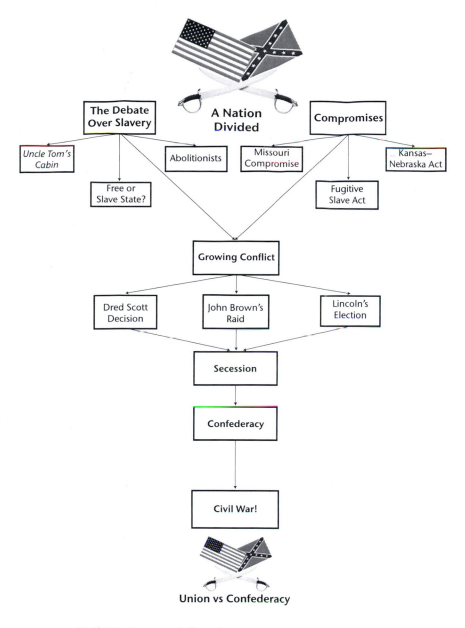

FIGURE 7.2 Civil War Structured Overview

Source: Permission of Taylor & Francis for authors Fordham, Wellman, Sandmann

Name: _____ Date: _____

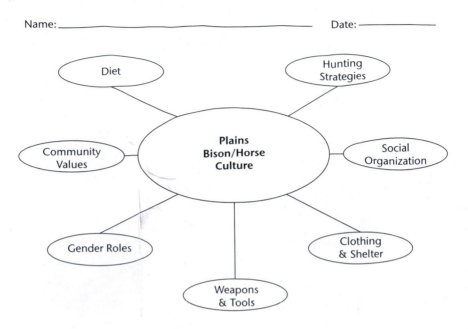

FIGURE 7.3 Bison Hunters Concept Web

Concept Maps and Murals

The Concept Map is a less formally structured way to present an overview of a topic. More free-form and organic than the graphics above, it can easily be extended in unanticipated directions. Concept maps are especially useful for literally mapping concepts, as the example by van Drie and van Boxtel (2003) demonstrates. They helped their students map the concept "communism," which was central to the course they were teaching (Figure 7.4). The students worked in pairs to map out major dimensions of the topic. As the students already were somewhat familiar with the topic, mapping it helped them activate background knowledge as well as identify what they still needed to know. Maps can be especially useful in history units that use a broad concept to help structure the content. Units on the Renaissance, the Industrial Revolution, or the Cold War immediately come to mind. While a teacher can introduce a concept map as an overview of a topic, it has added value when students build upon it as the unit unfolds. When completed it can help illustrate the connections students have made in an end-of-unit synthesis. Maps called Concept Murals are similar in format, but also use pictures to identify the topics.

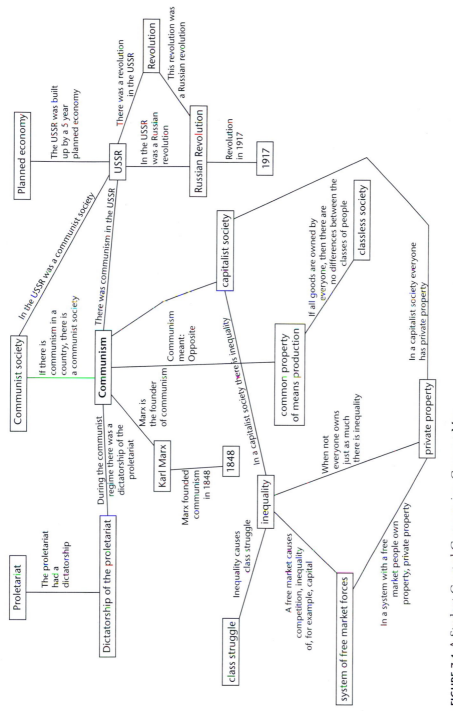

FIGURE 7.4 A Student Created Communism Concept Map

Source: Permission of the Historical Association, authors Carla van Boxtel and Jannet van Drie

Outlines and Timelines

Outlines and timelines are perhaps the most familiar formats for unit overviews. In a set of units designed to integrate socials studies and language arts instruction, Morin (2003) used an outline to introduce her fifth-grade students to US expansion into the Oregon Country. It presented the major points of the new topic on the overhead. She then walked her students through the outline, reading excerpts from the textbook and other nonfiction books to provide background knowledge about the topic. The students used the outline to construct an illustrated timeline of this phase of American expansion prior to investigating each aspect of the topic. Timelines, which we will discuss in Chapter 10, serve much the same purpose, with events, developments, and the dates on which they took place displayed along the horizontal axis.

Student-Created Overviews

While unit overviews typically are provided by the teacher, they can also be created by students. In a unit on Ancient Greece described by Richard Kellough and his colleagues (1996), the teacher on the first day assigned each of seven small groups a topic that was to be covered in the unit. Using the textbook and other classroom resources, the groups prepared brief oral reports. They presented these on the second day, with the rest of the class taking notes. On the third day, the students used their notes to make a timeline of the periods and events introduced. It provided both a survey of the topic and an opportunity to work on note-taking skills. Anita Downs (1993) briefly introduced her Middle Ages unit and then sent her fourth-grade students to the library to browse, read, and explore books on the topic. They recorded whatever they found interesting in spiral notebooks. The students used these notes the next day for an informal discussion about the period, which served as a student-led overview of the unit. With guidance from the teacher, such student previews may be even more productive than direct instruction. They involve students in the inquiry process from the outset.

Text Previews

Previewing text, a pre-reading strategy commonly used for reading comprehension, also can engage students in the overview of content. These are quick previews of a chapter or text passage that introduce students to what they are about to read. They focus on the main ideas of the content and on such text features as chapter title, subheadings, sidebars, illustrations, and captions or information otherwise called out in the text. To prevent the activity from becoming merely a recitation of what they had found, Diane Sanders asked her fourth-grade students to use their list to summarize what they were about to learn and to share that with the class (Robb, 2003, p. 307). To preview the content of a chapter, students at any grade level should do more than just skim through the material. Interacting with it helps build background knowledge and may well whet their interest in learning more about it.

Vocabulary Instruction

Introducing students to key vocabulary terms is another way to preview unit content. Vocabulary instruction involves more than learning the meaning of words. It helps students build background knowledge. It also can help students build a conceptual framework for the learning to come, as general or more abstract vocabulary terms often are important concepts (Marzano, 2004). Fortunately, we are well beyond the time when middle grades and high school teachers questioned whether "teaching reading" was their responsibility. It is widely recognized that subject-matter teachers are better qualified than anyone else to introduce students to their discipline's specialized vocabulary, text structures, and distinctive syntax or phrasing and word usage. The old dichotomy between "learning to read" (through literacy instruction) and "reading to learn" (through content instruction) has little meaning to teachers who recognize how closely the two are linked. This does not mean that secondary history and social studies teachers should be responsible for teaching basic word decoding skills. It means that they are well qualified to introduce students to the vocabulary and text reading and writing strategies specific to their discipline and subject-matter.

It is common wisdom that learning words in context is the preferred way to learn vocabulary. While this frequently may be the case, learning words in context requires multiple encounters through wide reading. In history classrooms, new vocabulary terms often are specialized and topic specific. "The exposure needed to learn these specialized [content-area] words is limited because they appear infrequently in texts" (Harmon & Hedrick, 2000, pp. 155–156). Even strong readers may need more than infrequent encounters to learn a new term. It is even less likely that struggling readers will learn very many specialized terms in context. Aaron Jackson (HLP) found that working with vocabulary in context was useful but insufficient for ill-prepared readers. Many of his sixth-grade students who were learning about the United States and Canada struggled with basic concepts, such as the difference between a continent and a country. Others did not know what the term "colony" meant. For these students, direct vocabulary instruction was essential for them even to begin understanding the content of the unit. However, as we will see below, Aaron did not rely on traditional "drill-and-kill" methods of vocabulary instruction. Like many teachers, he used a variety of strategies for direct vocabulary instruction.

Direct Teaching of Vocabulary

While not the only way to help students learn new words, direct vocabulary instruction often is the most effective way to do so in a content area. Research on student learning demonstrates that direct vocabulary instruction in academic subjects is effective (Beck & McKeown, 1991; Graves, 1987; Marzano, 2004). However, it must be done strategically. Current best practice in academic vocabulary instruction calls for teaching fewer and more useful words (Faulkner, 2010; Kelley, Lesaux, Kieffer, & Faller, 2010). Instruction should "target high-utility academic words" and "teach a small number of these words in depth" (Kelley, et al., 2010, p. 12). Focusing on linguistic properties of words, including Greek and Latin roots, may also facilitate history vocabulary learning (Harmon, Hedrick, & Wood, 2005; Vacca & Vacca, 2008). However, words that students are not likely to encounter more than once, especially archaic terms in primary sources, are not good candidates for vocabulary instruction. Effective vocabulary instruction also requires students to have multiple exposures to each word. It seems obvious that a few "high utility" terms frequently revisited are more likely to become part of a student's working vocabulary than more arcane or infrequently encountered words.

Content-area teachers are devoting more time at the outset of instruction to the direct teaching of vocabulary (Baumann, Ware, & Edwards, 2007; Donnelly & Roe, 2010; Farris & Downey, 2004). It has become, as Harmon and Hedrick (2000) observed, "an integral part of content learning" (p. 156). This can be accounted for, in part, by the focus on comprehension in reading instruction, which has brought content-area vocabulary into sharper relief. It is widely recognized that each subject area poses its own reading challenges, not the least of which are their distinctive vocabularies (Harmon, et al., 2005; Marzano, 2004; Readence, Moore, & Rickelman, 2000). Recognition of the conceptual load of many vocabulary terms has also contributed. Vocabulary is more than a matter of words, as many key terms (proper nouns aside) are labels for important concepts. In that respect, Marzano (2004) notes, "the research and theory strongly suggest that teaching vocabulary is synonymous with teaching background knowledge" (p. 35). Finally, students who lack the vocabulary of a discipline or subject-matter remain "outsiders" to its ways of thinking "and the concepts inherent in its terminology" (Readence, et al., 2000, p. 46). While history does not have a vocabulary as specialized as some content areas, its conceptual language is sufficiently different to make outsiders of most students.

How do teachers identify key words for vocabulary instruction? Every topic has specialized terms that will be obstacles to understanding for students who do not know them. Indentured servitude, nativist, gradual emancipation, secede, open range, tenement house, political machine, yellow journalism, and muckraking are a few obvious ones for American history. Words teachers select should have an essential link to the subject-matter. Marzano and Pickering (2005) recommend compiling discipline-specific word lists from state and national content standards. We encourage teachers to strike a balance between general terms or concepts and singular referent terms, such as proper names, legislative acts, battles, and place names. Focusing on concepts will help teachers align vocabulary instruction with the Big Ideas driving the unit, while more specific terms will help anchor students in a particular time and place. Once the important words are determined, teachers need to use focused and direct methods to help students make these concepts and terms part of their own vocabulary.

Direct vocabulary instruction needs to be deliberate, repetitious, and student engaging. Aaron Jackson (HLP) addressed key terms at the outset of a new unit, selecting words that occurred multiple times and that students were likely to encounter beyond that unit. He provided a basic definition of a term, but asked the students to restate it in their own words. He also helped them connect the new vocabulary term to words they already knew. As these terms came up in the course of instruction, he revisited these initial vocabulary activities. Like many teachers, Aaron moved away from dictionary definitions toward a more descriptive approach to teaching vocabulary. For example, the dictionary definition of the term "plantation" as a large self-sufficient farm in the pre-Civil War South, Harmon and Hedrick (2000) note, "does not capture the full meaning of the term. A more substantive description of *plantation* involves associations with southern life in pre-Civil War days and a southern economy based upon cotton and slavery" (p. 156). No less important, the descriptions should be in the students' own words. Dictionary definitions are static and fixed, to be learned once, if at all, and hopefully committed to memory. Student descriptions are a work in progress. They allow the meaning of a term to evolve over the course of instruction as students become more familiar with the concept that is being defined. They also are likely to be more easily retrieved from long-term memory.

For vocabulary instruction, teachers have found new uses for traditional techniques, such as study guides and flashcards. At the beginning of every unit, David Farrell (HLP) provided his students with a study guide that listed vocabulary terms and Essential Questions. The guide provided structure and focus to vocabulary learning, as students could refer back to it as they proceeded through the unit. However, students added their own explanations to the definitions he provided. He also gave students a word bank and allowed them to create flashcards called "grade makers." On these cards, the students defined, described, and explained in their own words each term on the vocabulary list. They could turn in the list for extra credit. The cards also led to better grades because Farrell encouraged students to use them on the unit test, both for the objective part and for the essay. They were expected to use the assigned vocabulary words in their essays. Similarly, Carin Barrett (HLP) used an Internet tool called Quizlet to provide her students with flashcards that had terms and definitions. After a first "cold-read" of an article, they worked in small groups to generate lists of words they were not familiar with. The full class then reviewed the words to ensure they understood the text. Barrett also utilized sentence starters to assess student understanding of what they had read.

Research demonstrates that creating visual or mental images of key vocabulary terms helps students remember them (Dewhurst & Conway, 1994; Johnson-Glenberg, 2000; Sadoski & Pavio, 2001; Schwartz & Heiser, 2006). Visualizing a word may include students reconstructing it in their mind or drawing a picture of the scene or the event the word represents. The image can also be a chart or graphic organizer. Aaron used images to describe new concepts or to connect new terms to words his sixth-grade students knew well. He found that this approach worked better than asking students to take vocabulary notes. The students included images in their interactive notebooks and Aaron displayed his own on the walls of the classroom. When he encountered a vocabulary word in the subsequent lessons, he drew attention to the term, bringing students back to their notes, and referencing the images on the walls. A sixth-grade unit on Ancient Greece described by Kellough, et al. (1996) included a "vocabulary scribble" in which students mined a textbook chapter for unfamiliar words, defined them, made a drawing for each word, and placed them in meaningful categories.

In her middle school classes that included many English Language Learners (ELL) students, Ann Putsche (HLP) engaged in daily vocabulary instruction that depended heavily on images. To help students learn words that were central concepts in the unit of study, she gave them a chart with four cells (Figure 7.5). In the first one, her students wrote the word to be learned. Putsche offered a simple definition for the word, which students working with a partner or individually restated in their own words, writing it in the "definition" cell. In the "graphic representation" cell, the students drew a picture or a symbol to help them visualize the concept. Finally, at the bottom of the chart they wrote a sentence that used the new term. Later in the class period, Putsche showed the students her own laminated photograph that illustrated the concept. Then she hung the photo and the term on the wall, where these remained as a visible reminder of the concept throughout the rest of the unit of study.

Engaging multiple senses and learning modalities also helps students learn new vocabulary terms, especially ELL students. Sheltered instruction in ELL incorporates a variety of approaches that include "emphasizing key points, defining vocabulary in context, and coupling talk with the use of gestures, drawings, graphs and charts" (Weisman & Hansen, 2007, p. 181). Teachers in ELL classrooms break vocabulary words into parts, paste words on paper around the classroom on word walls, and use multiple pictures. Such strategies also work well in more mainstream classrooms. Gabrielle Wymore's (HLP) students worked in groups of three to create a group vocabulary poster and applied Total Physical Response strategies to act out the meaning of words. They defined words in their own terms, provided an example, added a visual, used the word in a sentence, and created a physical demonstration of the term. Direct vocabulary instruction, like activating prior knowledge and checking for misconceptions, is essential to

| Name _____ Date _____ Period _____ |
| Terms and Names _____ Class _____ Chapter _____ |

1. word	3. graphic representation
2. definition _____ _____ _____ _____ _____	
4. sentence _____ _____ _____	

FIGURE 7.5 Concept Definition Chart

Source: Permission of Ann Putsche (HLP)

getting learning underway. This involves more than teachers having students copy dictionary definitions or referring them to glossaries. Students must have an opportunity to work with words, like the students studying the Middle Ages at an elementary school in Texas. These students "created vocabulary journals that recorded terms and definitions for the specialized words they were learning. The fifth graders often worked in small groups to brainstorm definitions, connotations, and implications of vocabulary terms. They displayed the results of their efforts on 'word walls' in their classroom and in the school's hallways" (Johnson & Janisch, 1998, p. 7). They internalized new words by spending time with them. Like the other activities that we have reviewed in this chapter, vocabulary building is an essential part of helping students know what lies ahead in the unit. We think time is well spent in previewing the learning to come.

References

Ausubel, D. P. & Robinson, F. G. (1969). *School learning: An introduction to educational psychology*. New York, NY: Holt, Rinehart & Winston.

Ausubel, D. P., Novak, J., & Hanesian, H. (1978). *Educational psychology: A cognitive view* (2nd edn.). New York, NY: Holt, Rinehart & Winston.

Baumann, J. F., Ware, D., & Edwards, E. C. (2007). "Bumping into spicy, tasty words that catch your tongue": A formative experiment on vocabulary instruction. *The Reading Teacher*, 61(2), 108–122.

Beck, I. L. & McKeown, M. G. (1991). Conditions of vocabulary acquisition. In R. Barr, M. Kamil, P. B. Mosenthal, & P. D. Pearson (eds.) *Handbook of reading research, Vol. II* (pp. 789–814). New York, NY: Longman.

Dewhurst, S. A. & Conway, M. A. (1994). Pictures, images, and recollective experience. *Journal of Experimental Psychology*, 20(5), 1088–1098.

Donnelly, W. B. & Roe, C. J. (2010). Using sentence frames to develop academic vocabulary for English learners. *The Reading Teacher*, 64(2), 131–136.

Downs, A. (1993) Breathing life into the past: The creation of history units using trade books. In M. O. Tunnell & R. Ammon (eds.) *The story of ourselves: Teaching history through children's literature* (pp. 137–145). Portsmouth, NH: Heinemann.

Farris, P. J. & Downey, P. M. (2004). Concept muraling: Dropping visual crumbs along the instructional trail. *The Reading Teacher*, 58(4), 376–380.

Faulkner, J. (2010). Reducing vocabulary to increase vocabulary: Student-centered vocabulary instruction for writing that makes a difference. *English Journal*, 100(1), 113–116.

Fordham, N. W., Wellman, D., & Sandmann, A. (2002). Taming the text: Engaging and supporting students in social studies readings. *Social Studies*, 93(4), 149–158.

Graves, M. F. (1987). The roles of instruction in fostering vocabulary development. In M. G. McKeown & M. E. Curtis (eds.) *The nature of vocabulary acquisition* (pp. 165–184). Hillsdale, JN: Erlbaum.

Hallden, O. (1994). On the paradox of understanding history in an educational setting. In Leinhardt, G., Beck, I. L., & Stainton, C. (eds.) *Teaching and learning in history* (pp. 27–46). Hillsdale, NJ and Hove, UK: Lawrence Erlbaum Associates.

Harmon, J. M. & Hedrick, W. B. (2000), Zooming in and zooming out: Enhancing vocabulary and conceptual learning in social studies. *The Reading Teacher*, 54(2), 155–159.

Harmon, J. M., Hedrick, W. B., & Wood, K. D. (2005). Research on vocabulary instruction in the content areas: implications for struggling readers. *Reading and Writing Quarterly*, 21, 261–280.

Johnson, M. J. & Janisch, C. (1998). Connecting literacy with social studies content. *Social Studies & the Young Learner*, 10(4), 6–9.

Johnson-Glenberg, M. C. (2000). Training reading comprehension in adequate decoders/poor comprehenders: Verbal versus visual strategies. *Journal of Educational Psychology*, 92(4), 772–782.

Kelley, J. G., Lesaux, N. K., Kieffer, M. J., & Faller, S. E. (2010). Effective academic vocabulary instruction in the urban middle school. *The Reading Teacher*, 64(1), 5–14.

Kellough, R. D., Jarolimek, J., Parker, W. C., Martorella, P. H., Tompkins, G. E., & Hoskisson, K. (1996). *Integrating language arts and social studies for intermediate and middle school students*. Englewood Cliffs, NJ: Prentice–Hall, Inc.

Lee P. (2005) Putting principles into practice: understanding history. In M. S. Donovan & J. D. Bransford (eds.) *How students learn: History in the classroom* (pp. 31–78). Washington, DC: National Academies Press.

Marzano, R. J. (2004). *Building background knowledge for academic achievement*. Alexandria, VA: Association for Supervision and Curriculum Development.

Marzano, R. J. & Pickering, D. J. (2005). *Building academic vocabulary: Teacher's Manual*. Alexandria, VA: Association for Supervision and Curriculum Development.

Morin, J. H. (2003). *Social studies instruction incorporating the language arts*. Boston, MA: Pearson Education, Inc.

Readence, J. E., Moore, W. D., & Rickelman, R. J. (2000). *Prereading activities for content area reading and learning*. Newark, DE: International Reading Association.

Robb, L. (2003). *Teaching reading in social studies, science, and math: Practical ways to weave comprehension strategies into your content area teaching*. New York, NY: Scholastic.

Sadoski, M. & Pavio, A. (2001). *Imagery and text: A dual coding theory of reading and writing*. Mahway, NJ: Erlbaum.

Schwartz, D. & Heiser, J. (2006) Spatial representations and imagery in learning. In R. K. Sawyer (ed.) *The Cambridge handbook of the learning sciences* (pp. 283–298). Cambridge: Cambridge University Press.

Vacca, R. T. & Vacca, J. L. (2008). *Content area reading: Literacy and learning across the curriculum*. Boston, MA: Pearson Education, Inc.

Van Drie, J. & van Boxtel, C. (2003). Developing conceptual understanding through talk and mapping. *Teaching History*, 110, 27–31.

Weisman, E. M. & Hansen, L. E. (2007). Strategies for teaching social studies to English-language learners at the elementary level. *Social Studies*, 98(5), 180–184.

PART IV
Building Historical Knowledge

Getting Learning Underway
*   Activate Prior Knowledge
*   Check for Misconceptions
*   Preview the Learning to Come
*   Address Vocabulary

Building Historical Knowledge
*   ***Build Factual Knowledge***
*   ***Compare Texts***
*   ***Analyze Text***
*   ***Analyze Perspectives***
*   ***Make Temporal and Causal Connections***
*   ***Create a Synthesis***

Applying Learning
*   Think About Change
*   Use Historical Perspectives
*   Analyze People's Perspectives

FIGURE 8.1 Teaching for Historical Literacy: Building Knowledge

8

COLLECT EVIDENCE

With some shared background knowledge, a Big Question in mind, and a sense of where they are headed, students are ready to explore a historical topic. As illustrated in Figure 8.1, Teaching for Historical Literacy: Building knowledge chart, on the facing page, the second phase of historical literacy focuses on the building knowledge phase of historical instruction. During the early stages of an investigation, students will spend much of their time collecting factual evidence, which in terms of historical thinking is the first step toward creating a historical account. We use the term "collecting evidence" intentionally to differentiate what they are doing from the aimless gathering of information. That is, students engaged in inquiry look for specific information that has some bearing on the Big Question they have asked. Persuasive, student-written accounts, Chauncey Monte-Sano (2010) notes, are based on factual evidence that is "specific, relevant, and significant" (p. 561). In this process, they will encounter and even take notes about information that turns out to be irrelevant or of little use in the end. Gathering and winnowing out information as they go is part of the inquiry process.

The emphasis on the memorization of facts in the traditional history pedagogy has cast a shadow over factual learning in history education. That is unfortunate, as facts are the boards, bricks, and building blocks of historical knowledge. Factual knowledge provides the foundation for the conceptual knowledge essential to historical literacy. Students cannot do without it and we should not minimize its importance in history instruction. Factual knowledge also has been associated with a lockstep learning sequence based on an assumption that higher-level thinking depends upon the mastery of factual information. Teachers who pursue such a "facts first" approach inevitably run out of time before they can engage students in more complex learning. That, too, is unfortunate, as constructing historical knowledge is not a linear process. As we shall see, it is a reiterative and recursive undertaking that can engage students in multiple kinds of learning at the same time. Students may need an understanding of concepts while still learning factual information. With some conceptual knowledge in hand, they may have to retrace their steps to learn new factual information to elaborate on what they know. Students also may need to acquire procedural knowledge when the need arises. There in no recommended sequence.

Factual and procedural learning in history classrooms go hand in hand. Paul's introductory lessons on Ancient Egypt emphasized factual learning, but did not exclude other kinds of learning. As Aulls (2008) observed, "Paul balanced the learning of knowledge about Egyptian history with knowledge about strategies for learning how to read, think, and talk about what was being learned" (p. 21). To organize and process the information they were gathering, Paul emphasized procedural as well as factual learning. He introduced a note-making strategy, a semantic map construction procedure, and a strategy for group study and reflection. The importance of explicitly teaching such learning strategies in social studies is well supported by research (Knight, Waxman, & Padron, 1989).

In teaching about the Civil War, Lyle, a teacher observed by Monte-Sano (2011), also combined conceptual and factual learning. "Learning history in Lyle's classroom was as much about learning to talk, read, write, and think historically as it was about the Civil War content," Monte-Sano observed (p. 240). To annotate text, Lyle's students "underlined words or wrote notes, questions, and ideas in the margins," and "judging by their course readers, most students annotated daily" (p. 224). As Lyle noted, "I want them to raise questions to themselves as they read whenever they're reading. ... I wanted to slow them down ... to have a dialogue with both themselves and the author" (p. 224). As Monte-Sano concluded, "The reference to 'a conversation' with the text indicated that reading in this class was not about gathering and seeking information, but rather about interacting with a text to construct meaning" (p. 225). Paul, the teacher in the paragraph above, also had introduced note making as a strategy for making connections and moving his students toward a conceptual understanding of the information they were learning.

Paul also had introduced his students to key concepts early in his unit on Ancient Egypt. He began the unit, Aulls (2008) observed, by providing his students with a conceptual framework for thinking about civilizations. It included such properties of civilization as the emergence of cities and places having a permanent food supply. He presented these basic concepts as just other kinds of factual information to be learned and remembered, as he knew that the students later on would need a conceptual vocabulary to categorize and make connections between the facts they were learning. Through discussion and note-taking as the unit progressed, he helped them internalize this information and deepen their understanding of the concepts.

Building factual knowledge requires students to develop skills of note-taking and note-making, to help them retain the information and make sense of the facts.

Like Paul, teachers in inquiry classrooms make a distinction between note-taking and note-making. Students take notes primarily to store information, although note taking during reading may also improve comprehension. Some teachers have students use sticky notes for jotting short comments on a page, although they should be restrained from what one teacher called "sticky madness" or the plastering of notes over the page (Angelillo, 2003). The same caution is appropriate for students who use highlighters indiscriminately. Other teachers have students take notes in a journal that they keep open as they read. Reading journals are especially useful for note-making, which is a reflective kind of note-taking.

Note-making and journaling ask students to reflect on the information that they are taking notes about. This may include elaborating on the concepts and ideas they had found in their readings and relating them to other things they have learned. As Aulls (2008) noted, "Paul was teaching note-making to have students make a record of facts, concepts, and ideas, and also to actively engage their attention to understanding what they read ... and to further develop all students' conceptual grasp of the general topics and their relationships to subtopics that elaborated their meaning" (p. 26). Fourth-grade students in a Texas elementary school who kept a journal when reading their textbook retained the information longer than students who did not use journals (Davis, Rooze, & Tallent, 1992). While reading journals can also serve this purpose, two-column note-taking formats are probably more common in inquiry classrooms. Perhaps the most widely used is the Cornell, two-column note-taking system. Faber and her colleagues reported that note-taking with the Cornell system in a ninth-grade world cultures class in a suburban Philadelphia school facilitated students' comprehension (Faber, Morris, & Lieberman, 2000). Students at Herbert Hoover High School in San Diego used the Cornell system across all subject areas to help raise the school's assessment results (Fisher, Frey, & Williams, 2002). HLP partner Michelle Pearson developed a version of two-column notes based on the Cornell Note model for use with her middle school students (Figure 8.2). This format encouraged her students to draw inferences about what they were learning as well as to make notes for future references.

Teachers as Sources of Information

Teachers are an important source of information for students in history classrooms. In teacher-directed instruction, teacher talk may account for as much as 80 percent of a lesson (Sharp, 2008). Not all of that involves the delivery of content information, as teachers also orally give instructions, clarify assignments, ask questions, and manage classroom behavior. Yet teachers do transmit a great deal of information through direct instruction. Teachers in secondary and higher education often use lectures for this purpose. Lectures can be an efficient way to summarize information and bring it to bear on a specific learning task. They can be most effective when kept brief, clearly focused, and designed to hold student

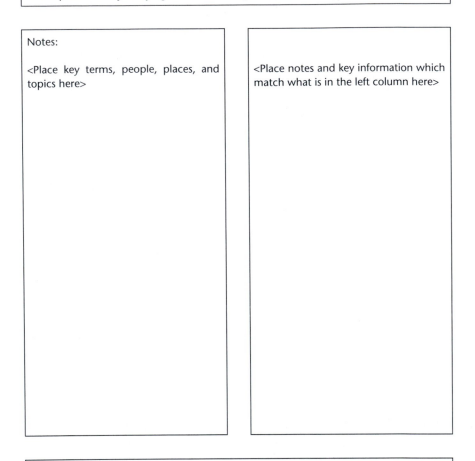

Topic:	Date:

Essential Question:
What question are you trying to answer with your research/study?

Notes:

<Place key terms, people, places, and topics here>

<Place notes and key information which match what is in the left column here>

Summary: (6-8 sentences MINIMUM) The most important facts and information within the notes that you have taken should go here in a **COMPLETE and CONCISE** summary. Make sure that the summary is readable and answers the essential question listed at the top of your notes.

Reflection: How and why do I know this? **Give specific examples.** Connect what you learn to your life, to other subjects, to what you have read.

FIGURE 8.2 Cornell Notes Modification

Source: Permission of Michelle Pearson (HLP)

attention. Even teacher questions frequently become occasions for delivering information. Recitation-type questions often serve as springboards for mini-lectures, prompting the teacher to elaborate on the students' less than satisfactory answers (Edwards, 1992). Teachers must be mindful that this kind of exchange might invite students to give the teacher the answer they think he is after, discouraging divergent thinking and real inquiry.

Teachers spend much time and effort outside the classroom preparing useful information for their students. Conscientious teachers read widely, watch documentaries, and keep up on the news searching for interest-catching materials. They create readings that are age appropriate, workable within the timeframe of a class period, and targeted toward their students. This requires editing texts, excerpting longer pieces, and paraphrasing difficult materials. The Historical Literacy Partnership teachers typically brought a wide variety of items into their classrooms. While we made no attempt to assemble an inclusive list, the teachers mentioned political cartoons, songs, music, art, maps, artifacts, photos of architecture, costumes, *Junior Scholastic* magazines, almanacs, atlases, *We the People* publications, *National Geographic* articles, book carts they had librarians assemble, as well as newspapers and magazines. They introduced these materials in a variety of ways.

When engaged in direct instruction, teachers in the HLP used a variety of strategies to sustain student interest. They personalized the content whenever possible, establishing connections between the topic and their own life experiences. They talked about books, newspaper items or online accounts that they read as a jumping off place into a topic. They encouraged student questions about their interests. Keeping lectures brief and illustrating them with pictures, charts, and maps helped teachers sustain student interest. They also varied their delivery by using the smart board and computer-assisted presentations. They read aloud excerpts from interesting primary sources. Some located online Advanced Placement study guides to share with their students. After assigning her students a quick Internet search to provide an overview of the Vietnam War, Carin Barrett (HLP) brought into her high school classroom primary sources, letters, artifacts, music, and newspaper articles. She arranged these items in "stations" on tables, which her students rotated among to find specific information.

Teachers may not always be fully aware of the role they play as deliverers of information. Social studies teachers interviewed by Frederick Smith and Karen Feathers (1983) explained that assigned readings accounted for most of the information their students received. However, their students reported that "teacher talking" contributed as much or more than the textbook and other readings (p. 352). The students saw the goal of the course primarily as remembering facts, dates, and names of presidents. The researchers concluded that this disconnect between teacher and student perceptions was a result of the students reading the assigned texts superficially to answer worksheet questions or avoiding them altogether. They relied mainly on what the teachers were telling them. The teachers underestimated their role as information providers and what that was communicating to their students about their own goals for the class.

Textbooks as Sources of Information

Even in an age of increasing presence of computers and Internet resources, textbooks remain ubiquitous in history classrooms. They are as commonplace as classroom desks and chairs. Teachers who do not organize instruction around textbooks still find them useful. Even while urging teachers to move beyond the textbook, David Kobrin (1996) noted that "Most middle and high school social studies teachers value the support a good textbook can provide." He observed that "Just the thought of doing without a text can be scary. After all, textbooks serve as a principal source of information in many classrooms" (pp. 3–4). In inquiry classrooms, they provide students with a common core of information. Donna Ogle and colleagues (2007) note that "textbooks have an important role to play" even in extended inquiry and thematic units. Providing overviews of topics and explaining how events and people "fit into the larger context," these authors observe, "The textbook provides a starting point and a reference to which students can return to clarify issues that arise as they engage with the more extensive and focused resources" (p. 26). Importantly, they provide students with the long sweep of history that is essential for breadth of content knowledge (Key, Bradley, & Bradley, 2010). Our project partners attested to the usefulness of textbooks as a good way of getting at central ideas; they are written by historians and they provide students with a common text. Many newer ones have online resource components. However, the HLP teachers also reminded us of the reality that not all classrooms have textbooks, that students are not always able to take textbooks home, and that even in classrooms that have fairly recent editions, students may not have a book for their individual use.

Despite their potential value, history textbooks have enjoyed a mixed reputation over the years—for good reason. While they can be a time-efficient way to organize the curriculum, teachers too often have allowed them to drive instruction. Sometimes they are not well written, and often they presume too much background knowledge on the students' part. The authoritative voice of the textbook can have the effect of demotivating students who are trying to reorganize information in meaningful ways. The textbook information is already organized, presumably by experts (Voss & Wiley, 1997), which can lead students to wonder why they would bother to figure things out for themselves.

While textbooks must be used deliberately and carefully in history classrooms, textbook assignments remain an important dimension of instruction. Paul relied heavily on the textbook as the jumping-off place for factual learning. Students in Paul's classroom spent about 30 percent of their time reading, taking notes from, and talking about the textbook (Aulls, 2008). Of course, textbooks are not the only sources of information in classrooms. Paul's students spent about 40 percent of their class time on project activities. For these projects, students used library resources, historical reference books, historical atlas, documentary films, and interviews with experts. In her fifth-grade classroom, Caroline C. Eidson used chapters from two textbooks to get her lessons on exploration and colonization underway (Tomlinson & Eidson, 2003). After her students had completed a short, assigned reading, they moved beyond the textbook to work with other materials at independent learning centers. Both teachers used textbooks, but did not allow textbooks to drive instruction.

Primary Sources

Primary sources are featured in much of the recent literature describing effective or highly promising practices in history classrooms (Aulls, 2008; Kobrin, 1996; Lesh, 2011; Wineburg, Martin, & Monte-Sano, 2011). These include first-hand accounts, historical photographs, and other documentary evidence. Some teachers rely more heavily on primary sources than any other texts for student reading. In Lyle's classroom, primary sources made up 82 percent of his reading materials, with 92 percent of classroom time devoted to them (Monte-Sano, 2011). However, teachers may be relying too much on primary sources, at the expense of other accounts. As Bain (2005) notes, source-based activities appear to be "synonymous with historical thinking in the US classrooms and on standardized exams" (p. 202). There is more to historical thinking than working with documents.

The reasons most commonly given for using primary sources are quite persuasive. They introduce students to the points of view of people of the time. Lyle justified his heavy reliance on documents by noting the insight they provided into the perspectives and motivation of historical actors. He explained, "I think you're giving them the head and the heart of somebody back then" (Monte-Sano, 2011, p. 219), which a textbook, however well written, could not provide. Such sources also typically include a level of detail for which textbooks or secondary accounts seldom have space. A ninth-grade world history teacher assigned primary sources as a supplement to other materials because they helped introduce students to the "strangeness" of the past. "The language, the subject-matter, the writing style, and the expressions demonstrate better than anything else how differently people thought, communicated, believed, and even acted in the past," observed Jada Kohlmeier (2005, p. 504). Primary sources, in brief, provide students with the close encounters with the past lacking in many other historical texts.

While primary sources are critical for engaging students in historical thinking, they can be problematic as sources of general background information. They are fragments of information, only "traces" or "leavings" of the past, as Thomas C. Holt (1990, pp. 13–14) explains. They often offer contradictory descriptions of what happened in the past. The detail that provides students with a glimpse at the complexity of any event in history can be overwhelming. Students also need a good deal of background knowledge to interpret a primary source and to place it in context.

Teachers need to use primary sources in targeted ways in order to make them useful for understanding the past. When working with their high school students, both Russ Brown and Carin Barrett (HLP) used the acronym OPVL—Origin, Purpose, Value, and Limitations helps students establish who made the document, when and where the document was created, why it was created, whether it was propaganda, and how balanced it was in terms of the information it offered. The process also asked students to think about whether the information was originally meant for the public. Carin prepared students to answer Document Based Questions by doing a quick identification exercise that answered basic who, what, when, where, and why questions. Her students learned to determine what the question was asking so they could try to categorize it properly in terms of what information a source could provide. Then they annotated the document in specific terms of the question being asked. For example, if the question required students to take a side, they would annotate the document by indicating which side it could be used to support and why. Cory Reinking (HLP) provided a study guide that his community college students found helpful for focusing their reading and analyzing primary sources. Cory's study guide questions built from basic to more advanced questions. For the discussion on John Locke's *The Second Treaties on Civil Government*, for example, the questions were ordered as follows (Figure 8.3).

Primary sources work well in conjunction with a textbook account that provides students with an overview of the larger historical context in which the documents were created. Primary sources are likely to be most productive when students work with multiple sources about a topic, including sources that contradict one another. Sam Wineburg and colleagues (2011) have compiled sets for such commonly taught topics as the Battle at Lexington Green, Abraham Lincoln and the slavery issue, Rosa Parks and the Montgomery bus boycott, and the Cuban missile crisis that provide students insight into multiple perspectives of key events.

Perhaps the most common place where teachers find primary sources are various sites on the Internet. Among the sites that we have found most useful and reliable are the Library of Congress, especially its American Memory collection therein; the National Archive and Records Administration; the Gilder-Lehman Institute; the Yale Avalon Site; and presidential libraries. Museums and historic sites offer interesting points of regional sources that can also be accessed online, such as Old Sturbridge Village, Plimouth Plantation; and the National World War Two History Museum in New Orleans. In addition to Internet sites, teachers have also found creative uses for local artifacts and nearby historic sites.

1. What is human nature according to Locke? How does he view humanity?
2. What type of society does Locke argue for (class, politics, economics, religion, military)?
3. Is this society feasible? What problems do you foresee with Locke's society?
4. Which theory could better control and order society, Machiavelli or Locke?

FIGURE 8.3 Study Guide Questions

Source: Permission of Cory Reinking (HLP)

Secondary Accounts

In addition to textbooks and primary source documents, students need access to secondary accounts. Secondary accounts are interpretations of what happened in the past, written later and by non–participants, including professional historians, journalists, and political and social commentators. Documentary films, videos, museum exhibits, and teacher-made presentations also are secondary accounts. Their great benefit is that they are more narrowly focused than textbook accounts and have the potential to offer multiple points of view. In elementary classrooms, secondary accounts for historical inquiry usually include biographies. In Debbie Stien's third-grade classroom, she used biographies to help her students make the transition from story books to nonfiction because "Biographies seemed like a natural bridge between the two genres, because they had some of the aspects of fiction, such as a character, but they were also nonfiction—based on facts" (Stien & Beed, 2004, p. 513). Whatever form they take or wherever they originate, secondary historical accounts are indispensable to historical inquiry.

Secondary accounts fill the gap between textbooks and primary sources. While textbooks only present an overview of a topic, usually the point of view of a single writer (or set of authors), primary sources provide unique and often multiple perspectives, but are fragmented accounts of what happened. Janet Angelillo (2003) argues that, "[In everyday life] we rarely search for information from textbooks, so it makes good sense that most of the content-based reading students do should come from nonfiction trade books" (p. 101). To interpret a primary source, students may need a context into which to place it that is more specific than a textbook can offer. It also helps for them to have some knowledge "of the ways others have made sense of it" (Husbands, 1996, p. 18). Well-chosen secondary sources can fulfill both needs. In recent years, they have taken a back seat to primary sources in history instruction.

Secondary accounts enable teachers to introduce the idea that historians "talk" to each other. "A preoccupation with primary historical evidence," Chris Husbands (1996) notes, "underplays the importance of secondary (accounts): no historian would embark on a historical investigation without considering what other historians had written" (p. 17). Through these accounts, historians disagree with, argue about, and revise the work of other historians. By comparing secondary sources or excerpts from them, students can consider how such accounts differ and ask questions about how an account reflects an individual historian's point of view or the time in which he or she wrote. Dan Rypma (HLP) provided his high school students with conflicting secondary accounts about the American Revolution by historians Howard Zinn, Gordan Wood, and Gary Nash. As they read, compared, and assessed these accounts, they used a graphic organizer to help them keep track of each historian's arguments and examples. By using multiple texts, Dan led his students beyond fact gathering and toward the analysis of arguments and interpretations. Writing their own accounts allowed students to join in this conversation.

Teachers have used secondary accounts to engage their students in historical investigation and inquiry in a variety of ways. Patricia Collins (1990) created a classroom research center of books and other materials to help her sixth-grade students investigate life in the Medieval period. Pamela Derson and Judy Costello introduced fourth-grade students to secondary sources with packets of information and books to supplement the textbook (Van Sledright & Frankes, 2000). Other teachers brought sets of "leveled" books for historical reading into the classroom, so called because the sets include books written at several, clearly identified reading levels (Ogle, et al., 2007). Linda Levstik and Keith Barton (1997) recommend that teachers collect sets of three or four books that represent both broad and more narrow aspects of the same topic to "help students move beyond an attachment to a single perspective" (p. 98). In such a manner, Liz Melahn (HLP) gathered a collection of individual books for students to use during the 80 minutes a week that she allowed for personal reading time. Her students showed increased motivation when they were allowed to select their own books. Their presentations based on these books reflected high levels of connection to the content being studied in class.

An eighth-grade teacher described by Donna Ogle and her colleagues (2007) used a jigsaw strategy involving multiple secondary accounts. She provided her students with three articles on the topic of women's rights, each written at a different reading level. The students previewed all three articles, choosing the one they could read most confidently. After reading, students met in expert groups, in which all students had read the same article, to decide on its most important points. Presenting these in a graphic overview, they explained the article to the rest of the class. Some teachers consider secondary accounts more authentic sources of information than textbooks. The way teachers use secondary accounts may be the most individualistic and extemporaneous aspect of history instruction, which may be one reason that it is not as well documented as the use of textbooks and primary sources (Angelillo, 2003; Bamford & Kristo, 1998; Lombard, 1996; Maxim, 1998).

Reading with Comprehension

Among the tools students need to construct historical knowledge, none is more important than being able to read history texts with comprehension. Reading for comprehension represents a fundamental change in reading instruction brought about by the Cognitive Revolution (Reynolds & Sinatra, 2005). It shifts the focus of reading from "word saying" or recognition and correct pronunciation to reading for meaning (Ryder & Graves, 1998). History students rely more on written texts than those in any other subject except language arts and literature. History is itself a language art consisting of multiple genres and grammatical structures, as functional linguists point out, depending on the purpose for which a historical text was written (Coffin, 2006).

To help students read for comprehension, reading specialists have developed a number of strategies that also are useful for reading history texts. They are based largely on techniques that proficient readers use to read for meaning. Strategies used before reading help students activate prior learning, engage their interest, and provide a purpose for reading. Strategies used during reading check for and deepen comprehension. After-reading strategies check for misunderstandings and help students retain what they have learned. Among the most effective of these strategies, according to a research study by the National Institute of Child Health and Human Development (2000), are activities that help students monitor their own comprehension, make connections within the texts being read, and relate text to background knowledge. While some students have learned such techniques on their own, many others do find instruction in reading strategies helpful (Willingham, 2006).

Many of the comprehension strategies used for story reading also help students read in the content areas, including history and social studies (Alvermann & Swafford, 1989; Schell & Fisher, 2007). Activating prior knowledge can help students better understand a passage in a history textbook by relating it to what they may already know. Introducing students to key terms before they begin a new textbook chapter can alert students to vocabulary that might otherwise pose problems. Checking for comprehension during reading and reading a text passage for the main idea are useful in the subject areas as well as for story reading. Moreover, some of these activities could be converted into more general learning strategies, either to help introduce students to a new topic or to deepen comprehension of difficult content. Generic comprehension strategies may be useful in content-area reading; however, they also have limitations.

This is largely because content area reading presents its own set of challenges. Many of the text structures and literary conventions that elementary students come to expect from reading stories do not apply to historical texts. History textbooks, according to Isabel Beck and Margaret McKeown (1994), are part of the problem because they make unwarranted assumptions about students' background knowledge and present text content that is not coherent. Even adept readers being introduced to history are likely to find the vocabulary, word usage, and structures of history texts unfamiliar and at times perplexing.

Another question concerning use of textbooks and other written text pertains to "how" teachers actually help students use and garner information from them. We are beyond the time when we can assume that all students come ready to read well within our discipline. Young students and struggling readers at whatever grade level may need help with textbooks as well as other historical accounts and documents. As Shanahan and Shanahan (2008) explain, "Most students need explicit teaching of sophisticated genres, specialized language conventions, disciplinary norms of precision and accuracy, and higher-level interpretive processes" (p. 43).

Textbooks often pose challenges for young students, who are used to the more friendly narrative style of fiction. Allen (2000) notes that "Textbook reading is the most difficult kind of reading and is the one most often given to students to read independently." She continues, "Fiction depends on readers' identifying with interesting plots, dynamic characters, exciting resolutions, and memorable descriptions to hold their interest. Textbooks rely on graphs, charts, pictures, historical events, and scientific descriptions to sustain the reader's attention" (p. 128).

The long-established Survey, Question, Read, Recall, and Review (SQ3R) method has been helpful to readers in Kelly Long's courses (Robinson, 1946). This technique leads students through the full range of reading comprehension steps for before, during, and after reading. As students become more familiar with this process over time, it becomes one of the metacognitive strategies that they automatically enact before reading. In the first step students look over the reading assignment, observing pictures, graphics, bold type font, highlighted words, italics, captions, and so on. The next step is to question. Although students might consider end-of-the-chapter questions, it is more effective if they ask their own questions at this stage, reflecting upon their own prior knowledge and beginning to make connections. The practice of learning to turn bold-faced headings into questions will be helpful to students as they approach writing tasks as well. During the recall phase, students are essentially pausing to write brief summary statements in their own words in order to keep track and make sense of what they are reading. During this recall, they consider the questions they posed and how the reading is helping them answer these. During the review stage, students take time to actively reflect upon the notes they have taken. Long encourages her students to take a final step to make a short summative statement about the entire reading assignment and its key ideas.

The presence of many English Language Learners in history classrooms means that history teachers at every grade level should be prepared to address second language acquisition problems. Assigning less reading is not a constructive alternative. As Donna Ogle and colleagues (2007) argue, struggling readers "need to be surrounded by *more* rather than less material on the topics being taught.

They need to be enticed into reading and writing in as many ways as possible." As they also note, "Only by reading regularly will they develop fluency with the content, vocabulary, and style of academic writing" (p. 27). As well as using comprehension strategies, the authors recommend: providing easy reading materials for struggling readers as an entry into a topic; making multiple texts available to increase the frequency with which they will encounter new vocabulary words; and placing them in jigsaw groups with texts written at different reading levels. Teachers can help many of these students increase their reading proficiency simply by making the effort to find appropriate texts.

Teachers in every content area must understand that learning to read involves more than students being able to decode words. It is an on-going task that changes as students advance through the grades. Content-area teachers, as Carol Lee and Anika Spratley (2010) note, are "much better positioned to analyze these sources of difficulty ... than those typically teaching generic remedial reading courses in high schools. History teachers are also more likely to understand the ways in which helping students to pay attention to and make sense of these kinds of text difficulties are intimately linked to history reasoning and content" (p. 9). We must, Wineburg (2005) insists, "think of ourselves, first and foremost, as reading teachers, no matter what area of the social studies we teach" (p. 664). We do not go quite that far. We think of ourselves and our colleagues in schools and universities primarily as history teachers, which includes helping students read history texts for understanding and meaning.

Teachers help students with specialized reading in the content area by reading aloud, and not only to younger students and struggling readers, although this strategy certainly helps poor readers focus on content rather than on decoding words. Kathryn Button (1998) read nonfiction history trade books in her second grade classroom, although the books were beyond her students' reading level. It contributed to their store of factual knowledge "inasmuch as young children can listen with comprehension to texts beyond their reading level. ... These experiences can stretch young readers and prepare them for future encounters with challenging texts" (p. 23). More capable readers are also introduced to the syntax of historical writing when listening to reading aloud. "By hearing nonfiction read aloud, children begin to internalize these structures," Barbara Moss, (2003) notes. She explains that "Consequently, they become better able to comprehend these structures as they read and model them in their own writing" (p. 57).

High school students also benefit from having historical accounts read to them (Allen, 2000). High school teacher Lori Davis (HLP) attested to the positive impact of reading aloud to her students in both her advanced and regular courses. Sometimes she engaged them by reading short segments from a nonfiction book over an extended period of time. She also read to students early in the year and gradually moved toward having students in the class read individual paragraphs after which they stopped to discuss what had just been read. Russ Brown (HLP) read opening paragraphs to students in his high school history classes to grab their attention before turning them to the task of reading for themselves.

Reading aloud also lets teachers model how to read history texts for comprehension. While reading aloud to her fourth-grade students from *Cassie's Journey*, a book of historical fiction, Rhoda Coleman stopped frequently to encourage her students to think about the historical period in which the story was set (Levstik & Barton, 1997). Pausing periodically for questions and discussion also enables teachers to check student comprehension of the material. Reading is a core competency in the history classroom and one that history teachers can address in a variety of innovative and content enriching ways. Reading must remain a central part of the history classroom.

References

Allen, J. (2000). *Yellow brick roads: Shared and guided paths to independent reading*. Portland, ME: Stenhouse Publishers.

Alvermann, D. E. & Swafford, J. (1989). Do content area strategies have a research base? *Journal of Reading*, 32(5), 388–394.

Angelillo, J. (2003). *Writing about reading*. Portsmouth, NH: Heineman.

Aulls, M. W. (2008). Developing students' inquiry strategies: A case study of teaching history in the middle grades. In B. M. Shore, M. W. Aulls, & M. A. B. Delcourt (eds.) *Inquiry in education, Vol. II: Overcoming barriers to successful implementation* (pp. 1–49). New York, NY and London: Lawrence Erlbaum Associates.

Bain, R. B. (2005) They thought the world was flat. In M. S. Donovan & J. D. Branford (eds.). *How students learn: History in the classroom* (pp. 179–213). Washington, DC: National Academies Press.

Bamford, R. A. & Kristo, J. V. (1998). *Making facts come alive: Choosing quality nonfiction literature K-8* (pp. 259–264). Norwood, MA: Christopher-Gordon Publishers, Inc.

Beck, I. L. & McKeown, M. G. (1994). Outcomes of history instruction: Paste-up accounts. In M. Carretero & J. F. Voss (eds.) *Cognitive and instructional processes in history and the social sciences* (pp. 237–256). Hillsdale, NJ and Hove, UK: Lawrence Erlbaum Associates.

Button, K. (1998). Linking social studies and literacy development through children's books. *Social Studies and the Young Learner*, 10(4), 23–25.

Coffin, C. (2006). *Historical discourse: The language of time, cause and evaluation*. London: Continuum.

Collins, P. J. (1990). Bridging the gap. In N. Atwell (ed.) *Coming to know: Writing to learn in the intermediate grades* (pp. 17–31). Portsmouth, NH: Heinemann.

Davis, B. H., Rooze, G. E., & Tallent, M. K. (1992). Writing-to-learn in elementary social studies. *Social Education*, 56(7), 393–397.

Edwards, T. (1992). Teacher talk and pupil competence: A response to section 4. In K. Norman (ed.) *Thinking voices: The work of the National Oracy Project*. London: Hodder & Stoughton.

Faber, J. E., Morris, J. D., & Lieberman, M. G. (2000). The effect of note taking on ninth grade students' comprehension. *Reading Psychology*, 21(3), 257–270.

Fisher, D., Frey, N., & Williams, D. (2002). Seven literacy strategies that work. *Educational Leadership*, 60(3), 70–73.

Holt, T. C. (1990). *Thinking historically: Narrative, imagination, and understanding.* New York, NY: College Entrance Examination Board.

Husbands, C. (1996). *Historical forms: Narratives and stories. What is history teaching? Language, ideas and meaning in learning about the past.* Buckingham, UK: Open University Press.

Key, L., Bradley, J. A., & Bradley, S. (2010). Stimulating instruction in social studies. *Social Studies*, 101(3), 117–120.

Knight, S. L., Waxman, H. C., & Padron, Y. N. (1989). Students' perceptions of relationships between social studies instruction and cognitive strategies. *Journal of Educational Research*, 82, 270–276.

Kobrin, D. (1996). *Beyond the textbook: Teaching history using documents and primary sources.* Portsmouth, NH: Heinemann.

Kohlmeier, J. (2005). The impact of having 9th graders "do history". *History Teacher*, 38(4), 499–516.

Lee, C. D. & Spratley, A. (2010). *Reading in the disciplines: The challenges of adolescent literacy.* New York, NY: Carnegie Corporation.

Lesh, B. A. (2011). *"Why don't you just tell us the answer?" Teaching historical thinking in grades 7–12.* Portland, ME: Stenhouse Publishers.

Levstik, L. S. & Barton, K. C. (1997). *Doing history: Investigating with children in elementary and middle schools.* Mahwah, NJ: Lawrence Erlbaum Associates.

Lombard, R. H. (1996). Using trade books to teach middle level social studies. *Social Education*, 60(4), 223–226.

Maxim, D. (1998). Nonfiction literature as the "text" of my intermediate classroom: That's a fact. In R. A. Bamford & J. V. Kristo (eds.) *Making facts come alive* (pp. 247–258). Norwood, MA: Christopher-Gordon Publishers.

Monte-Sano, C. (2010). Disciplinary literacy in history: An exploration of the historical nature of adolescents' writing. *Journal of the Learning Sciences*, 19(4), 539–568.

Monte-Sano, C. (2011). Beyond reading comprehension and summary: Learning to read and write in history by focusing on evidence, perspective, and interpretation. *Curriculum Inquiry*, 41(2), 212–249.

Moss, B. (2003). *Exploring the literature of fact: Children's nonfiction trade books in the elementary classroom* (pp. 56–61). New York, NY and London: Guilford Press.

National Institute of Child Health and Human Development. (2000). *Report of the National Reading Panel. Teaching children to read: An evidence-based assessment of the scientific research literature on reading and its implications for reading instruction* (NIH Publication No. 00-4769). Washington, DC: US Government Printing Office.

Ogle, D., Klemp, R., & McBride, B. (2007). *Building literacy in the social studies.* Alexandria, VA: Association for Supervision and Curriculum Development.

Reynolds, R. E. & Sinatra, G. M. (2005) The cognitive revolution in scientific psychology: Epistemological roots and impact on reading research. In J. M. Royer (ed.) *The cognitive revolution in educational psychology* (pp. 13–39). Greenwich, CT: Information Age Publishing.

Robinson, F. P. (1946). *Effective study.* New York, NY: Harper and Brothers.

Ryder, R. J. & Graves, M. F. (1998). *Reading and learning in content areas* (2nd edn.). New York, NY: John Wiley and Sons.

Schell, E. & Fisher, D. (2007). *Teaching social studies: A literacy-based approach.* Upper Saddle River, NJ: Pearson, Merrill Prentice Hall.

Shanahan, T. & Shanahan, C. (2008). Teaching disciplinary literacy to adolescents: Rethinking content-area literacy. *Harvard Educational Review*, 78(1), 40–59.

Sharp, T. (2008). How can teacher talk support learning? *Linguistics and Education*, 19, 132–148.

Smith, F. R. & Feathers, K. M. (1983). Teacher and student perceptions of content area reading. *Journal of Reading*, 26(4), 348–354.

Stien, D. & Beed, P. L. (2004). Bridging the gap between fiction and nonfiction in the literature circle setting. *The Reading Teacher*, 57(6), 510–518.

Tomlinson, C. A. & Eidson, C. C.. (2003). *Differentiation in practice: A resource guide for differentiating curriculum, grades 5–9*. Alexandria, VA: ASCD.

Van Sledright, B. A. & Frankes, L. (2000). Concept-and strategic-knowledge development in historical study: A comparative exploration in tow fourth-grade classrooms. *Cognition and Instruction*, 18(2), 239–283.

Voss, J. F. & Wiley, J. (1997). Developing understanding while writing essays in history. *International Journal of Educational Research*, 27(3), 255–265.

Willingham, D. T. (2006). The usefulness of *brief* instruction in reading comprehension strategies. *American Educator*, 30(4), 39–50.

Wineburg, S. (2005). What does NCATE have to say to future history teachers? Not much. *Phi Delta Kappan*, 86(9), 658–665.

Wineburg, S., Martin, D., & Monte-Sano, C. (2011). *Reading like a historian: Teaching literacy in middle and high school history classrooms*. New York, NY: Teachers College Press.

9

ANALYZE AND EVALUATE

Imagine a classroom in which students are gathering information about a historical topic or period. Let's say that they are investigating the bloody encounter between Boston townspeople and British troops on the evening of March 5, 1770. While taking notes from their textbook and other materials, these students are doing more than collecting information. They are analyzing what they have found out as they gather it. How trustworthy is Paul Revere's depiction of the incident in his famous engraving? Do the contemporary accounts by the townspeople of Boston that their teacher has provided them tell the full story or are there other possible perspectives? What about the British soldiers' point of view? They also are evaluating the information they have at hand. Is it sufficient to make a compelling argument about the causes of the Boston Massacre or should they look for more? Which pieces of information are relevant? Several students, no doubt, are wondering why they are doing this assignment in the first place. This hypothetical classroom allows us to make several observations about analysis and evaluation in historical learning.

As the above scenario demonstrates, analysis and evaluation are virtually inseparable from building factual knowledge. It begins with students trying to make sense of what they are learning. This scenario involves students in thinking critically about sources, their reliability, and their relevance. We think of historical analysis and evaluation as a form of procedural knowledge rather than as a generic skill. Critically weighing historical evidence involves knowledge specific to the discipline of history. This is a kind of learning that can be deepened and expanded rather than a mental habit that is acquired and locked in.

The literature on history education has emphasized three kinds of critical historical analysis. Although these are sometimes overlapping in practice, they merit separate attention. Teachers are likely to be most familiar with comparative analysis, which is widely practiced in K-16 history classrooms. It is concerned with similarities and differences in historical settings and situations. Research suggests that these mental operations are "basic to human thought" (Marzano, Pickering, & Pollock, 2001) and "indeed, they might be considered the 'core' of all learning" (p. 14). A second type, textual analysis, has also received a great deal of attention in the scholarly literature. The literature has focused especially on the critical reading of primary sources, as observed in the scenario above. The third kind of analytical thinking that is central to historical learning is the analysis of perspectives. It involves the close reading of historical evidence and accounts to identify the point of view embedded in them. Perspective analysis goes beyond the detection of bias. It is an attempt to account for that bias. We will examine each kind of analytical thinking in turn.

Teachers have found journals or learning logs useful at this stage of learning. These typically are notebooks dedicated to this subject in which students work on concept webs, maps, and lists, or note what they are doing and what they are thinking about it, depending on the assignment. Blake's (1990) upper elementary students used logs to "focus on, compare, and classify information," which helped them "capture it on paper where they can see and respond to it" (pp. 53–54). Journals also are useful formative assessment tools for evaluating learning in progress. Teachers do not always grade them, although grades may serve a purpose. For his university course, Steffens (1987) noted that "the success of journals in history classes depends, perhaps unfortunately, on the student's realization that they 'count'." He used such broad criteria as regularity of entries, length, and appropriateness to judge "a continuous involvement with the course material throughout the semester" and to assign letter grades (p. 226).

In his high school US history course, Mark Sass (HLP) required his students to keep a journal. He used it primarily as a formative assessment tool, monitoring the notebook entries to "locate any misconceptions before they manifest themselves on [formal] assessments." He learned quickly that effective journaling depended on well-structured assignments. At the beginning of the semester, he gave the students a great deal of latitude as to what they wrote about. He found out a lot about the personal interests of his students, which was valuable, but little about what they were learning in the course. Thereafter, he used writing prompts focused on "specific historical issues," which gave him useful feedback about their struggles with historical learning. Several students continued to write about themselves but learned to place their stories in a historical context. They drew parallels and made connections between the past and their own lives—an unanticipated benefit of teen-age journaling. Incidentally, Mark kept a journal of his own, which provided a continuing assessment of his own teaching.

Comparative Analysis

Of the three analytical strategies considered here, comparative analysis is the most encompassing. It provides a framework as well as a process for historical inquiry by setting up a comparison of two or more developments, events, or historical actors. Students use this framework when they are asked to compare Federalists and Anti-Federalists, the Union and the Confederacy, or the First and Second New Deals. The framework provides an obvious setting for investigating conflicts in the past that are grounded in different interests and perspectives. As the focus on similarities and differences can be more or less inclusive, it also addresses the competing demands of depth and breadth of instruction. Comparative history lessons might investigate one development across several civilizations or do a more in-depth comparison of two of them. We will look at examples of various ways teachers use comparative analysis in their classrooms.

Units on ancient civilizations often use a comparative framework for historical analysis. In a survey of ancient cultures, Dan Rypma (HLP) worked with high scool students to compare basic characteristics of civilizations rather than doing a full-blown study of each. As they read and researched, students created a chart to keep track of different cultures, with six categories or characteristics of a civilization (Table 9.1). These included urbanization, organized religions, record keeping and writing, monument building, division of labor, and organized government. The students expanded the chart by adding civilizations and assessing them according to these comparative categories. At the end of the unit they used a Venn diagram to show comparisons of two or three civilizations and what they thought were the most important characteristics of each.

As Dan's chart illustrates, teachers can effectively use graphic organizers to help students conduct comparative historical analysis. When teaching for historical breadth, comparative timelines can also be used to compare historical events in

TABLE 9.1 Ancient Civilizations Comparison Chart

Criteria	Place		
	Egypt	Mesopotamia	India
Urbanization			
Organized religions			
Record keeping and writing			
Monument building			
Division of labor			
Organized government			

Source: Permission of Dan Rypma (HLP)

multiple places. Other graphic organizers that help develop higher levels of analysis include the multi-column, multi-line matrix, Venn diagrams, and similarities-and-differences charts. The comparison matrix is useful for comparing multiple (three or more) instances. It is widely used because it can be adapted easily to different grade levels. For example, the San Diego (CA) County Office of Education created a graphic organizer for a sixth-grade world history unit on ancient civilizations (Schell & Fisher, 2007, p. 128). The graphic lists characteristics across the top including physical geography, economic factors, religion, social life, and leadership. The vertical column lists different ancient civilizations such as India, Egypt, and China. This makes it easy for students to see how civilizations differed.

Comparative analysis is especially useful for teaching world history, a subject in which both breadth and depth of understanding are important. With only two weeks remaining in her school year, Alecia Ford, a sixth-grade teacher, had not yet begun to teach the Enlightenment (Secules & Ford, 2006). While she had time only for a broad overview, she did not want to sacrifice depth entirely. She wanted her students to know that the Enlightenment was a period of change throughout Western societies, but that it played out differently in different places. Her solution was to divide her class into groups to complete a content matrix that they could then use to explore the topic in more conceptual depth.

At the beginning of the unit, Ford divided her class into five groups, assigning each a nation at the time of the Enlightenment. Relying mainly on the textbook, the students searched for information related to: type of government, who wielded power, major events related to the topic, important people, colonies founded (if any), dominant beliefs or new ideas, and whether the country experienced a political revolution. On the chart, these questions provided the column headings across the top. The countries involved (England, France, Spain, Russia, and America) were listed down the left side of the page. It helped the students understand the topic and how the Enlightenment was similar yet different from one place to another. The chart also was a useful source of information later on, when it came time for the class to draw conclusions about the Enlightenment.

The HLP partners used comparative analysis in a variety of world history units. Their students have compared colonization and imperialism, the two world wars of the twentieth century, the Reformation and the Enlightenment in different nations, and the anti-slavery movement. In her ninth grade world history course, Shelley Reffner began a unit on comparative revolutions by asking students to define the term "revolution." Once they agreed upon the criteria, the students compared different revolutions with which they were familiar, including the American, French, Russian, and even Industrial Revolutions. Having an agreed upon set of criteria, they were able to look for commonalities as well as distinctive characteristics of each example. This inquiry approach also prepared them to revisit and refine their definition of a revolution.

Teachers of US history are no less resourceful in their use of comparative analysis. A comparative unit on American colonial history is an old stand-by. In his unit on Colonial American society, Bob Jansen organized instruction around a 3 × 3 matrix, "with Northern, Middle, and Southern colonies across the horizontal axis and social-cultural life, economics, and government down the vertical axis" (Van Sledright, 1997, p. 40). With this schema in mind, the students used the textbook and teacher-provided handouts to map out the significant regional differences in colonial America. Van Sledright (1997) who observed Jansen's class, concluded that students were able to construct a conceptual understanding of colonial society in less time than the students in a second, more traditional classroom in which a teacher provided more detailed factual information.

A variety of US history topics lend themselves to comparative analysis. David Farrell (HLP) used comparative analysis in the study of the Progressive era. He used a set of common and oppositional events, positions, and documents to help his high school students examine issues pertaining to the era. For example, he used pro and anti-imperialist speeches and writings during a study of Imperialism. In a freshman level survey course, to examine transitions from pre-World War Two to post-World War Two US culture, Kelly Long's students used Venn diagrams and similarities-and-difference charts at both the beginning and the end of the unit. Initially, comparisons focused on events at a general level. As her university students engaged in further investigation by reading, viewing, and listening to lectures outside of class, and then working with primary sources and discussing their learning during class sessions, they added detail to the similarities and differences charts, and then drew from these to complete a three-way Venn diagram. These comparative activities engaged them in historical analysis of sources and prepared them to offer short written responses. These comparative and analytical exercises prepared them to create a synthesis assignment at the end of the unit.

Deciding which differences and similarities to compare also allows teachers to sharpen the focus of historical investigation and inquiry. In one New York elementary classroom, students addressed the question of whether British colonization resulted in progress for everyone. They did this by comparing the experiences of Native Americans, European Americans, and African Americans and by creating poster panels on each of the three groups. The assignment helped students understand the very different impact of colonization on the groups of peoples involved (Libresco, 2005). Such charts in the form of a matrix with columns and lines also help students compare multiple cases or examples of a historical development or of change over time. Teachers often refer back to wall charts that remain visible in the classroom as the unit or course progresses.

Textual Analysis

Written texts play a major role in the history classroom. How students interact with texts is critical to historical learning. We have emphasized the importance of their being able to read for comprehension, but that is only the beginning. They must also be able to critically analyze the texts that they read. Critical literacy begins with students understanding the difference between textbooks, secondary accounts, and primary sources. Even students who know the difference may not understand how to evaluate these different sources. In studies in which high school students used a variety of history texts, Wineburg (1991a, 1991b) found that they tended to regard primary sources, just like textbooks, as one more source of information. Some viewed textbooks as more reliable because they seemed more authoritative. Students need to understand the strengths and limitations of each, and the different challenges that each presents for a critical reader. Here we will look at strategies for critically analyzing textbooks and primary sources, the two most commonly used texts in history classrooms.

Textbooks are the most ubiquitous of the texts found in history classrooms, and perhaps the least well understood. Textbooks certainly are not primary sources, but neither are they like most secondary accounts by historians. They are surveys or summaries of what the writer or team of authors extracted from other historians' accounts about what happened. Textbooks are tertiary accounts. Conscientious history textbook writers try to present a consensus of historians' views about a topic, which is one reason they often lack a distinctive authorial "voice." While they are not the whole truth, they are authoritative in the sense that they usually are written or edited by or bear the stamp of approval of academic historians. Textbook publishers also hire editorial fact-checkers to be as certain as they can that a textbook has accurate information. They are the most reliable historical reference sources in most classrooms.

Although students may not know enough to question the scholarship on which a textbook rests, they can at some level be critical textbook readers. They can recognize that there is an author behind the authoritative text and decide what the author wants them to know. They can question what may have been left out of the account and how effective the author was in communicating what he had to say. Perhaps the best-known strategy for critically reading history textbooks is Isabel Beck and Margaret McKeown's (2006) "Questioning the Author." This involves students interacting with the text by asking questions about the meaning of the text and discussing the author's ideas. Ms. Bobeck, a teacher observed by Chauncey Monte-Sano (2008), created prompts that helped students read their textbook for comprehension and to identify the perspective or point of view from which the author was writing. For example, one prompt asked for a one-paragraph summary of the author's main argument about a topic and the information used to support it.

Using multiple textbooks to help his community college students develop confidence to challenge the authority of a text, Cory Reinking (HLP) helped to move his students from mere fact gathering to more analytical thinking, by noting the perspectives reflected by differing textbook authors. At the beginning of their study of the Atlantic System and the rise of the bourgeoisie, he asked students to write one question that they wanted to know about the Atlantic System. They wrote another question about what they thought they *needed* to know to answer the major conceptual question: How did the bourgeoisie become the most powerful class in Europe? Thereafter, he had students work in groups of three to four. Each group was given a different world history textbook to answer the more narrow questions: "Who were the bourgeoisie in the seventeenth and eighteenth centuries? How did they acquire wealth? How did they impact the Atlantic world?"

After students worked in teams, Reinking listed key words or phrases on the board as they called out answers from their textbook about how the Atlantic System formed. Students heard and saw that the different textbooks offered different perspectives and reflected different key ideas or topical focus. For example, while one textbook included many personal stories, images of people, and primary sources, others emphasized economic factors and had few embellishments. All conveyed a different viewpoint about an important historical development. Moving beyond merely gathering factual information, students reinforced their conceptual and procedural knowledge though discussion that helped them see history, and textbooks, as a collection of arguments, intellectual positions, accounts, and perspectives that can and should be questioned like any other source of information.

Textbooks are not the only materials in a classroom that require careful analysis. Much of the professional literature about the critical reading of history texts is focused on the analysis of primary sources and public documents. The consensus is that using primary sources effectively requires a good deal of direct instruction. In the first place, students must understand that a primary source differs from other texts by being a first-hand account written at the time of an event, and not just another account about the past. Otherwise, students tend to focus on the "literal meaning of documents," Monte-Sano (2011) observed, paying little attention to the kind of source, "unless explicitly instructed to do so" (p. 216). Moreover, reading a primary source for comprehension requires a different set of strategies than students are likely to be familiar with from reading fiction or other nonfiction texts. While teachers go about this in different ways, the best-known approach is Sam Wineburg's heuristics for primary source analysis.

From observations about how historians approach sources, Wineburg created a three-part strategy that includes sourcing, corroboration, and contextualization. He describes these as "sense-making activities, for they help their user resolve contradictions, see patterns, and make distinctions among different types of evidence" (Wineburg, 1991b, p. 77). Sourcing means determining who wrote a document, the time and place in which it was created, and how this might influence the perspective from which it was written. Corroboration involves comparing multiple documents with each other to check for discrepancies and contradictions. Contextualization refers to placing the source in the larger historical context in which it was written and in which the events mentioned in it took place. We will look at each in turn.

Implementing Wineburg's strategies presents different kinds of challenges. Of the three, sourcing is the simplest and most skill-like. To source a document, students only need to look for the author's name, and its place and date, which are often provided by the editor of the document. While deciding the influence these may have had on the perspective of the document is more problematic, students have little difficulty with the mechanics of sourcing. That is not necessarily the case with its companion strategies. In his research in a high school history classroom, Avishag Reisman (2012) found that "Sourcing became habitual in all of the treatment classrooms. … Contextualization and corroboration, by contrast are intertextual strategies that require one to draw connections to prior knowledge or between multiple texts. Such processes are more difficult to model with discrete, concrete behaviors" (p. 104). Jeffrey Nokes, Janice Dole, and Doug Hacker (2007) found that contextualizing sources presented problems for high school students. The strategy was either too difficult for them or they lacked the background knowledge to place the events in context. Using literacy strategies effectively, as Moje (2008) notes, "is, to a large extent, dependent on knowing something about the subject" (p. 102). While knowledge is important, we must not lose sight of the reason we want students to work with primary sources. We want them to use source documents, as Charles Perfetti, Anne Britt, and Mara Georgi explain, to develop "an ability to reason about historical topics—to place them in more than one context, to question the sources of a historical statement, to realize that more information is needed to reach a conclusion, and so on" (1995, p. 5). These reasoning traits are part of the historical thinking process. The use of primary sources, like any other text or teaching material, is to help students better understand how that process works.

The careful selection of primary sources is of critical importance. As Bruce Lesh (2011) points out, the selection of sources "make or break any investigation of the past" (p. 56). The sources teachers select must correspond to the broader question being investigated, be written in accessible language, and provide information that helps students place the document in context. Good use of sources requires selecting examples that support the claim. Lesh recommends that teachers use no more than four to six sources, read them ahead of time, combine visual and written sources, and help students with difficult vocabulary words.

The Library of Congress resources proved quite useful for Liz Melahn's (HLP) students in a non-traditional high school during a unit on Jamestown because she had confidence in the reliability of this Internet source and the documents found within it. Liz arranged her class into small groups, each of which worked with a small collection of documents, different from another group's. As they read or viewed, students wrote on butcher paper what they noticed about their sources. They next wrote "I wonder…" and eventually formed a statement about the topic based on the information they had taken from the sources. Next, students went on a "gallery walk" to other tables and selected a document from that set that might either support or change their own analysis of the historical situation. Thereafter they had small group discussions about what they chose and why. Moving beyond comparative textual analysis, students need to also be engaged in comparing points of view.

Perspective Analysis

Analyzing points of view is about recognizing that people of the past viewed things from different perspectives. The Essential Question for perspective analysis is how did people view it at the time? Analysis of viewpoints goes beyond identifying the author and when and where a text was created. Perspective analysis requires a good deal of background knowledge. In the discussion that follows, we move beyond analyzing the intellectual perspective of authors of secondary accounts to discuss ways that students can be asked to reconstruct the perspective of the individual involved in or commenting on the events at the time, as reflected in primary source documents. Typically, it is the point of view about a key event or issue that is central to the larger development being studied. Perspective analysis works well with topics rife with conflict and tension (Riley, 1998). It typically requires comparing several texts.

Teachers engage students in examining different points of view in several ways. Take, for example, the events leading up to the American Revolution. British ministers of colonial affairs clearly had views about managing the Empire that were different from those of colonial merchants, landowners, and taxpayers. Lyle assigned informal writing prompts that focused student attention on the perspectives of the historical actors involved in the Constitutional Convention (Monte-Sano, 2011). In working with high school students, Dan Rypma (HLP) gave his students primary source documents representing perspectives of different historical figures involved in the American Revolutionary War. They examined these documents and sought to determine why the author would have held the viewpoint he or she did given their time, position, race, class, gender, and social status.

Perspective analysis differs from activities focused on evoking historical empathy, yet at times, comparative points of view will reveal something about the emotions of a person from the past. Students can work with these emotional traces from the past in the same way that they work with assertions of a person's thinking about some conflict or event in the past. Just as students can observe the thinking of historical actors by examining their written words, so too, historical actors sometimes used emotional language to tell others what they felt. Yet emotional perspectives can be more ambiguous and difficult to decipher. They might require further steps in the inquiry process.

For example, historian Doris Kearns Goodwin (2005) recounts the story of a letter from President Abraham Lincoln to General George Meade that he closed with "I am deeply vexed." Vexed is likely not a word contemporary students would use, and so they might need to conduct an inquiry about the meaning of the word in Lincoln's time while exploring reasons Lincoln might have arrived at such a feeling. An inquiry activity could help them understand that Lincoln was dismayed after Meade failed to pursue Lee at the close of the battles of Gettysburg, and thereafter, they might ask what actions Lincoln took based on that feeling. Students might be interested to inquire about what Meade thought and felt, and why he chose to disregard an order from his Commander-in-Chief. The awareness that people in the past had strongly held ideas and strongly felt emotions can deepen students' understandings of differing points of view and may help them to feel more connection to subjects they are investigating.

Recognizing that people of the past felt emotions, and analyzing how these influenced the actions of historical figures, helps us remember that perspectives are not disembodied abstractions. They are points of view held by men and women who lived through and had feelings about the controversies of their time. They can only be explained by examining the life experiences of those who held these views. Consequently, perspective analysis involves a level of biographical examination, in search of explanation as well as information. Lyle wanted his students to look closely at conflicting perspectives about the slavery issue as a cause of the Civil War, and to do that he involved his students in examining individual actors and their points of view. To steer their inquiry in that direction, he posed the following questions: "What were the perspectives of abolitionist and supporters of slavery?" "What were the perspectives of politicians on sectional issues?" and finally, "How did these perspectives clash?" He was careful to select readings appropriate for these mid-range questions and "Every reading offered a clue to the overarching inquiry" (Monte-Sano, 2011, p. 219). How students responded was up to them, but Lyle's questions focused their attention on conflicting perspectives about slavery as a causal factor in the coming of the Civil War.

To explore perspectives on the slavery controversy, Lyle focused eight of the nine short writing assignments on the analysis of points of view. Lyle also engaged his students in creative biographical writing by having them write one-page "political profiles" of leaders involved in the sectional controversy of the 1850s (Monte-Sano, 2011, p. 230). They included such diverse points of view as William Lloyd Garrison, the Women's Anti-Slavery Convention, John C. Calhoun, and William Fitzhugh. After having written about several individual perspectives, students brought this information together in an imaginary debate between pro-slavery and anti-slavery advocates (Monte-Sano, 2011). Students considered what it was about a person's life experience and situation that shaped his or her views. Lyle also guided his students' reading of several primary sources and their reflective writing was based on these materials in much the same way. For example, the writing prompt for Frederick Douglass' Independence Day speech in 1841 asked: "What is he aiming to do in this speech?" "How do you suppose he believed that this address would further and strengthen the abolitionist cause?" Chauncey Monte-Sano (2011, p. 219) noted "All these questions guided students' reading of primary documents," toward consideration of an individual's perspective. Robert Bain (2000) asked his students to write nonfiction stories to create a narrative structure for understanding historical episodes. "It enables teachers and students to explore the voice of the storyteller and to retell a story from multiple perspectives," he noted (p. 341).

Teachers have used a variety of techniques to have students write about and analyze differing perspectives. Biographical profiles have been used by teachers to investigate historical figures and situations. During the study of the interwar period, Liz Melahn (HLP) had students in her world history course create "Facebook" profiles for various dictators and other key figures of this period. This activity helped her students examine perspectives and personalities of the selected figures. University students in Kelly Long's class created social network profiles for three important and lesser known historical figures from units in American history. Rather than doing the next step online, Long's students shared their profiles during class. Selecting one of their historical actors, they moved about the classroom, introducing themselves to others, and in Facebook terms, "friended" or "unfriended" those they encountered. Each time they did a new introduction, they began by revealing their friend list. Students were engaged and had fun. More importantly, they learned about historical figures and developed an understanding of how actors in the past might have joined forces or opposed others around a historical dispute. The discussion at the end of the activity allowed students to describe the differing perspectives of which they had become aware.

Other teachers pose very specific questions that call for close reading of the texts. Ms. Bobeck provided her students with explicit and detailed instructions for analyzing primary sources (Monte-Sano, 2008). For a selection the *Narrative of the Life of Frederick Douglass*, she asked them to look at specific passages, to determine what these demonstrated about the status of slaves and how the system maintained power over them. She then asked students to consider Douglass' purpose in including such information in his account. For opposing viewpoints in primary sources on Indian removal by Andrew Jackson and Theodore Freylinghuysen, she asked them to identify what each author meant by "civilized" and "savage," as well as to summarize their arguments for or against removal.

Perspective analysis is essential to help students move toward higher levels of historical analysis. Tracy Brady's (HLP) university students analyzed primary sources to explore different perspectives before writing a formal essay. During their study of the Cherokee removal and the Trail of Tears, Tracy's students selected three documents that supported removal and three documents against removal of Native Americans. As they analyzed the removal policy, they considered the when, where, for whom, and to what purpose the document was written. Finally, they took a position on the policy based on the perspective of a figure from that time period. Brady found that this examination of diverse perspectives helped her students to feel more engaged with the topic and therefore they tended to write longer, more persuasive essays supported with ample evidence from sources to advance a position they felt strongly about.

To help high school students examine the past through multiple perspectives, Russ Brown (HLP) used a variety of short texts in his International Baccalaureate courses. These small books draw together source documents that present a variety of perspectives on issues such as World War Two. After reading and analyzing assigned documents on topics in the books, students were able to write in an informed manner about a variety of perspectives held at the time of the events under examination. To help students gain a more personal insight into a challenging question about the buildup to World War Two in Germany, Long used a jigsaw activity to analyze how or why German citizens would have supported the Nazi party during the 1930s. In groups of seven, each student read a one-paragraph character vignette of an individual within a demographic sector in German society in the interwar period (Good, 1968). Each short paragraph describing a point of view contributed to students' understandings of the multiple views, challenges, and grievances of citizens in Germany during the interwar period. High school and university students can do perspective analysis, as the above examples demonstrate, but what about elementary students? For younger students to entertain an account for a point of view that is not their own seems more problematic. In his research in two elementary classrooms, Matt Downey (1994, 1995) found that perspective analysis was a difficult task for most fifth-grade students. Students in the school in the more affluent neighborhood who had better writing skills were more successful than those in the inner-city classroom who were less proficient. In her research, Nancy Dulberg (2002) found that students in the upper elementary grades "can and do engage in historical thinking, including historical perspective-taking, some of the time" (p. 40). Perspective analysis, she concluded, has to be seen in a developmental perspective. Students at a concrete operations stage of development may not do it as well as more mature students, but can do it inconsistently and in ways appropriate for their level of thinking. We should not expect as much from elementary students, but must acknowledge what they can do as learning in progress.

The three kinds of analysis we have examined are a step beyond gathering evidence. Such analysis asks students to take a critical look at the information they have at hand. It is a step toward synthesizing what they know into an explanation that addresses the unit's Big Question. But the students are not there yet. Between analysis and interpretation lies another critical step: connecting what they know in meaningful ways, the phase of historical inquiry that we will examine next.

References

Bain, R. B. (2000). Into the breach: Using research and theory to shape history instruction. In P. N. Stearns, P. Seixas, & S. Wineburg (eds.) *Knowing, teaching, and learning history: National and international perspectives* (pp. 331–352). New York, NY: University Press.

Beck, I. & McKeown, M.G. (2006). *Improving comprehension with questioning the author.* New York, NY: Scholastic Teaching Resources.

Blake, M. (1990). Learning logs in the upper elementary grades. In N. Atwell (ed.) *Coming to know. Writing to learn in the intermediate grades* (pp. 53–60). Portsmouth, NH: Heinemann Educational Books, Inc. and Concord, Ontario, Canada: Irwin Publishing.

Downey, M. T. (1994). After the dinosaurs: Children's chronological thinking. Paper presented at annual meeting of the American Educational Research Association, New Orleans.

Downey, M. T. (1995). Perspective taking and historical thinking: Doing history in a fifth-grade classroom. Paper presented at the Annual Meeting of the American Educational Research Association, San Francisco, CA.

Dulberg, N. (2002). Engaging in history: Empathy and perspective-taking children's historical thinking. Paper presented at the Annual Meeting of the American Educational Research Association, New Orleans, LA.

Good, J. M. (1968). *The shaping of western society: An inquiry approach.* New York, NY: Holt, Rinehart and Winston, Inc.

Goodwin, D. K. (2005) *Team of Rivals: The Political Genius of Abraham Lincoln.* New York: Simon & Schuster.

Lesh, B. A. (2011). *"Why don't you just tell us the answer?" Teaching historical thinking in grades 7–12.* Portland, ME: Stenhouse Publishers.

Libresco, A. S. (2005). How she stopped worrying and learned to love the test … sort of. In E.A. Yeager & O. L. Davis (eds.) *Wise social studies teaching in an age of high-stakes testing: Essays on classroom practices and possibilities* (pp. 33–49). Greenwich, CT: Information Age Publishing.

Marzano, R. J., Pickering, D. J., & Pollock, J. E. (2001). *Classroom instruction that works.* Alexandria, VA: Association for Supervision and Curriculum Development.

Moje, E. B. (2008). Foregrounding the disciplines in secondary literacy teaching and learning: A call for change, *Journal of Adolescent & Adult Literacy*, 52(2), 96–107.

Monte-Sano, C. (2008). Qualities of historical writing instruction: A comparative case study of two teachers' practices. *American Educational Research Journal*, 45(4), 1045–1079.

Monte-Sano, C. (2011). Beyond reading comprehension and summary: Learning to read and write in history by focusing on evidence, perspective, and interpretation. *Curriculum Inquiry*, 41(2), 212–249.

Nokes, J. D., Dole, J. A., & Hacker, D. J. (2007). Teaching high school students to use heuristics while reading historical texts. *Journal of Educational Psychology*, 99(3), 492–504.

Perfetti, C. A., Britt, M. A., & Georgi, M. C. (1995). *Text-based learning and reasoning: Studies in history.* Hillsdale, NJ and Hove, UK: Lawrence Erlbaum Associates.

Reisman, A. (2012). Reading like a historian: A document-based history curriculum intervention in urban high schools. *Cognition and Instruction*, 30(1), 86–112

Riley, K. L. (1998). Historical empathy and the Holocaust: Theory into practice. *International Journal of Social Education*, 13(1), 32–42.

Schell, E. & Fisher, D. (2007). *Teaching social studies: A literacy-based approach*. Upper Saddle River, NJ: Pearson, Merrill Prentice Hall.

Secules, T. & Ford, A. (2006). Divide and conquer: Detecting patterns that explain the big picture. *Social Education*, 70(2), 89–92.

Steffens, H. (1987). Journal in the teaching of history. In T. Fulwiler (ed.) *The journal book* (pp. 219–226). Portsmouth, NH: Boynton/Cook Publisher.

Van Sledright, B. (1997).Can more be less? The depth-breadth dilemma in teaching American history. *Social Education*, 61(1), 38–41.

Wineburg, S. (1991a). On the reading of historical texts: Notes on the breach between school and academy. *American Educational Research Journal*, 28(3), 495–519.

Wineburg, S. (1991b). Historical problem solving: A study of the cognitive processes used in the evaluation of documentary and pictorial evidence. *Journal of Educational Psychology*, 83(1), 73–87.

10

MAKE CONNECTIONS

Let's go back to that hypothetical classroom in which students are investigating the Boston Massacre. Students are collecting, analyzing, and evaluating contemporary accounts from townspeople and British soldiers who on March 5, 1770 witnessed that incident. They discover that tensions between citizens and soldiers had escalated in recent weeks, that off-duty soldiers and local day laborers competed for jobs on Boston's waterfront, and that heckling British soldiers had become a favorite pastime of some Bostonians. They need to explain why these developments led to the fatal event of that evening. Students investigating this event as a significant turning point need to extend the range of their investigation in order to establish connections between the people and events leading up to that violent encounter. Doing so represents the difference between their memorizing information presented in a textbook and building historical knowledge of their own.

Making connections and seeing patterns are central to building any kind of conceptual knowledge. "Understanding is itself the realization that what is separate in ignorance is connected in knowing," John Biggs (1999) notes. He continues by observing that "Cognitive growth lies not just in knowing more, but in the restructuring that occurs when new knowledge becomes connected to what is already known" (p. 73). In building historical knowledge, connection making is essential for explaining why something happened. The goal of building historical knowledge, as Kathryn Spoehr (1994) notes, "is to generate explanations ... by extracting patterns and commonalities from a collection of data." Problem solving in history "does not call for accumulation of declarative facts, but discrimination and informed judgment about the relationships between parts of that knowledge base" (p. 79). Simply stated, connections have explanatory power.

The importance of making connections can be demonstrated by what happens when students fail to do so. A case-in-point, Jere Brophy and Bruce Van Sledright (1997) observed elementary students during a history unit on the plains Indians. These students knew that plains Indians hunted bison, lived in tipis, and used travois to move their belongings from one place to another. Yet many of them failed to link the Indians' nomadic way of life with their hunting and gathering economy. They had "only limited grasp of abstractions such as the notion of a hunting and gathering society or explanations such as the reasons why nomadic tribes kept moving or lived in tipis" (1997, p. 119). That is, tipi dwelling and travois using could have been a matter of personal choice or cultural inheritance. By not making those connections, students failed to understand that the plains Indians' various activities were aspects of a coherent way of life. Students, even young students, can comprehend temporal and causal relationships, as we shall see below.

Historical thinking involves two kinds of connection making—temporal and causal. Temporal reasoning means placing events in their place in time and in chronological order. It provides the answers to "what?" and "when?" questions. Causal thinking involves identifying causes and consequences. It addresses the "how?" and "why?" questions of historical inquiry. The goal of causal thinking is an explanatory synthesis. In the history classroom, a synthesis is the answer to the Big Question posed at the outset of instruction. For students who have been analyzing and evaluating information, arriving at a synthesis is a big leap. Connection making is an intermediate step, not that it always takes place in a linear fashion. The connecting links that students discover as they are learning are the stepping stones toward a synthesis. Reaching that goal requires making both temporal and causal connections.

Temporal Connections

Historical understanding for students begins with making temporal connections. Putting events in chronological order is the most rudimentary form of historical knowledge. "The ability to sequence is a fundamental feature of historical understanding," Sydney Wood (1995) states, and without it "the past is chaos" (p. 11). Teachers help students make order out of that chaos by posing one of the essential or middle-level questions that we introduced earlier: What was the sequence of events? It is fundamental to historical thinking in several ways. Through a sense of time, Wood adds, "we are helped to interpret our own lives, to understand current issues, and to make sense of the man-made landscape" (p. 11). Alan Hodkinson's (2003) research suggests that chronological understanding helps students to store historical information and retrieve it from long-term memory. "If we take our historical past to be a vast cloakroom," he states, "historical time becomes the coat pegs which enable individual coats to be extracted and examined with ease" (p. 34). Temporal relationships also provide the nexus for thinking about causation, as we shall examine later on. "Without a grasp of the concept of time," Tim Lomas and Gordon Richard Batho (1993) note, "there can be no real understanding of change, development, continuity, progression and regression" (p. 20).

Timelines

The principal tool that teachers have used to help students understand chronological order is the timeline. Its great advantage is that it enables students to visualize a sequence of events. Placing dates along a line divided into equal segments (years, decades, centuries) makes the abstract concept of chronology more concrete. The more teachers exploit the graphic dimensions of a timeline, the more effective it tends to be. In their primary school, Rory McIlroy (2011) and her colleagues decorated the main corridor of their school with an oversized timeline. Its sheer visual impact, she noted, "brings history alive and challenges our perceptions daily" (p. 10). A second-grade teacher created a well-illustrated timeline to help her students place the "Famous Americans" emphasized in her curriculum in chronological order (Fallace, Briscoe, & Perry, 2007). Differences in individual's clothing helped students understand the distance between the periods in which they lived. Still other teachers have built kinesthetic dimensions into timelines. "Many pupils benefit from physical activities which require them to stand on a timeline and 'move about in history', gaining a sense of how far it was from one date to another by simply walking across the timeline" (Dawson, 2004, p. 21). When studying the Cold War, Carin Barrett (HLP) had students form human timelines and cluster around events. Then they explained why they clustered together and why they ordered themselves as they did.

Illustrated timelines are especially useful for young students. Research suggests that elementary-grade students rely heavily on visual cues in chronological thinking. Keith Barton and Linda Levstik (1996) found that young students who were asked to arrange images in chronological order depended on such cues. By using such characteristics as hair styles, clothing, and technology to distinguish temporal distance from the present, even very young students could place most images in correct chronological order. In interviews with fourth-grade students, Matt Downey (1994) found that students' grasp of chronology depended heavily on visual cues. While the fourth-grade students whom he interviewed knew relatively little about Abraham Lincoln, they could place him after the colonial period but before modern times by the clothing he wore, especially his tall, silk hat. The differences in clothing in the Famous Americans timeline referred to earlier not only helped the students differentiate between the times, but also provided cues for understanding what those times were like. We suspect that students of all ages and grade levels can benefit from such visual cues.

In addition to the sequence of historical events, timelines introduce students to temporal concepts and the vocabulary of time. While the dates on a timeline represent chronological order, the division of time into decades or periods introduces the notion of interval. Divisions within a timeline can also help students visualize the idea of duration, especially extended timelines that encompass several historical periods. That understanding can be enhanced by color-coding periods of time—blue for the Age of Exploration, green for the Colonial Period, red for the American Revolution. A timeline that fails to make such concepts obvious is a recipe for confusion, such as the one that an inspector of schools in Britain found in a classroom. It consisted of a series of pictures representing events from the Age of the Dinosaurs to a current-day World Cup competition. Each image bore a single date, with events evenly spaced. The visual message that it conveyed was that the Age of the Dinosaurs began shortly before the appearance of humans and lasted no longer than a modern-day sports event (Maddison, 2011).

Timelines are multipurpose tools. They also help teachers introduce historical concepts, such as causation, consequence, and significance. The placement of events on a timeline can create discussions about causal relationships. By questioning why events were included or left off a teacher-made or textbook timeline, teachers can raise questions about judgments made about significance. Having students construct their own timelines necessarily raises questions about significance. They must decide what events of the period being studied were the most significant or worthy of inclusion and explain why they included some rather than others (Tripp, Basye, Jones, & Tripp, 2008). While timelines are effective graphic organizers, they also can support historical learning in less visible ways.

Students can also use timelines to demonstrate their understanding of change and continuity. In a unit on the Medieval period, Yosanne Vella (2011) asked students in her school in Malta to trace the ebb and flow of Christian and Islamic influence by adding color to a timeline. The shift from orange (Christian) to green (Islamic) represented change, with lighter shades of one color or the other representing continuity during periods of change. Christine Matthie's (HLP) students worked in small groups to create posters on flip-chart paper. Each group depicted one set of events and historical actors. They lined these portrayals up along walls in the hallway outside her classroom to create a gallery walk timeline.

After recognizing that his community college students needed a better grasp of historical chronology, Cory Reinking (HLP) created an effective review and engagement activity for his Western Civilization course. His students worked in groups of four, and used a giant sticky pad meant for business presentations. They had twenty minutes to create a timeline (without using dates) that linked the Age of Discovery to the liberal revolutions in the late-eighteenth to early-nineteenth centuries. They used thought bubbles and connected as many vocabulary terms from the course as possible to link the two events. A group presenter explained to the class why each event was connected and how they linked the beginning and ending events. Cory awarded one point for each vocabulary term from the course that they linked effectively. This allowed him to understand their interpretation of events and what they found to be the most significant in the course, as well as to correct errors in their historical chronology.

Texts as Timelines

While we usually think of timelines as visual displays, much of ordinary historical thinking and writing is organized like a timeline. Chronology provides the organizational structure for a variety of kinds of historical texts. Diaries, memoirs, and autobiographies usually are verbal timelines, with a "this happened, and then that happened" structure. So, too, are those biographies and history textbooks that do little more than present a sequence of events. Such texts essentially are fleshed-out chronologies or chronicles rather than interpretative biographies or histories, as they recount or retell what happened rather than interpret or explain why things happened as they did in the past. Linguists have identified three kinds or "genres" of historical writing, classifying texts according to the function or purpose they serve (Coffin, 2004; Schleppegrell, 2004). Caroline Coffin (2006) lists them as recording, explaining, and arguing genres. At the most rudimentary or recording level, students write about the past by stringing events together along a timeline. They focus on temporal connections. More advanced students add causal connections that produce more interpretative accounts. The most proficient writers construct arguments that make a case for one interpretation over another.

Although the chronological recount or report represents the simplest form of historical reasoning, it needs to be explicitly addressed in the classroom. While it likely is linked both to language and to mathematical development, "chronological understanding can be accelerated through clearly-targeted teaching and learning strategies" (Dawson, 2004, p. 15). Helping students construct chronologies is the first step in nurturing their historical thinking. They do not consistently apply familiar, everyday temporal concepts to distant historical situations, with the result that their view of the past may be "closer to a collage of events than to historical narrative" (Blow, Lee, & Shemilt, 2012, p. 28). Sarah Gadd (2009) discovered this in the historical narratives written by her high school students. Many included whatever they happened to know about, producing accounts that "did not make chronological sense" (p. 40). History to them was simply whatever they remembered that had happened in the past, even if the events had no apparent connections between them. We suspect that this level of historical naiveté is quite common.

How do we teach chronological thinking? The storyboards that Blow, and colleagues (2012) used to investigate students' chronological thinking surely also have classroom applications. They asked students to place cards containing short segments of text in chronological order. Students could do so by using dates in the text or by making inferences based on internal evidence. Teachers could use them to help students sort out a critical sequence of events or as a summative assessment where chronological order is important. Storyboards also lend themselves to writing activities. The authors of the above study included a writing assignment by asking students to write about "what must have happened in the gaps between the cards" (p. 28). Shelley Reffner (HLP) used graphic organizers and timelines to reinforce chronology, and then had her students make storyboards pertaining to empires of China and India. At the end of the unit students created a mosaic using "Tiles of Knowledge" that reflect the connections they made about the topics by the end of their study.

Writing activities play an obvious role in teaching about chronology. For many elementary teachers, the step beyond the timeline is autobiographical writing. In her studies of secondary students in Australia, Coffin (2004, 2006) found that the historical writing of younger students (11–13 year-olds) consisted mainly of chronological recounts about the past. They reported events in their own lives (autobiographical recounts), wrote reports about the lives of historical characters (biographical recounts), and constructed the sequence of happenings that led up to a historical event (historical recounts). We suspect that the same is likely true for upper elementary and middle-grade students (grades 4–5, 6–9) in the United States. Writing as chronological recounting probably describes entry-level historical writing for most students everywhere.

To help students develop chronological thinking, they need to become sensitive to the language we use to express temporal relationships. In her study, Coffin (2006) found that in recounting events students relied mainly on four devices. Like most student writings about the past, theirs included language denoting duration ("for nearly half a century") and identifying the beginning, continuing, or ending phases of a development ("finally, in 1939, when Germany attacked Poland") (p. 105). However, students writing at the recounting level were far more likely to use "sequencing and setting" terms than those who had advanced to more complex kinds of writing. That is, recounts relied heavily on dependent clauses introduced by temporal conjunctions ("when," "after") (p. 103) and on setting events in time ("in 1931"; "at the beginning of the twentieth-century") (p. 104). Matt Downey found that some of his university-level students used strings of sentences to convey chronological development, with little or no attempt to link together the thoughts behind them. These serial thoughts seldom made causal connections or argued a point of view, which they could have done by adding temporal conjunctions.

Causal Connections

After temporal connections, the most fundamental relationships in historical thinking are causal links. Causal reasoning is the way historical thinkers explain why events happened that result in change. It begins with students posing another middle-level or Essential Question: What or who made it happen? The notion of causality is "pivotal to historical meaning-making," Coffin (2006) notes. It is not so much what happened in the past that fascinates historians, but "why did it happen, and why did it have the influence it did" (p. 11). To be sure, temporal and causal connections are closely related, as sets of chronological relations are implicit in the very notion of causation. "When someone knows a historical topic, what is known is the causal-temporal relations that are the core of the story" (Perfetti, Britt, & Georgi, 1995, p. 7). In other words, events happen because of antecedent developments or decisions by people. It is often the case, Martha Howell and Walter Prevenier (2001) state that "historians select information and order it chronologically precisely to demonstrate ... the causal relationships between events described" (p. 128). Also, it is causal reasoning, especially the student's construction of causal chains of events, "that make the story coherent and memorable" (Perfetti, et al., 1995, p. 7). Stories with causal links are easier to remember than recounts that rely on temporal connections alone.

To help students make causal connections, teachers must introduce them to the language of causality. We signal causal links, as we do temporal connections, by the way we use language—especially causal conjunctions, phrases, and verbs. Charles Perfetti and colleagues (1995) provide a succinct example of such word use: "So, for example, the United States wanted to have a canal *because* faster transcontinental movement would aid commerce and *because* military deployment would be improved. And the United States had to negotiate with Colombia *because* Panama was part of Colombia; but *then* Colombia rejected the treaty, and *then* Panama had a revolution and, *as a result*, the United States could negotiate with Panama" (p. 6). We are not suggesting that history teachers need to become linguists or grammarians, but that they should help students become attentive to the everyday language of historical discourse.

To understand causation, students must first grasp the idea that causes and consequences are not links forged in the past waiting to be discovered. They are relationships that historical thinkers establish between events to make sense of what happened. Establishing causation is the clearest reflection of the interpretative nature of history. It involves making judgments about how things are connected, including that some causal links are more significant or have more explanatory power than others. To decide how important slavery was as a cause of the Civil War requires weighing it against other contributing factors. The strength of this judgment call lies in the weight of the evidence and in how persuasively this case can be argued. It may also depend upon the choice of the thinking-writing genre used to make the case, which we will explore below.

Research suggests that causal reasoning, like chronological thinking, must be explicitly taught. In a study of ninth-graders, Jesus Dominguez and Ignacio Juan Pozo (1998) wanted to know if causal thinking emerged naturally from factual and conceptual instruction about a historical topic or if it had to be taught. Three groups of students in a high school received different kinds of instruction about the French Revolution: content instruction (factual and conceptual), instruction in content and in making causal connections, and instruction in historical reasoning only. Given a list of events and conditions leading up to the Revolution, the students were asked to analyze the relative significance of the causes and explain cause-and-effect relationships. The group that received both factual and conceptual instruction *and* instruction about making causal connections significantly outperformed the others in explaining causal relationships. The researchers found that the teaching of facts and concepts was essential, but not sufficient for students to be able to explain why events take place. They concluded that "no learning of causal explanation takes place unless it is expressly taught" (p. 358).

Understanding how World War Two and pre-war mobilization led to development of a military industrial complex was an important causal link in Kelly Long's US university-level history survey. To show impact on urban development and demographic shift across the nation, she used comparative maps that reflected population distribution before and after World War Two, the development of nuclear and military industries in the so-called Gun Belt, and the emergence of the Sun Belt. Students later drew on other source documents to connect these shifts with the development of the interstate highway system and the rise in private automobile ownership.

Making causal connections is an essential step in historical knowledge building. Students in Russ Brown's (HLP) high school class made causal connections by annotating timelines. Part of their annotations related to causality, wherein students had to explain why the event was important by arguing that it caused another event to take place. For example, the Munich Agreement led Hitler to think he could continue to take over more territory without opposition, ultimately resulting in World War Two. As a formative assessment, David Farrell (HLP) had his high school students create a flowchart activity on Herbert Hoover's responses to the Great Depression. Students' charts used arrows to show how events interrelated, demonstrating that the Depression had multiple causes. The activity responded to Essential Questions from the unit that required students to make claims about cause, effect, and significance. When Cory (HLP) had his community college students in a Western Civilizations course work together to explain how the Age of Discovery led to the liberal revolutions in the late-eighteenth to early-nineteenth centuries, they created a flow chart that illustrated the causal relationships. Making causal connections provides the link students need to make arguments, to stake claims about significance of past events, and to offer interpretations in their own historical accounts.

Creating a historical account is part of the back and forth process of knowledge building, not an isolated event. The finished account will present what students have learned, but producing it will help them discover what they still need to know. The point is nicely illustrated by a writing assignment in a middle-school classroom described by Richard Kellough and his colleagues (1996). The students were engaged in writing biographies of Sojourner Truth. "The learning sequence is not read, then write," the observer noted. "Rather it is write a little ... then find out a little. Write some, learn a little more, write some more, and so on" (p. 400). Writing an account, in other words, is a process, not a single event. The process, in turn, depends upon the kind of account students write. The biographies mentioned above were narrative accounts, which we will look at first.

Narrative Accounts

Narrative accounts represent a bridge between chronological recounts and causal explanations about the past. A narrative is a story, a nonfiction story in the case of historical writing. "Learning history," Perfetti and colleagues (1995) state, "includes learning a story. It is far from everything that constitutes learning history. It is merely the minimum standard ... of whether a student has attained competence in historical topics" (p. 4). Narrative accounts are not all alike. Like their literary cousins, historical narratives come in different sizes. If a historian's book-length manuscript were comparable to a novel or a scholarly article to a short story, a student-created narrative is likely to be a very, very short story. It could be an account of the Boston Massacre of a few paragraphs in length, a poster presentation in which the student talks the audience through a topic, or a longer essay or paper.

Writing a narrative account is the easiest way for students to link temporal and causal thinking. Creating a narrative, Caroline Coffin (2004) explains, "gives students practice in explaining rather than simply recording past events, but significantly it does this without students losing the iconic form of a timeline as a scaffold for text construction" (p. 279). In other words, the causal explanation unfolds along with the temporal narrative. While writing narrative accounts can help students, even younger students, link chronology and causality, it also can be problematic.

In the first place, the narrative format may constrict students' thinking about causality. It encourages a tendency among novice historical thinkers to reason in single causal chains rather than in more complex causal structures (Perfetti, et al., 1995). Teachers reinforce such simple views of cause–effect relationships if they teach only chronological explanations of events. It also is called the "billiard ball model" (Coffin, 2004, p. 261), in which one event caused another, which, in turn, led to a third, which resulted in still another and so on. Dominguez and Pozo (1998) found that students had a "strong tendency ... to represent causal relationships as a chain sequence. ... We may well conclude that, if not for the express intervention of the teacher, the majority of pupils at the end of compulsory secondary education will see history as a series of events placed one after the other ... in other words, related like the days of the week" (pp. 358–359). It is the opposite of multiple causation in which events are linked more like a web than like a chain. In academic circles, mono-causal explanations are frowned upon, with multiple causation explanations being the gold standard. "Events have multiple causes: nothing in history is so simple as to have a single, isolated cause,"

James Woodcock (2011) reminds us, and he adds, "History as it happens is an infinitely tangled web of cause and effect, of reinforcement and negation, reflection and refraction, acceleration and hindrance" (p. 125). As narratives are all about one thing leading to another, they reinforce the novice's preference for causal chains. A single causal thread also tends to give sequences of events a sense of inevitability. It could only have happened this way.

Narratives also tend to privilege personal agency over abstract forces in causal thinking. In the unfolding of a narrative, individuals and groups typically play more obvious roles than do abstract forces, which are often expressed as social science concepts (technological change, nationalism, ethnocentrism). Students, especially younger students, seem more likely to think in humanistic or personal rather than in social scientific terms (Carretero, Jacott, Limon, Lopez-Manjon, & Leon, 1994; Hallden, 1986). Historians, Ola Hallden notes (1997, 1998), draw upon both traditions, focusing on individuals in a humanistic fashion, but placing them within broader, social science-like contexts. Students, on the other hand, "seem to have both feet in the humanities, thus leaving out the impersonal structures altogether" (1997, p. 205). In other words, students tend to "personalize" the past, ascribing causation to the mental and emotional states of individual agents, and sometimes attributing mental states to social and political institutions, as in "Sweden regards" and the "Soviet Union wants" (Hallden, 1998, p. 134). Attributions of personal agency are especially characteristic of younger students. In a study by Mario Carretero and others (1994), sixth- and eighth-grade students attributed Columbus' sailing to personal motives, while tenth graders and older students placed greater emphasis on the economic conditions of the time. The narrative form, at the very least, does not discourage this way of thinking among novice historical thinkers.

The obstacles that narrative accounts present are not insurmountable. The best antidote to a narrative account's narrowing of thinking may simply be presenting students with additional narratives. In her secondary school classroom, Gadd (2009) presented a unit on Britain and India in the nineteenth century as a series of "small stories" about historical characters, events, and episodes. The students then wove these together into a larger story that linked small-story events. In his university course, Matt Downey's students constructed multiple timelines for a period of Colorado history, which they had to link together in an end-of-unit essay. In both cases, linking several narratives created opportunities for students to find multiple causes. As these activities engaged students in constructing a synthesis of a historical period, we will examine them in more detail in the synthesis chapter.

Explanatory Accounts

With the narrative account providing a somewhat limited view of causation, history educators have for the most part favored a more productive alternative.

The most common strategy used both for research about students' causal reasoning and for classroom instruction is a problem-solving model in which students write an explanatory account. These writings also answer the Essential Question, "how do we explain what happened?" Explanatory accounts differ from a story-like narrative in that the timeline is replaced by a more analytical framework. For example, Dominguez concluded a unit on the French Revolution by giving his ninth-grade students a list of events and conditions preceding that event (Dominguez & Pozo, 1998). Their assignment was to identify factors that were causally related to that event (and to exclude non-causes), to analyze their relative significance, and to identify the causal relationship. He also asked the students to do counter-factual analysis ("if the event had not happened …"), which often is included in this model. The students' written explanatory accounts were then scored on a four-point scale depending on how adequately the students connected the events selected as causes. The scale ranged from "no causes, only facts," and "a series of undifferentiated facts," to "partial connections between causes", and "full connections between causes" (pp. 350–351).

Strategies that help students develop causal explanations are plentiful. In studying the World Wars, Russ Brown's (HLP) students used graphic charts to identify causes of World Wars One and Two, as well as the conditions that led to Hitler & Stalin coming to power. Students' comparison charts identified causes that were similar and different for these events. Tracy Brady's (HLP) university students described five factors that led to FDR's election in 1932. These included immediate, intermediate, and long-term causes such as Hoover's failed economic policies, Al Smith's bringing immigrant voters into the Democratic Party in 1928, and the historic identification of the Republican Party with big business. Short essay explanations showed interconnections between these causal factors.

Teachers in Britain, where teaching about causation is an objective embedded in the National Curriculum for England, have further developed this problem-solving model. They often use a card sort by which students prioritize and categorize causes. The students identify the causes listed on the cards by their importance, long-term/short-term duration, and by social science categories. Requiring students to consider long-term causes counterbalances the tendency that many have to see the most immediate causes as the most important (Clark, 2001). Sorting causes into social, political, religious, economic, and other categories helped students place human agency in broader and more formal contexts. Some teachers engage students in debates and discussions prior to their writing an explanatory account, including discussions of the language commonly used to express causation (Clark, 2001; Evans & Pate, 2007). These activities culminate in a written account or oral report in which students weigh the significance of the several possible causes.

As causal reasoning itself is difficult for many students, teachers have found that scaffolding is essential (Howells, 1998). That includes creating diagrams that help students visualize patterns of causation (Chapman, 2003). However, as

Jennifer Evans and Gemme Pate (2007) discovered, too much scaffolding tends to inhibit students' thinking. Their students were more creative and flexible in their thinking when they created their own causation cards, instead of using a teacher-made set. For his beginning secondary students, Vaughn Clark (2001) relied heavily on their verbal skills, which were more highly developed than their writing abilities. His students broke into small groups to discuss individual causes and reported orally to the whole class, which critiqued each report. After responding to the criticism, each group orally presented its final account in an essay format. "The whole class becomes a team building an essay, and each group of six is a mini-team working on a paragraph. ... Following each presentation by each group, the whole class is the given an opportunity to reflect upon the strengths of the talk" (Clark, 2001, p. 29). The presentations were even more effective when videotaped, which permitted more leisurely student reflection.

What kind of teacher-provided scaffolding do students need to make causal connections? In their study of university undergraduates, James Voss and Jennifer Wiley (1997) asked students, who were divided into three groups, to rate the importance of a series of statements taken from various sources about the Irish potato famine. Their purpose was "to test the hypothesis that students would write better essays if they first indicated the importance of the specific items of textual information" (p. 257). Those students who rated potential "causes" before they wrote their essays increased the number of causal connectives in the narrative and history essay groups compared to those who did the rating afterwards. However, it tended to depress the number of connections made by the argument group, with those who had not thought about individual causes being less constricted and ranging further afield in their writing. The researchers' conclusion was that it helped those who were least likely to think of causes on their own, but constrained those who were most wide-ranging.

Explanatory writing (and oral presentation) uses language in a characteristic way, which effective teachers incorporate into their lessons. Most obviously, we use different words to express cause and effect. As Coffin (2004) notes, "there are lexical sets for each side of the 'causal coin' (*factors, reasons*, and *causes* on one side and *results, outcomes, consequences* on the other)" (p. 283). While explanatory accounts use causal conjunctions also common to the narrative form, they rely more heavily than narratives on causal verbs ("bring about," "led to," or "resulted in") and causal nouns ("reason, factor, outcome, consequence") (Coffin, 2004, pp. 263–264, 273). To help students write causal arguments, Evans and Pate (2007) used a variety of scaffolding activities. Among them were sentence starters ("The ultimate reason …"); word banks, including lists of conjunctives ("As a result of," "additionally"); and helper sheets of tips on writing good essays. Clark (2001) had his students brainstorm words related to key causal terms. "What matters is that they gain confidence in using the vocabulary orally and that the vocabulary choice is associated with thinking" (p. 28). Opposite we have created a vocabulary table that includes some commonly used causal conjunctions, verbs, and nouns (Figure 10.1).

The Language of Causation	
Causal Conjunctions	**Causal Nouns**
Because	Reasons
As a result of	Causes
Then	Results
Therefore	Factors
Due to	Outcomes
Consequently	Consequences
Causal Verbs	
Brought about	
Led to	
Resulted in	
Caused by	
Produced by	
Stemmed from	

FIGURE 10.1 The Language of Causation

While the language of causation is not confined to the use of such targeted vocabulary terms, and to look only for them would do a disservice to more articulate students, students do need to be taught to use language that reflects causation. Teachers need to be alert to the language that students use in causal accounts and students need to know how to use words that help them achieve rather than defeat their purposes. Narrative and explanatory accounts are high-level writing tasks for students. They are important opportunities for students to put their own understandings forward. They are building blocks to an even higher level task, which is that of synthesis, which we take up in the next chapter.

References

Barton, K. C. & Levstik, L. (1996). "Back when God was around and everything": The development of children's understanding of historical time. *American Educational Research Journal*, 33(2), 419–454.

Biggs, J. (1999). *Teaching for quality learning at university: What the student does*. Buckingham, UK: SRHE and Open University Press.

Blow, F., Lee, P., & Shemilt, D. (2012). Time and chronology: Conjoined twins or distant cousins. *Teaching History*, 147, 26–34.

Brophy, J. E. & Van Sledright, B. A. (1997). *Teaching and learning history in elementary schools*. New York: Teachers College Press.

Carretero, M., Jacott, L., Limon, M., Lopez-Manjon, A., & Leon, J. A. (1994). Historical knowledge: Cognitive and instructional implications. In M. Carretero & J. F. Voss (eds.) *Cognitive and instructional processes in history and the social sciences* (pp. 357–376). Hillsdale, NJ: Erlbaum.

Chapman, A. (2003). Camels, diamonds and counterfactuals: A model for teaching causal reasoning. *Teaching History*, 112, 46–53.

Clark, V. (2001). Illuminating the shadow: Making progress in causal thinking through speaking and listening. *Teaching History*, 105, 26–33.

Coffin, C. (2004). Learning to write history: The role of causality. *Written Communication*, 21(3), 261–289.

Coffin, C. (2006). *Historical discourse: The language of time, cause and evaluation*. London: Continuum.

Dawson, I. (2004). Time for chronology? Ideas for developing chronological understanding. *Teaching History*, 117, 14–24.

Dominguez, J. & Pozo, I. J. (1998). Promoting the learning of causal explanations in history through different teaching strategies. In J. F. Voss & M. Carretero (eds.) *International review of history education, Volume 2: Learning and reasoning in history* (pp. 344–359). London and Portland, OR: Woburn Press.

Downey, M. T. (1994). Historical thinking and perspective taking in a fifth-grade classroom. Paper presented at the Annual Meeting of the College and University Faculty Assembly of the National Council for the Social Studies, Phoenix, AZ.

Evans, J. & Pate, G. (2007). Does scaffolding make them fall? Reflection on strategies for developing causal argument in Years 8 and 11. *Teaching History*, 128, 18–29.

Fallace, T. D., Briscoe, A. D., & Perry, J. L. (2007). Second graders thinking historically: Theory into practice. *Journal of Social Studies Research*, 31(1), 44–53.

Gadd, S. (2009). Building memory and meaning: Supporting Year 8 in shaping their own big narratives. *Teaching History*, 136, 34–41.

Hallden, O. (1986). Learning history. *Oxford Review of Education*, 12, 53–66.

Hallden, O. (1997). Conceptual change and the learning of history. *International Journal of Educational Research*, 27(3), 201–210.

Hallden, O. (1998). On reasoning in history. In J. F. Voss & M. Carretero (eds.) *International review of history education. Volume 2, Learning and reasoning in history* (pp. 272–277). London and Portland, OR: Woburn Press.

Hodkinson, A. (2003). "History howlers": Amusing anecdotes or symptoms of the difficulties children have in retaining and ordering historical knowledge? Some observations based on current research. *Research in Education*, 70, 21–36.

Howell, H. & Prevenier, W. (2001). *From reliable sources: An introduction to historical methods*. Ithaca, NY: Cornell University Press.

Howells, G. (1998). Being ambitious with the causes of the First World War: Interrogating inevitability. *Teaching History*, 92, 16–19.

Kellough, R. D., Jarolimek, J., Parker, W. C., Martorella, P. H., Tompkins, G. E., & Hoskisson, K. (1996). *Integrating language arts and social studies for intermediate and middle school students* (pp. 396–405). Englewood Cliffs, NJ: Prentice-Hall, Inc.

Lomas, T. & Batho, G. R. (1993). *Teaching and assessing historical understanding*. London: Historical Association.

Maddison, M. (2011). Developing pupils' chronological understanding: The view from Ofsted. *Primary History*, 59, 8–9.

McIlroy, C. (2011). A view from the classroom. *Primary History*, 59, 10.

Perfetti, C. A., Britt, M. A., & Georgi, M. C. (1995). *Text-based learning and reasoning: Studies in history*. Hillsdale, NJ and Hove, UK: Lawrence Erlbaum Associates.

Schleppegrell, M. J. (2004*). The language of schooling: A functional linguistics perspective*. Mahwah, NJ and London: Lawrence Erlbaum Associates, Publishers.

Spoehr, K. T. (1994). Enhancing the acquisition of conceptual structures through hypermedia. In K. McGilly (ed.) *Classroom lessons: Integrating cognitive theory and classroom practice* (pp. 75–101). Cambridge, MA and London: MIT Press.

Tripp, L., Basye, C., Jones, K., & Tripp, V. (2008). Teaching and learning with time lines. *Middle Level Learning*, Supplement to *Social Education*, 72(4), 4–7.

Vella, Y. (2011). The gradual transformation of historical situations: Understanding "change and continuity" through colours and timelines. *Teaching History*, 144, 16–23.

Voss, J. F. & Wiley, J. (1997). Developing understanding while writing essays in history. *International Journal of Educational Research*, 27(3), 255–265.

Wood, S. (1995). Developing an understanding of time-sequencing issues. *Teaching History*, 79, 11–14.

Woodcock, J. (2011). Causal explanation. In I. Davies (ed.) *Debates in teaching history* (pp. 124–136). London and New York: Routledge.

11
SYNTHESIZE

A synthesis brings many separate elements together into a coherent whole. A historical synthesis weaves evidence and accounts into an explanation for why something happened the way it did. This is what historians set out to do when they undertake a historical investigation. They also revise other historians' work to provide more persuasive explanations. That these historical syntheses are tentative, open to dispute, and subject to revision is what makes history an interpretative discipline. To help students understand this and to create syntheses of their own that are grounded in evidence and are persuasive should be the goal of history instruction.

Constructing a synthesis is the capstone of historical learning. It is the culmination of the process that began with a Big Question, which led to activating prior knowledge, and then to collecting, analyzing, and connecting historical information. A synthesis represents the position a student takes in response to that Big Question, as well as an explanation that weaves together several strands of historical thinking. As a documented historical narrative or argument (Account and Evidence), it will attempt to explain why something happened (Causation and Agency), the sequence of events (Time and Chronology), and the perspectives of those involved (Perspective Analysis). It will assess its impact at the time (Change and Continuity) and its importance to us (Significance). As a learning task, a synthesis represents a convergence of both historical content and conceptual disciplinary thinking.

In a constructivist classroom, a synthesis is the product of student thinking. It is not a pre-packaged explanation to be committed to memory, whatever guidance a teacher or a textbook may have provided along the way. A synthesis is, as Daniel Callison (1999) notes, "a structure or pattern not clearly there before, either new to the student or on an original research level new to the human knowledge base" (p. 39). The element of originality makes synthesizing different from merely listing information or, in Marlene Scardamalia and Carl Bereiter's (1987) phrasing, "knowledge telling." Otherwise, Kathleen M. Young and Gaea Leinhardt (1998) note, "the writer essentially lists what she or he knows about a topic through a semistructured memory dump." Synthesizing, on the other hand, is "knowledge transformation, in which the writer generates, analyzes, and restructures what she or he knows about a topic into a coherently integrated argument, explanation or description" (p. 29). It is the difference between "knowing about" and "reasoning with" content (p. 31). To reason historically at the level of synthesis is to address historical change and to explain why it took place.

We must treat the creation of syntheses as an explicit goal of history instruction. Teachers have always used synthesis-like assignments, but not always in the way that we propose here. Unit projects, research papers, and essay questions on tests are likely to require students to synthesize knowledge. The quality of the connections they make may even be weighed in the grade for the assignment. But we suspect that such assignments primarily are used to assess *how much* students have learned rather than *how well* they have interpreted or explained it. The best evidence for this lies in the professional literature itself. Reports of the explicit teaching of synthesis are like Sherlock Holmes' curious incident of the dog that did not bark. They are conspicuous for their absence, with a few notable exceptions (Monte-Sano, 2011). Consequently, this chapter is more heavily dependent on academic research studies or on teachers' action research projects than the reports of effective classroom practice that we have hitherto relied heavily on.

The format that students use for a synthesis depends on the nature of the project, the students' interests and the teacher's expectations. Written presentations probably are the most common. However, Callison (1999) suggests a number of other generic formats, including alternative forms of communication (posters, critical essays, newspaper articles), plans of operation (scripts, lesson plans), and abstract relationships (including working hypotheses). Syntheses can be "conducted over a range of challenges, from a quick microlevel to a very large scale and complex creation task" (p. 40). These could include student-made computer-based projects, dramatic enactments or readings, or multi-media presentations. However, to focus on format is to miss the point. What matters most is the kind of thinking involved in creating a synthesis, which is thinking that extends beyond the reshuffling or summarizing of someone else's conclusions. In this chapter, we emphasize three basic approaches to synthesis making. These include creating a historical narrative, producing an expository or explanatory account, and presenting a historical argument (Coffin, 2006; Voss & Wiley, 1997a; Young & Leinhardt, 1998).

Synthesis as Narrative

A common approach is to present a synthesis as a historical narrative or story. It also may be the approach that students are most comfortable using. "Narrative is how most of us understand most of the world around us most of the time," Sean Lang (2011, p. 24) noted, arguing for more storytelling and writing in history classrooms. A narrative synthesis is essentially a student's telling of a story. "Rather than teaching them [students] to be consumers of stories," Thomas Holt (1990) observes, "we might better develop their critical faculties by letting them create stories of their own" (p. 12). Writing such a synthesis would, of course, ask them to do more than tell a simple "first this and then that" kind of story. It would need to include causal links and to determine the significance of various influences. "Good stories are complex, with rich connections, events that play multiple roles, and multilayered interpretations," Perfetti, Britt, and Georgi (1995, p. 3) point out. The narrative form allows students to move beyond temporal thinking to at least rudimentary causal reasoning.

However, as we also have seen, the synthesis-as-story approach also has inherent problems. The narrative form tends to constrict students' causal reasoning. It reinforces their tendency to think in terms of single causal chains rather than of the causal webs required for a complex story. Historians overcome this by drawing upon their extensive knowledge of a period or topic as well as their professional expertise. They weave together multiple strands of a story, present the different perspectives of historical actors, and use professional judgment to weigh various causal influences. Students are much less well prepared to do this. Familiarity with the narrative form may not help them much and may even be an obstacle to more analytical thinking. We need to explore ways that teachers can scaffold instruction to help students meet this challenge.

Synthesis as Multiple Stories

In her high school classroom in Britain, Sarah Gadd (2009) confronted this challenge by organizing instruction around multiple stories. The existing curriculum presented Britain and India during the Victorian era as an overarching narrative or pre-determined story that students were expected to learn. The problem was that by failing to link key events and developments, the students came away with disconnected learning that gave them little sense of Victorian Britain as a coherent period. To find a solution, Gadd transformed the unit into an action research project. She broke up the 12-lesson unit into a series of shorter developments, with the students creating their own smaller stories about each. For the unit's concluding activity, they had to connect these multiple stories as a larger, coherent narrative. "The final outcome was an individually written historical narrative knitting together the history of Britain and India during a 70-year period, in whatever way pupils found meaningful" (Gadd, 2009, p. 36).

She hoped this would enable students to create their own synthesis of the period, show them that history is "constructed," not "found," and allow her to learn more about how students "make meaning through narration" (p. 37). That, in turn, might help her to find better ways to deepen students' understanding both of this historical period and of historical thinking.

From this admittedly limited study, Gadd learned a great deal about the role that both "received" and "constructed" narratives can play in historical learning. She even had to create a new vocabulary to describe the different ways her students created larger narratives from the smaller stories she had provided them. The most successful was the "blended narrative" (Gadd, 2009, p. 41) that a student named Paul created by juxtaposing disparate facts and pieces of stories into his account. More common were "concurrent narratives" (p. 39) in which students wove separate stories and story fragments together. Sometimes a dominant story (not always the same one) formed the core, with fragments of stories linked to it. Other students interlaced smaller stories, moving from one to another and then back again. Still others wrote essays focused on side stories, but implied the existence of a central story, with occasional references to it. Not all students were so successful. Some final essays presented largely disconnected stories or "fractured narratives" (p. 40). She also discovered that the emphasis on narrative writing enabled students to do interesting things with historical content, including creating their own narrative structures. By telling their own overarching stories, her students developed a greater interest in broader historical trends than she had anticipated. However limited the study, Gadd's classroom research provides the rest of us with a model for continuing this kind of inquiry and a point of departure for thinking further about narratives as student-made syntheses.

In her unit on the South during the Civil War, Tracy Brady (HLP) used an approach similar to the above. Her university students read several mini-biographies of people living in the Confederacy, including those of a slave, a planter on a large plantation, a Confederate soldier's widow, and a poor, white southerner. Their assignment was to synthesize these accounts to create a picture of the south during the war. Drawing on multiple accounts helped them write a better synthesis.

Synthesizing Multiple Timelines

History courses that emphasize topics pose special problems for synthesizing knowledge. A topical organization tends to promote piecemeal learning, with each topic having its own chronology. Gadd's students had "struggled to retain and transfer knowledge across topics and themes, making meaningful connections difficult (Gadd, 2009, p. 36). Matt Downey faced a similar problem in his university-level Colorado history course for future elementary teachers. He presented it topically because that is the way Colorado history is taught in the schools. The unit on frontier settlement begins with the Gold Rush of 1859, then the development of gold and silver mining, followed by topics on farming and ranching, Indian removal, railroad building, and town and city life. The mining of precious metals—a story about gold rushes, instant millionaires, and raucous mining towns—provides the most popular narrative for the period. However, it is only marginally useful, as it relegates farmers, railroad workers, and everybody else to the status of bystanders. Downey's problem was to get students to see this period not as a series of disjointed topics or a mining era with assorted hangers-on, but as a period of economic and social development in which several groups of actors played equally important roles.

His solution was to organize the late-nineteenth-century unit around multiple timelines with a culminating assignment asking students to write a narrative that wove these timelines together. The four topics for which they completed timelines included gold and silver mining, farming and ranching, railroad building, and Indian removal. Each topic was the focus of one week of instruction during the four-week unit, with students constructing a timeline of significant events and developments for each topic. In addition to the instructor's lectures, they drew upon information from the textbook, assigned secondary readings, primary sources and historical photographs. To make the task of synthesis writing more manageable, the final assignment was divided into two chronological periods (1859–1871 and 1871–1890). That is, students wrote a two-part essay, making connections between the timelines for each period.

Instruction focused on historical content, except for two practice-writing assignments. During the last two weeks of the unit, students wrote one-to-two-page exit-ticket essays that asked them to connect two (first essay) and then three (second essay) timelines for the earlier period. The assignments also served as formative evaluations for Downey, who returned them at the next class period with brief written critiques. After reading the second assignment, he prepared a handout that emphasized the importance of temporal and causal conjunctions and causal verbs and phrases when establishing causal connections. On the day of the unit test, students were given 45 minutes to write their syntheses. To help them focus on connection making rather than remembering what to connect, the students were allowed to use their completed timelines as notes.

The students' essays varied substantially in knowledge of content, quality of historical thinking, and in how well they connected timelines. They ranged in length from two to five pages. Not surprisingly, students with the best command of the material, who brought substantial and accurate factual knowledge to the task, also made the most connections. However, except for the thinnest presentations, the way most students organized their essays was remarkably similar. They used either a "main story–satellite stories" approach or they combined several mutually supporting stories. Essays for the first period (1859–1871) most frequently used the Gold Rush as a dominant narrative, with events from the other timelines playing supporting roles. That is, farmers and ranchers provided food for the miners; railroads reduced the cost of transporting ore; and new gold and silver discoveries created pressure to remove Indian tribes. The essays for the latter period (1871–1890), which lacked a single compelling narrative, consisted of several more-or-less equal stories. One or more of the events within each story was connected to at least one other story, but no one timeline dominated the narrative. While the main story-satellite stories approach produced a more coherent narrative, they also resulted in the simplest and least thoughtful timeline connections. Connecting co-equal stories seemed to require more reflection and deliberate thought.

How students connected and synthesized information in the timelines within these narrative structures also varied. A number of the least well-developed essays seldom did more than make temporal connections within a timeline, with causal links either left out or implied. These took the form of "this happened and then that happened" narratives, sometimes with "this led to" serving as an ambiguous link between them. Other connections described simultaneous developments between timelines, often with a phrase introduced by "as" and with each referred to in the same sentence. For example, "As people rushed to the Continental Divide, the Utes were removed from the area." The use of passive voice implies that the two developments were connected, but the sentence does not make it explicit or describe the process. The most effective responses were explicitly causal connections across timelines, as in "Railroads made both mining and farming more efficient by reducing the cost of transportation." Multiple connections of this kind often were most succinctly made in concluding summaries. As one student ended her essay by noting that, "Overall this shows the connections between the miners following the gold into Colorado and the farmers following the miners, which caused conflict with the Indians forcing the government officials to remove the Indians. The removal of the Indians led to the [expansion of] farming and opportunity for transportation." Other students accomplished the same purpose with an introductory paragraph that laid out the connections they planned to make.

Synthesis as Exposition

Another approach to creating a synthesis relies on an expository presentation. It differs from a narrative synthesis by abandoning the timeline in favor of a more analytical text structure. That is, it develops an explanation by drawing from an array of supporting factual information regardless of its chronological order. Expository prose is probably familiar to most history students as it is the prose in which history textbooks and informational texts are often written. Most of the writing tasks that students are assigned in history classrooms, such as identification questions, reports, and research papers, also ask for expository writing. The expository prototype in classrooms in the United States is the five-paragraph essay, which usually is introduced in the elementary grades. It can provide a useful scaffold for younger or less able students (De La Paz, 2005), although advanced students may find its rigid structure confining.

In his high school US history course, Lyle concluded a unit on opposing views on slavery during the pre-Civil War period by assigning a synthesis essay (Monte-Sano, 2011). He wanted his students to explain how perspectives on slavery differed and were a contributing factor to the outbreak of the war. Lyle had his students read a series of primary sources, analyze them carefully in class, and write about each source. He then critiqued each source essay. The writing assignments gave the students experience recognizing perspectives and using historical evidence. It helped prepare them to write synthesis essays with evidence-based conclusions supported by the analysis of perspectives.

An expository synthesis does not have to be a written report or essay. We used an earlier example of discussions based on a content matrix that Ford used to help her sixth-grade students learn about the Enlightenment (Secules & Ford, 2006). Her students, working in small groups, reported on this development in different European nations, while she recorded the information on a wall chart. As they constructed the chart, the students discussed similarities and differences in the Enlightenment between various countries. In the final days of the unit, they looked for commonalities and exceptions, which generated further discussions about connections between changes in government, belief systems, and other aspects of society. Their discussions led to a shared class synthesis about why the Enlightenment happened when it did and why it had different results in different places. Instead of memorizing lists of facts or accepting a textbook's definition of the term, the authors reported, "these sixth grade students literally constructed their own understanding" of "why this period is called the Enlightenment" (p. 91). It was accomplished largely through discussion.

Teachers in the United States have used Document Based Question (DBQ) assignments to engage students in constructing syntheses. Introduced by the College Board as part of its Advanced Placement (AP) test in 1973, the DBQ has become a familiar fixture in many inclusive as well as AP high school classrooms (Rothschild, 2000). In a typical BDQ, students are given a set of short passages from primary sources presenting different perspectives on a historical topic. A prompt asks them to interpret the documents and to advance an explanation or argument. For example, "'From 1781 to 1789, the Articles of Confederation provided the United States with an effective government.' Using the [eight] documents *and your knowledge of the period* [italics added], evaluate this statement" (Young & Leinhardt, 1998, p. 34). While a DBQ may only ask students to construct an explanation or argument based on the documentary evidence at hand (Monte-Sano, 2010), it also may, like the example above, ask students to synthesize a broader knowledge base.

To investigate how high school students respond to a synthesis assignment, Young and Leinhardt (1998) observed a high school Advanced Placement class taught by a teacher they identified as Sterling. As the course was focused on the

AP exam, she emphasized such test-taking skills as addressing the question, interpreting (not paraphrasing) the documents, and developing a plan for a coherent essay. Sterling taught history not as factual information to be regurgitated on the test, but as "a way of reading and writing about events in the past. All history is interpretation" (p. 33). She emphasized the students' role as interpreters of the past. "You are the author," she would tell them. "It's your essay. ... You are the author. I cannot emphasize that enough" (p. 35). During in-class instruction and in written comments on practice essays, she explained that as authors they needed to transform and integrate their historical knowledge rather than just list what they knew. Students, Young and Leinhardt agreed, "cannot simply 'tell' what happened in the period or what the documents literally 'say.' Rather, they need to transform their knowledge and the documents to explain, evaluate, analyze, and argue aspects of a critical historical topic" (p. 35).

The essays, which Young and Leinhardt (1998) analyzed, produced mixed results. Most students began making little more than lists of information, with a few making more complex causal links and arguments. Thereafter, the pattern of development was uneven, with more students writing less list-like essays, but not consistently. The problem, the authors concluded, was the lack of explicit instruction in academic literacy. While Sterling had provided excellent history instruction, engaging the students in the discipline rather than in memorizing content, "students received no instruction or explanation while engaged in the task itself. Sterling had students practice writing under time constraints that allowed for very little unpacking or analysis of the task. ... When producing written arguments and explanations, students needed to manage the entire task themselves; to produce coherent linear text; and to do so without having student or teacher models or coaching" (p. 59). They concluded that explicit instruction and modeling about how to write to synthesize information from different perspectives would have improved the students' arguments and deepened their conceptual knowledge of the topic.

Synthesis as Historical Argument

Still another approach to historical synthesis asks students to make an argument. To make a historical argument is to make a case for a particular interpretation of the past. This is, students must explain why their argument is the best or most complete explanation for why past events turned out as they did. This is surely the most demanding of the three alternatives that we have explored, but also the one most likely to lead to complex causal explanations. In research with university students, Jame F. Voss and Jennifer Wiley (1997a, 1997b; Wiley & Voss, 1996, 1999) compared the results of students using different writing formats to make causal connections. Students learning about the Irish potato famine were divided into three groups, with those in each group assigned to write either "a history," "a narrative," or "an argument" about why significant changes took place in

Ireland during the 1840s. The researchers evaluated the students' work on how they organized their essays, completeness of the accounts, and the number of conceptual and causal connections. Students writing arguments out-performed the other groups. The authors further concluded that students who wrote arguments using multiple sources were least likely to engage in "knowledge-telling" and more likely to use information in a "knowledge-transforming" way than those using a textbook (Wiley & Voss 1996). Argumentation, the authors concluded, involved more mental processing and critical thought. Such assignments also are likely to have other benefits. "By writing their own arguments, students may begin to see that history is not just about learning names and dates, but an on-going debate about what those facts may mean" (Voss & Wiley, 1997a, p. 264). Whether secondary or elementary students would have produced similar results is an open question, but we suspect that they would. Wiley and Voss' students organized the information to make the strongest argument instead of producing collective or list-like statements of fact. "They would need to select the text contents that they felt were important to the position they were taking and would need to integrate such information to develop their argument" (Wiley & Voss, 1996, p. S64). While the quality of arguments may differ, students of any age should be able to meet the challenge.

That does not mean that students can be left to their own resources, as research suggests that argumentative historical writing must be explicitly taught. In a study in a middle school classroom conducted by Susan De La Paz (2005), students in the experimental group learned an argumentative writing strategy, with the control-group students fending for themselves. The writing strategy was based on the mnemonics STOP and DARE. The first prompted students "to **S**uspend judgment, **T**ake a side, **O**rganize (select and number) ideas, and **P**lan more as you write." They wrote journal entries describing their own past attempts to persuade someone and read persuasive articles that might serve as models. The second mnemonic included other elements of argumentative writing, advising students "to **D**evelop a topic sentence, **A**dd supporting ideas, **R**eject an argument for the other side, and **E**nd with a conclusion" (p. 146). To help students apply it, the cooperating teachers modeled how to compose introductory and concluding paragraphs of a five-paragraph argument. They engaged the students in independent practice by having them apply the strategy to various historical topics. Finally, the students composed arguments taking sides in two controversial events—the Indian Removal Act of 1830 and the US–Mexican War. This carefully structured process produced significant gains for the experimental students, who "wrote longer and more persuasive papers containing more arguments and more accurate historical content" (p. 152). A later study by De La Paz and Mark Felton (2010) in an eleventh-grade history classroom produced similar results.

Neither should we assume that instruction in argumentative writing can be taught separately from content instruction. As Chauncey Monte-Sano (2010) concluded from his research, "Although generic argumentation is a necessary component of historical writing, it alone is not sufficient." A student synthesis may display skill in argumentation "while revealing fundamental flaws in historical thinking" (p. 560). For an argumentative historical synthesis to be effective, it must include both. Perhaps the ideal solution is for language arts and history teachers to coordinate instruction, as was the case in the middle-grades program in which De La Paz (2005) conducted research. Each student in that northern California school was placed with a single team of teachers responsible for the four major subject-matter areas, permitting the Language Arts and the Social Studies teachers to plan instruction together. Where such collaboration is not possible, as in most high schools, teachers must teach literacy in their respective content areas.

Similar tools helped students in Dan Rypma's (HLP) high school class develop arguments based on primary sources. During his unit on the American Revolutionary War, Dan combined approaches that incorporated taking a position in a debate, as well as individual written work. Students used graphic organizers to keep track of key ideas, events, quotations and different historian's accounts. Then they filled out a debate organizer guide, in which they outlined support for a class debate that included author's name and quotation. After that debate, individual students wrote their argumentative essays.

We conclude this discussion about synthesis by emphasizing that recent research on students' historical thinking demonstrates the value of integrating history and literacy instruction in the history classroom. It goes without saying that the first requirement for students to think at the level of historical synthesis is knowledge about the events or developments concerned. However, that is not sufficient. Students also need explicit instruction in academic literacy, as Young and Leinhardt (1998) concluded. We must help students learn how to make the complex conceptual links required for higher-level thinking. This must include instruction in how to use language to serve that purpose, with due emphasis on the appropriate use of conjunctions and verbs as well as history's specialized vocabulary. Students also need to consider what kind of presentation best suits their purpose: a narrative; an explanation; or an argument? We need to increase students', and our own, level of awareness that historically literate people do not only reason historically about what happened, when, and where. They also can organize and use language in purposeful ways.

Synthesizing Like a Historian

The synthesizing activities described in the above sections of this chapter engage students in complex forms of historical reasoning that is like what historians do. Yet they also have a common shortcoming, as they do not reflect all that historians do when they conduct investigations and synthesize what they have learned. Students tend to approach historical study, Stuart Greene (1994) notes, from an "archivist tradition," viewing history as "a cumulative science based on the amassing of facts." Historians, on the other hand, assume that history is "an act of judgment made on the basis of historical evidence and a historian's interpretive framework that guides his or her selective attention" (p. 92). That framework is a complex layering of their interpretation of the data, knowledge of what others had written about the period, and understanding of how the world works. To think like historians, Greene concluded, students needed to justify their own conclusions by reconciling their interpretation with "what others have said, citing sources as both intellectual and social touchstones" (p. 95). In other words, historical syntheses are not created in an intellectual vacuum, but within the context of other and often conflicting interpretations.

As history teachers, we have been remiss in providing students with this historiographical framework. They should at least have some inkling of how others have dealt with the historical questions they are investigating. The textbooks that teachers have traditionally relied on rarely introduce differing historical interpretations. They are tertiary sources, digests of information that are more like reference books than historical monographs. The new pedagogy, which is heavily dependent on primary sources, also typically does not address this need. Consequently, not only are students shielded from historiographical controversy, but they are also only partially introduced to how historians work and think. History is not only an interpretative discipline; it is also an interactive one in which historians engage in discussions with one another.

What is missing are the secondary historical accounts that historians frequently consult, often rely upon, and sometimes use as a point of departure when creating their own historical explanations. Students need models of how historians have thought about the big historical questions that they themselves are investigating. Publishers have over the years provided such materials for university history courses, beginning with Prentice-Hall's *Problems in American History* (Leopold & Link, 1957). It departed from the traditional source-book format by including historians' interpretations for topics such as Jacksonian Democracy, Causes of the Civil War, and the Progressive Movement. A more recent example of this genre of supplementary materials is Greenhaven Press's *Opposing Viewpoints in American History* (Cozic, 1996), which included both primary sources and historical essays about major topics of US history. The problem is that extensive excerpts from scholarly books and articles present too heavy a reading load for most pre-collegiate students. They need briefer, interpretative essays that take pro and con positions on historical questions or that summarize historical scholarship about key topics in US and world history.

References

Callison, D. (1999). Synthesis. *School Library Media Activities Monthly*, 15(10), 39–46.

Coffin, C. (2006). *Historical discourse: The language of time, cause and evaluation*. London: Continuum.

Cozic, Charles P. (Ed.) (1996) *Opposing viewpoints*. San Diego: CA, Greenhaven Press.

De La Paz, S. (2005). Effects of historical reasoning instruction and writing strategy mastery in culturally and academically diverse middle school classrooms. *Journal of Educational Psychology*, 97(2), 139–156.

De La Paz, S. & Felton, M. K. (2010). Reading and writing from multiple source documents in history: Effects of strategy instruction with low to average high school writers. *Contemporary Educational Psychology*, 35, 174–192.

Gadd, S. (2009). Building memory and meaning: Supporting Year 8 in shaping their own big narratives. *Teaching History*, 136, 34–41.

Greene, S. (1994). The problem of learning to think like a historian: Writing history in the culture of the classroom, *Educational Psychologist*, 29(2), 89–96.

Holt, T. C. (1990). *Thinking historically: Narrative, imagination, and understanding*. New York, NY: College Entrance Examination Board.

Lang, S. (2011). Debates: Narrative in school history. *Teaching History*, 145, 24.

Leopold, Richard W. & Link, A. S. (Eds.) (1957) *Problems in American History*. Englewood Cliffs, NJ: Prentice-Hall, Inc.

Monte-Sano, C. (2010). Disciplinary literacy in history: An exploration of the historical nature of adolescents' writing. *Journal of the Learning Sciences*, 19(4), 539–568.

Monte-Sano, C. (2011). Beyond reading comprehension and summary: Learning to read and write in history by focusing on evidence, perspective, and interpretation. *Curriculum Inquiry*, 41(2), 212–249.

Perfetti, C. A., Britt, M. A., & Georgi, M. C. (1995). *Text-based learning and reasoning: Studies in history*. Hillsdale, NJ and Hove, UK: Lawrence Erlbaum Associates.

Rothschild, E. (2000). The impact of the document-based question on the teaching of United States history. *History Teacher*, 33(4), 495–500.

Scardamalia, M. & Bereiter, C. (1987). Knowledge telling and knowledge transforming in written composition. In S. Rosenberg (Ed.) *Advances in applied psycholinguistics; Vol. 2 Reading, writing, and language learning.* (pp. 142-175). Cambridge: Cambridge University Press.

Secules, T. & Ford, A. (2006). Divide and conquer: Detecting patterns that explain the big picture. *Social Education*, 70(2), 89–92.

Voss, J. F. & Wiley, J. (1997a). Developing understanding while writing essays in history. *International Journal of Educational Research*, 27(3), 255–265.

Voss, J. F. & Wiley, J. (1997b). Conceptual understanding in history. *European Journal of Psychology of Education*, 11(2), 147–158.

Wiley, J. & Voss, J. F. (1996). The effects of "playing historian" on learning in history. *Applied Cognitive Psychology*, 10 (special issue), S63–S72.

Wiley, J. & Voss, J. F. (1999). Constructing arguments from multiple sources: Tasks that promote understanding and not just memory for text. *Journal of Educational Psychology*, 91(2), 1–11.

Young, K. M. & Leinhardt, G. (1998). Writing from primary documents: A way of knowing in history. *Written Communication*, 15(1), 25–68.

PART V
Applying the Learning

Getting Learning Underway
* Activate Prior Knowledge
* Check for Misconceptions
* Preview the Learning to Come
* Address Vocabulary

Building Historical Knowledge
* Build Factual Knowledge
* Compare Texts
* Analyze Perspectives
* Make Temporal and Causal Connections
* Create a Synthesis

Applying Learning
* **Think About Change**
* **Use Historical Perspectives**
* **Analyze People's Perspectives**

FIGURE 12.1 Teaching for Historical Literacy: Applying Historical Knowledge

12

APPLY HISTORICAL KNOWLEDGE

A history unit begins by activating students' prior knowledge, checking for misconceptions, and providing an overview of the learning to come, but how should it end? As illustrated in Figure 12.1, Teaching for Historical Literacy, on the facing page, the third phase of historical literacy focuses on applying historical knowledge. History units typically conclude with a summative assessment, but that takes place after instruction is over. How should teachers bring instruction to a close? A recent social studies strategies manual offers one possibility: reviewing the major concepts introduced during the unit and asking students to summarize what they have learned (Ogle, Klemp, & McBride, 2007). The three-part reading instruction model suggests another way. It concludes with a phase called "after reading," which includes strategies for deepening students' understanding of a text and enhancing long-term retention (Schell & Fisher, 2007). The idea of an "after learning" phase for history instruction makes sense. However, the activities in both of the above examples are redundant or out of sequence in a classroom in which students have already synthesized much of what they have learned. How would a teacher appropriately bring instruction to a close when the goal is to help students become historically literate?

A historically literate person should be able to see connections between the past and the present. To help students do that, history instruction should provide opportunities for them to apply what they have learned to better understand themselves, the society around them, and the larger world in which they live. We also suspect that knowing how to make such connections, like most kinds of learning, requires explicit instruction. While helping students see the relevance of the past can be done during the course of instruction, an equally appropriate time is at the end of a unit. We recommend that teachers conclude instruction by setting aside a class period or two for this purpose.

Let us make clear at the outset that linking past to present is different than reading the present into the past. The latter is called "presentism," a fallacy of ahistorical reasoning that recreates the past in our own likeness. While professional historians abhor presentism, many do believe that we can learn from the past by learning about the past. William McNeill (1985) argued that historical knowledge teaches students about the uncertainties of life. "What if we have to learn to live with uncertainty and probabilities, and act on the basis of the best guesswork we are capable of? Then, surely, the changing perspectives of historical understanding are the very best introduction we can have to the practical problems of real life" (p. 1). Among a litany of ways the past helps students understand the real world, Paul Gagnon (1988) included "by learning how they resemble and how they differ from other people, over time and space ... [and] to be prepared for the irrational, the accidental in human affairs" (p. 44). Teaching about how societies change, Peter Stearns (1998) says, "requires more juxtaposition between past and present than much history teaching now allows. Students need to spend serious time with contemporary history, to talk about current changes, trace their roots into the past, and apply previously learned patterns of change to contemporary phenomena" (p. 291). The question is not whether connecting past to present is worthwhile, but what are the best ways to do it.

To help students apply historical knowledge to their own times, teachers must first make the task manageable. What are some practical ways for students to apply their historical knowledge to their present-day situation? As indicated in Figure 12.1 we suggest three possibilities. In the first place, students can apply what they have learned about change to their own lives. In addition, they can place the present in historical perspective by using analogies. Finally, students can use what they have learned from analyzing the perspectives of historical actors to better understand their own contemporaries. How successfully students can do any of these is, like historical literacy itself, a relative matter. It will be more challenging for younger than for older students, and neither likely will do it as well as professional historians. In this chapter, we will explore how teachers can help students apply their historical knowledge in each of the above ways.

Thinking about Change

History is about how societies change over time. "History is in fact the only subject that takes social change as its principal subject," Stearns (1998) notes. We are not suggesting that students wait until the end of a unit to think about change, as this idea is central to historical learning. It should be made clear from the outset that a unit is exploring what, how, and why things changed during the period under investigation. In her high school unit on the Industrial Revolution, Abigail Gable explained at the beginning that it was more than an economic revolution, as "it had incredible implications down the road for political and social change" (Brooks, 2013, p. 67). Formative assessments should touch base from time to time with what students are learning about change. Providing opportunities for students to think about change along the way should make time spent at the end of the unit discussing its implications for the present far more productive. It also raises the middle-range or Essential Question of historical significance: How important was this change or development to us today?

In their world history course at Carnegie Mellon University, M. Miller and Stearns (1995) explicitly made change the focus of instruction. They created an activity that asked students to identify major changes in one of the societies included in the course over an extended time period: 1750–1914. The students filled in a matrix that included Political, Economic, Social, and Cultural categories along the vertical axis, with Basic Features at the Beginning of Period, Basic Features at End of Period, Key Changes, and Key Continuities across the horizontal axis on top. Breaking change down into different dimensions made the task more manageable, while the labels across the top asked students to identify specific changes and to keep continuity as well as change in mind.

Such an activity could serve different purposes. In the Carnegie Mellon course, the matrix provided a springboard for further learning. After filling it in, students used it for more complex analyses of change, including comparisons between different societies and for causal analysis. Causal questions are critical to a meaningful discussion about change and about the contemporary ramifications of that change. Why did change take place in some aspects of a society, but not in others? Why did change take the direction it did? What accounts for the resistance to change? Secondary school students might spend more time identifying than accounting for changes; simply completing the matrix might be a sufficient task for elementary students. The question remains: how can what students learn about change in the past deepen their understanding of the present?

In the first place, a study of historical change can help disabuse students of the notion that change is a uniquely modern phenomenon. Having to cope with change does not distinguish us from our ancestors. We differ only in kinds of change and the manner in which we deal with them. That being the case, we need to learn what we can from past instances of change. What role did individuals play in bringing it about, as opposed to broader, more impersonal forces? What can we learn from the way individuals, groups, or the larger society responded to changes? This may require students to revisit the historical accounts that they produced and review the assumptions they made about causation. To apply those insights to the present, they also need time to think about events today that they associate with change.

A fruitful discussion explicitly addresses the changes taking place in the students' world today. Students might do that by constructing a matrix for the present. It should be created early in the school year or academic semester. Revisiting it over the course of study, tweaking or refining it as students give it more thought, will help them keep the present as well as the past in mind. The object is not only to find similarities between past and present, but to establish categories of change that help students distinguish between areas or kinds of change and continuity.

Present-day changes are not all of the same magnitude or immediacy to students' lives. Those that most deeply affect them are likely to be quite up-close and personal. A family is going through a divorce. A parent has lost his or her job. A good friend has moved to another city. Whenever possible, teachers should help students place changes in their lives in larger social and historical contexts. A search for causes may suggest that the loss of a job is not an isolated instance, but a result of change in production methods, globalization, or the latest economic downturn. Regional and international migration has historically been one of the consequences of shifting economic opportunities. Best friends and close relatives have historically moved to other places. The point is to help students find kinds of change in the past that may help them recognize and shed light on change in their lives or those of family and friends.

The purpose of looking at change then and now is to help students understand the persistence and complex nature of change. It requires reflection about causes and consequences rather than memorizing facts or learning lessons from the past. The consequences of change include how people have coped with change over time. Looking at what is happening in students' own lives and time provides a magnifying glass for examining change. We can also help students understand some of the problems involved in interpreting change. At the very least, they should learn to take the long view of the past as well as up-close glimpses, avoid attributing change to single causes, and appreciate the role of continuity in human affairs.

Focusing on change has implications for the broader curriculum. "A good history program," Stearns notes, "must thus present recurrent exposure to different kinds of change" (1998, p. 290). It should have a balance of social history (change in families, demography), economic history (work systems, technology), political history (political institutions and behavior), and the history of ideas (fundamental values and popular beliefs). A student's investigation of change should include different magnitudes of change, "from formal revolutions or cultural or economic transformations," Stearns adds, "to more subtle combinations of change and continuity." Likewise, students should have experience with different patterns of causation, including "some balance between top-down causation (including due consideration of the role of individual 'greats') and causation emanating from ordinary folk." To that, we would add structural change as well as causation through personal agency. The point is to help students "move through some of the analytical subsets of the phenomenon of historical change and become aware of what these subsets are so they can identify them in recurrent treatments" (p. 291). In other words, students need tools for thinking about and coming to grips with change as a phenomenon in human society.

Using Historical Perspective

A second purpose for students spending time reflecting on what they have learned is to help them place the present in historical perspective. "Historical perspective differs from history," Lawrence (1984) explains, "in that the object of historical perspective is to sharpen one's vision of the present, not the past" (p. 307). While historical perspective is focused on the present, it may also suggest possibilities for the future. "One cannot know the future," she adds; but by examining a development over time "one can get some idea of whether one is watching a mountain stream or a glacier" (p. 310). Trends may suggest possible futures, but the predictive value of historical thinking is marginal at best. The principal reason to engage students in using historical perspective is that history, as John S. Wills (1996) points out, "speaks to the present. It helps us understand the role of the past in shaping current events" (p. 370).

There are at least two ways to think about historical perspective. In one sense of the term, we place the present in perspective by taking a holistic view of the past. This perspective provides what John Tosh (2008) calls an "oblique illumination of the present." The value of looking at the past this way lies not in what we find that is similar to the present, but "precisely in what is different from our world. … It opens up other worlds with different preconceptions and different ways of doing. At the very least, this offers a measure of detachment from our own world; but, more than that, it allows us to evaluate our world from another position." That is, the past provides us with "a set of counter images" from which to compare the present (pp. 28–29). Counter-intuitive though it may be, seeing different worlds in the past can give us a better sense of the world in which we live. By providing multiple versions over time of who we are not, historical perspective can make us more fully aware of who we are.

The farther the past is removed from the present, the stronger the sense of "otherness" a historical perspective provides. That is, the more distant, the more the past seems like a foreign country. Abigail Gable, a teacher observed by Sarah Brooks (2011), found a powerful metaphor to help her students understand the grip that religion had on people's minds in the Middle Ages. "It's this idea of questioning the status quo, which to us is such an ingrained part of our intellectual tradition because we are post Enlightenment babies. But in the Middle Ages, you really lacked a sense of skepticism" (p. 176). Knowing that we are post-Enlightenment, post-Age of Exploration, and post-Industrial Revolution babies helps keep the past at a distance. As Gable's course progressed, the perception of otherness diminished. She explained to her students during the second semester that "the people of Western Europe resemble us much more. The middle class culture becomes dominant. … The ebb and flow of their lives resemble more our modern life" (pp. 177–178). A holistic historical perspective presents the past not so much as different in kind, but rather, in degree.

There is a second way to think about historical perspective, which uses the past to hold up a mirror that magnifies the present. This mirror takes the form of analogies in which we find similarities between now and then. That is, we use one aspect of the past to shed light on a similar aspect of the present. This use of past-present analogy gives us a close-up rather than a distant view. If the whole past were analogous to the present and not different from it, it would cease to be the past. To say it another way, this kind of historical perspective emphasizes continuity rather than change. By focusing on similarities, we look for what has in some recognizable form endured over time.

Using historical analogies presents a number of challenges. In the first place, the past is not a storehouse of ready-made "lessons" waiting to be applied to the present. George Santayana's warning that "Those who cannot remember the past are condemned to repeat it," oversimplifies the problem (1905, p. 284). Learning from the past is not only a matter of remembering, but also of interpreting what happened. Those who remember the past are in danger of misreading it, as making past-present analogies is a risky business. Teachers of recent US history can help students appreciate this by revisiting the false analogies that have so often bedeviled American foreign policy—most notably the Munich–Vietnam analogy. While history teachers have less at stake than foreign policy-makers, they and their students should be equally careful not to misread the past.

We suspect that teachers are most likely to use the second or analogy-making kind of historical perspective rather than the holistic view. Connecting past to present more easily helps students "see the relevance of history to their lives" (Brooks, 2014, p. 70). Africa's present-day problems, one state curriculum guide points out, "are rooted in Africa's past" (Georgia Department of Education, 2008, p. 1). A study of the Holocaust helped a teacher shed light on the 1994 Rwandan genocide (Boix-Mansilla, 2000). A Los Angeles teacher attempted to use the pre-Civil War experience of African-American slaves to place the 1992 riots in her city in perspective (Wills, 1996). Teachers also use historical analogies to find the historical roots of contemporary problems and issues. Historical knowledge, writes McNeill (1989), "is a supremely useful tool for understanding current affairs, minimizing misunderstandings and facilitating wiser decisions than are possible for those who lack historical knowledge" (p. 157).

While teachers and history educators agree that historical analogies can be useful tools, there seems to be no consensus about how to use them. Instructional strategies described in the professional literature vary widely (Brooks, 2014). A high school teacher observed by Stephanie van Hover and Elizabeth Yeager (2003) lectured to her students about what was relevant about the past as just another set of facts to be learned, "rather than allowing students to draw their own connections between past and present" (p. 225). Some teachers rely heavily on open-ended inquiry, leaving students to think of analogies on their own. Others strike a balance between the two, through a guided inquiry approach. For example, a middle-grades teacher observed by Michelle Anderson (2011) used writing prompts to engage students in writing-to-learn assignments that addressed past-present connections. "Have the civilizations we have been discussing [been] similar to ours?" this teacher asked. "Do you see Greek influence in our world today" (p. 109)? Classroom discussions are useful in getting students to think about connections, allowing them to hear other points of view, to challenge the teacher's analogies (Wills, 1996). Discussions in which students deliberately challenge each other's analogies can play a valuable role, as false analogies are one of the hazards of learning about the present from the past (Brooks, 2014; Saye & Brush, 2004).

Teachers have encountered no shortage of pitfalls in making past-present analogies. One common error is to reverse the analogy by reading the present back into the past. For example, a middle-grades teacher that Brooks (2014) observed attempted to use his expertise on student bullying by projecting the roles of bullies, victims, and bystanders into historical situations. To ask students to view English settlers at Jamestown as either school bullies or bystanders is presentism at its most extreme. Recreating a completely familiar past defeats the purpose of historical inquiry. Another danger is to find superficial similarities in situations that are fundamentally different, as did Judy, a Los Angeles teacher observed by Wills (1996). She happened to be teaching about the Civil War, when the riots following the 1992 Rodney King trial erupted in that city. Wanting to capitalize on the moment, she drew an analogy between slavery in the 1860s and the everyday experience of African Americans in 1992. Doing so left her eighth-grade students thoroughly confused, as they knew that in the US slavery no longer existed. Such clutching for similarities "too easily overlooks the difference between their circumstances and ours; it also discounts the processes of change and development which have taken place in the meantime" (Tosh, 2008, p. 61). Identifying superficial similarities can also lead to asserting causal relationships where none exist. A student in the ancient history class observed by Anderson (2011) did just that, noting that without Greek theater "TV shows and movies wouldn't exist today" (p. 47). Drawing analogies between the present and the past does not mean rummaging through the past searching for similarities. It means looking for evidence that illustrates instances in which the present is an unfolding of the past.

Effective historical analogies help students understand the present by uncovering continuities. These are what Tosh (2008) calls "the longer term trajectories which structure so much of the world around us" (p. 8). The way things are today, McNeill (1985) notes, "descends from the way they were yesterday and the day before that … institutions that govern a great deal of our everyday behavior took shape hundreds or even thousands of years ago" (p. 1). By calling attention to the supposed similarities between slavery and modern-day race relations, the teacher in Los Angeles missed an opportunity to emphasize the persistence of discrimination and marginalization in American society based on race. On the other hand, Linda Strait, a teacher observed by S. G. Grant (2003) helped her white, middle-class students see the connection between issues raised by the Civil Rights Movement and their own lives. As one white, middle-class student reflected, "Me, being where I'm living now and, and the race I am ... I think that I'm probably a privileged American" (quoted in Grant, 2003, p. 73). By dwelling on racial discrimination and civil rights, we are not suggesting that persistent social problems are the only continuities that need to be placed in historical perspective. History is a mansion with many rooms.

In using the past to address present-day concerns, teachers must also help students find analogies that resonate with them. Their present-day concerns may be quite different from the teacher's. Dave Neumann (2010) kept this in mind while looking for modern-day parallels to the women's movement in antebellum America. He first thought about such modern-day equivalents as the possibility of a woman running for president or the underrepresentation of women in Congress. But he questioned whether such analogies would interest his eighth-grade students, who could not vote and were not much interested in politics. He settled instead on their perception of gender differences. He asked his students to consider how the arguments for and against women's rights and suffrage in the 1840s related to their own ideas about differences between genders, other than physical ones. That was a question "never far from the concerns of adolescents," but also one that "effectively links the antebellum world to today by identifying a basic—and important—question these eras share in common" (p. 185). It was a good decision, even though it was not his first choice.

Expecting students to use historical perspective to connect the past to the present has implications for textbook writers and curriculum developers. For students to see continuities over time, the curriculum must provide the information needed. "One reason that Judy's focus on the experiences of African Americans as slaves was less than successful in achieving her goals," Wills (1996) noted, "was because African Americans were virtually absent from the rest of U.S. history" (p. 380). After being mentioned in the Colonial Period, they had dropped out of Judy's pre-Civil War US History curriculum. American Indians no doubt received similar sporadic attention. Consequently, her students associated the injustice that African Americans experience with slavery, not as a feature of race relations in the United States. To Judy's students, the end of slavery meant the end of injustice. "The way to include diverse groups is to place them in many different times and places and to study them as historical actors with political voices" (p. 380). In other words, understanding of historical continuity depends on students' encountering continuing themes that provide a coherent past and that connect the past to the present. For students to see how the past and present are causally linked, the curriculum and the textbooks students use must provide them with the connecting threads.

Analyze People's Perspectives

Students can also put historical learning to use by applying what they have learned about perspective analysis. This use of the term "perspective" refers to the kind of historical thinking in which students try to account for the perspectives of historical actors. Although introduced as part of the analysis phase of historical knowledge construction, perspective analysis has broader application. The idea that people often make decisions based on their own preconceptions, assumptions, and values is a concept that transcends historical periods. As procedural knowledge, it is a tool that can be applied to the present as well as the past. Such analysis also has a metacognitive dimension, as students need to ask themselves how well they understand another person's perspective and what they still need to know about it. Such thinking is not only useful in interpreting past events. It also has explanatory power in the present and in the students' own lives.

The discipline of history does not have a monopoly on perspective taking. Perspective differentiation is a process in human development that begins quite early. According to psychologists who work in the area called theory of mind research, children distinguish between points of view from about the age of four (Wimmer & Perner, 1983). It is part of a child's social development that is further refined over time, as children are taught both at home and in school to recognize and respect other points of views. While perspective analysis in history classrooms may be reinforcing a basic developmental and learning process, we think it does more than that. It also has a causal component. Historical analysis focuses on understanding why people have different perspectives.

Understanding why people's perspectives differ is useful to students in many ways. "Active and thoughtful participation in a democratic society often requires exercising complex multidimentional thinking: to 'see through the eyes of another' in the spheres of social, moral, and civic relations," Dulberg (2002, p. 44) notes. Knowing why other people see the world as they do helps us better understand the culturally diverse world in which we live. Knowing how other people's perspectives are shaped by their cultural and social experience can also contribute to self-knowledge, helping students see themselves more clearly. It does for self-understanding what the historical perspective of seeing "otherness" does for understanding the present. It should also promote self-inquiry. "Why do I act as I do?" "Why do I feel strongly about this or that?" Having to explain oneself has greater potential for social growth than unthinking acceptance. However, we suspect that applying perspective analysis to present-day situations, like most aspects of learning, does not happen on its own. It must be explicitly addressed through classroom instruction. Such instruction should affirm in students a value of historical inquiry, and understanding of how and why we investigate the past. We seek to be literate about history so that we use it in informed and thoughtful ways to address the challenges and opportunities of the present.

References

Anderson, M. R. (2011) Connecting the past to the present: Student meaning making in a middle school world history classroom. Doctorate of Education dissertation, University of Pittsburgh.

Boix-Mansilla, V. (2000). Historical understanding: Beyond the past and into the present. In P. N. Stearns, P. Seixas, & S. Wineburg (eds.) *Knowing, teaching and learning history: National and international perspectives* New York, NY: New York University Press. (pp. 390-418).

Brooks, S. (2011). Historical empathy as perspective recognition and care in one secondary social studies classroom. *Theory and Research in Social Education*, 39(2), 166–202.

Brooks, S. (2013). Teaching for historical understanding in the advanced placement program: A case study. *The History Teacher*, 47(1), 61–76.

Brooks, S. (2014). Connecting the past to the present in the middle-level classroom: A comparative case study. *Theory & Research in Social Education*, 42(1), 65–95.

Dulberg, N. (2002). Engaging in history: Empathy and perspective-taking children's historical thinking. Paper presented at the Annual Meeting of the American Educational Research Association, New Orleans, LA.

Gagnon. P. (1988). Why study history. *Atlantic Monthly*, November, 43–66.

Georgia Department of Education. (2008). Seventh grade unit 10: "Connecting Africa's past with Africa's present, p. 1. GeorgiaStandards.Org, accessed October 20, 2014.

Grant, S. G. (2003). *History lessons: Teaching, learning, and testing in U.S. high school classrooms.* Mahwah, NJ: Lawrence Erlbaum Associates, Publishers.

Lawrence, B. S. (1984). Historical perspective: Using the past to study the present, *Academy of Management Review*, 9(2), 307–312.

McNeill, W. H. (1985). Why study history. *American Historical Association: the Professional Association for all Historians*. Retrieved from http://www.historians.org/pubs/archives/whmcneillwhystudyhistory.htm

McNeill, W. H. (1989). How history helps us to understand current affairs. In P. Gagnon & The Bradley Commission on History in Schools (eds.) *Historical literacy: The case for history in American education* (pp. 157–169). New York, NY: Macmillan Publishing Company.

Miller, M. M. & Stearns, P. N. (1995). Applying cognitive learning approaches in history teaching: An experiment in a world history course. *History Teacher*, 28(2), 183–204.

Neumann, D. (2010). A different way of viewing history teaching: Balancing competing intellectual challenges, *Social Education*, 74(4), 184–188.

Ogle, D., Klemp, R., & McBride, B. (2007). *Building literacy in the social studies.* Alexandria, VA: Association for Supervision and Curriculum Development.

Santayana, G. (1905). *Reason in common sense.* London: Archibald Constable & Co. Ltd.

Saye, J. W. & Brush, T. (2004). Promoting civic competence through problem-based history learning experiments. In G. E. Hamot, J. J. Patrick, & R. S. Leming (eds.) *Civic learning in teacher education* (vol. 3, pp. 123–145.). Bloomington, IN: Social Studies Development Center.

Schell, E. & Fisher, D. (2007). *Teaching social studies: A literacy-based approach.* Upper Saddle River, NJ: Pearson, Merrill Prentice Hall.

Stearns, P. N. (1998). Goals in history teaching. In Voss, J. F. & Carretero, M. (eds.) *International review of history education, Volume 2: Learning and reasoning in history* 281–293). London and Portland, OR: Woburn Press.

Tosh, J. (2008). *Why history matters.* Basingstoke, Hampshire: Palgrave MacMillan.

Van Hover, S. D. & Yeager, E. A. (2003). "'Making' students better people?" A case study of a beginning history teacher. *International Social Studies Forum*, 3(1), 219–232.

Wills, J. S. (1996). Who needs multicultural education? White students, U.S. history, and the construction of a usable past. *Anthropology & Education Quarterly*, 27(3), 365–389.

Wimmer, H. & Perner, J. (1983). Beliefs about beliefs: Representation and constraining function of wrong beliefs in your children's understanding of deception. *Cognition*, 69, 1–34.

INDEX

Note: Page numbers in **bold** are for figures, those in *italics* are for tables.